*Childly Language*

# REAL LANGUAGE SERIES

*General Editors:*

**JENNIFER COATES**, Roehampton Institute, London

**JENNY CHESHIRE**, Queen Mary and Westfield College,
 University of London, and

**EUAN REID**, Institute of Education, University of London

---

# Childly Language:

## Children, Language and the Social World

Alison Sealey

*An imprint of* **PEARSON EDUCATION**

Harlow, England · London · New York · Reading, Massachusetts · San Francisco · Toronto · Don Mills, Ontario · Sydney
Tokyo · Singapore · Hong Kong · Seoul · Taipei · Cape Town · Madrid · Mexico City · Amsterdam · Munich · Paris · Milan

**Pearson Education Limited**
Edinburgh Gate
Harlow
Essex CM20 2JE
England

and Associated Companies throughout the world

*Visit us on the World Wide Web at:*
www.pearsoneduc.com

First published 2000

© Pearson Education Limited 2000

ISBN 0-582-30779-1 CSD
ISBN 0-582-30780-5 PPR

*British Library Cataloguing-in-Publication Data*
A catalogue record for this book is available from the British Library

*Library of Congress Cataloging-in-Publication Data*
Sealey, Alison.
  Childly language : children, language, and the social world / Alison Sealey.
    p.   cm. — (Real language series)
  Includes bibliographical references and index.
  ISBN 0-582-30780-5 (ppr) — ISBN 0-582-30779-1 (cad)
  1. Children—Language.  2. Socialization.  I. Title.  II. Series.

LB1139.L3 S334 2000
372.6—dc21                                                     99–047483

Set by 35 in 10/12pt Janson
Produced by Pearson Education Asia Pte. Ltd.
Printed in Singapore

# Contents

# Author's **Acknowledgements**

I am grateful to the University of Warwick for facilitating the writing of the manuscript by granting me a period of study leave. Some of the research described in Part III was funded by the Nuffield Foundation under the Social Science Small Grants Scheme, as a project on 'The role of spontaneous spoken language in the social relationships of six 8 and 9 year old children'. Initial transcription of the tapes was financed by COBUILD. I am very grateful to the children and their friends and families for their participation; all names have been changed. I am also indebted to the respondents to the elicitation survey described in Part III. In the course of researching for and writing this book I have been in contact with a range of people from whom I have learned a great deal. I should like to thank a number of people for their help and advice as I have been getting to grips with corpus linguistics, including: Ylva Berglund, Sebastian Hoffmann, Jean Hudson, Susan Hunston and Ramesh Krishnamurthy. Some of the collocational data presented in Chapter 3 was provided by the corpus linguistics group at the University of Zurich, to whom I am also very grateful. Some of the data and ideas presented in the book were introduced as conference and seminar papers and I am grateful to participants for their responses. I would also like to thank a number of people who have given their time to read drafts of one or more chapters of the book, providing me with constructive comments and sometimes engaging in lengthy discussions about the content. They include: Ylva Berglund, Bob Carter, Sheena Gardner, Jean Hudson, Susan Hunston, Derek Layder, Barbara Mayor, Richard Pearce, Leslie Stratta, Theo van Leeuwen, Sylvia Winchester. Bob Carter and I have written together about realist social theory and sociolinguistics, and Chapter 5, in particular, reflects this collaboration. I would like to acknowledge here the debt I owe to his intellectual companionship and continuing support.

# Publisher's **Acknowledgements**

We are grateful to the following for permission to reproduce copyright materials:

Solo Syndication for headline 'Queen in mercy bid for drug girl' in *Daily Mail* 29.10.96 & extracts from the article 'Head closes his school in battle over one boy' in *Daily Mail* 29.10.96; Express Newspapers plc for headline & extracts from the article 'One boy closes school' in *The Express* 19.10.96. © Express Newspapers; Independent Newspapers (UK) Ltd for various headlines and extracts taken from *The Independent* during 1996; Oxfam Publishing for material from the Oxfam Advertisement.

For Bob and Leon

# Discourses of Childhood

# Introduction to **Part I**

*Childhood, we might venture, is that status of personhood which is
by definition often in the wrong place.*

(JAMES et al. 1998: 37)

This book is concerned with relationships between language and 'children':
that is, people who fall clearly into the category of 'children', as the term is
routinely used in English at the present time. I suggest that there is a significant but relatively under-researched period in people's lives when they
are active, creative and socially effective, but are also unequivocally classified
as belonging to the stage in the lifespan designated 'childhood'.

I assume that you, the reader, are an adult, not a child. The statement of
this assumption also presupposes some further claims: that there are two
such categories as 'adult' and 'child'; that they are meaningful and distinct
from each other; and that you, the reader, will have no trouble deciding
whether my assumption about the category to which you belong is correct. I
shall begin by exploring briefly how assumptions like these are involved in
the language of several public texts.

If you live in the UK, you are very likely to have read the following text,
because it is displayed in public places around the country:

(1)  PROTECT CHILDREN: DON'T MAKE THEM BREATHE YOUR SMOKE

This instruction is to be found on the large hoardings which advertise cigar-
ettes in the UK. The simple text rests on several presuppositions which are
not particularly surprising or controversial, but I want to make them explicit
because of their relevance to what follows. Although it concerns children,
this text is addressed not to them but to adults who may find themselves in
the company of children. One obvious point is that the reader is positioned
as a smoker, by the inclusion of this sentence in an advertisement for cigar-
ettes and by the phrase 'your smoke'; status as a smoker is legitimate for
adults but not for children. Secondly, the two main verbs are both imperatives, implying 'you, the reader' as agent of the action to be taken, again not
unusual in public notices. In this case, the object of both verbs, 'protect' and
'make', is 'children' (pronominalized as 'them' in the second clause). So the

implied reader of this public text is an adult and is in a position to affect children, with a choice between 'making' them do things and 'protecting' them. The text does not specify what the reader is instructed to protect them from (world knowledge and familiarity with similar warnings supplies 'serious damage to health' or 'cancer'), but the collocation of 'child' and 'protect(ion)' is current in public discourse.

Here is another example of a public notice:

(2)   PARENTS. BUILDING SITES ARE DANGEROUS. PLEASE KEEP
      YOUR CHILDREN AWAY

The intended readers of this text (displayed outside a building site) are explicitly identified as 'parents'. When we read a notice like this in the normal course of going about our business, we process it rapidly, but I want to pause briefly now to consider its semantics. From the point of view of hyponymy, or relationships of inclusion, all such notices are, of course, implicitly addressed to people, who form the 'superordinate' category of human beings. It is possible to subdivide this category in many ways, depending on the context and the purpose of communication. Often the subcategories are antonyms; for example 'male' = 'not female' and vice versa. The lexeme 'child' is interesting as a subcategory of 'human being', because it is possible to place it in a contrasting relationship with each of two other lexemes, (i) 'adult' and (ii) 'parent'. In relation to (i), membership of one category logically precludes membership of the other ('adult' = not child). In relation to (ii), however, one can simultaneously be *both* someone's child (son/ daughter) *and* someone else's parent (father/mother). English speakers reading or hearing the word 'child' have to infer which meaning of 'child' is salient from the context. In text (2), the use of 'parents' as an address term suggests that the relationship appealed to is that of begetter/offspring, but the instruction only applies to a parent-reader whose offspring is not-adult. It is of course possible for an individual to belong to both the 'child' category in (i) and the 'parent' category in (ii), but there is serious social stigma surrounding the phenomenon of child-parents.

The imperative in the second sentence of (2) is again a verb of which children are the object. The text presupposes that parents can – and should – take responsibility for where their children are. The simple declarative first sentence 'Building sites are dangerous' may seem to present new information, but is presumably not interpreted in this way in context. Places in this category present a danger to anyone, although it is a humanly-constructed danger, and those responsible for the notice have privileged knowledge and experience which mitigates the danger to them. A further presupposition is that it is children rather than adults who might be attracted to this kind of public space, so the notice serves as a reminder of what the responsible parent is expected to know, and should make sure that their children know.

I said above that all public notices are implicitly addressed to human beings as a superordinate category. One qualification of this is that written language is by definition addressed to people who are literate in the language used. (Iconic symbols seek to overcome any potential incomprehensibility of some signs: stylized silhouettes of a man or a woman on public toilets, for example.) Many children will be able to read the sign in text (2): should they find themselves unaccompanied and tempted by the interest of a building site, it reminds them of the kinds of things adults communicate to each other about them and where it is permissible for them to be. Text (3) was seen in a clothes store whose display windows were easily accessible from inside the shop:

(3)    IMPORTANT NOTICE. PLEASE DO NOT ALLOW CHILDREN TO PLAY IN
       THE WINDOWS. THANK YOU

Again, it is children's behaviour which is the focus of the text, but, again, the implied reader is an adult. The verb 'allow' alludes to a similar established relationship of responsibility for children by adults to that implied in the previous texts. Two inferences are possible from the injunction embodied in this 'important notice': one is the protection of children from the risk of being hurt by playing in this space, the other is the damage they might do – to property or to other people. So this public text exemplifies the idea that children can cause negative things to happen, and that adults should prevent this.

Two other public proscriptions relating to children reinforce the image of child as nuisance in a public space. The first appears in the window of an electrical wholesale store:

(4)    NO PRAMS
       CHILDREN
       BIKES
       PETS
       ALLOWED

Here, although safety might be a motive for the notice, children are nevertheless grouped with other potential encumbrances which adult customers might take into the store with them unless instructed otherwise, and the notice again strongly implies an adult reader, as none of the other items with which 'children' are listed could conceivably interpret the text for themselves.

Variations on the following restriction of children's occupation of public space are quite often seen in small neighbourhood shops. This one was displayed in a sweet shop:

(5)    ONLY 2 SCHOOL CHILDREN AT A TIME ALLOWED IN THE SHOP

Here the readers are presumably children themselves, although they are addressed only indirectly in this third-person construction, which would be hard to formulate in the second person. The result is a prohibition which coincidentally avoids the impoliteness potentially associated with negative imperatives ('do not . . .'). The modification of 'children' by 'school' denotes one of the few subcategories to which children as social actors can typically belong. 'Schoolchildren' contrast with children of other ages (not 'pre-schoolers' and not 'school-leavers'), but in this context its defining function is probably the category of child who is out in the world away from the family and its disciplinary influence: it seems unlikely that the shopkeeper would enforce the prohibition if a mother brought her three young children into the shop together, whether or not they were identifiable, by a uniform perhaps, as 'schoolchildren'.

The final text appears outside a play area attached to a large store:

(6)   CHILDREN HAVE TO BE AT LEAST 3 YEARS OF AGE AND 3FT–4FT
      WITHOUT SHOES.

In this case, membership of the category 'child' is insufficient to determine who is allowed and who is denied access to a particular public space. Children are further categorized in both temporal and spatial terms – by age and by height.

Although what I have said about these examples may seem obvious, the taken-for-granted nature of their presuppositions will perhaps be clearer if they are rewritten to incorporate different assumptions. This approach is often used in stylistic analysis to demonstrate the contrast between different linguistic choices and the relationship of lexical or grammatical choices to different genres. (See, for example, Carter and Nash 1990; Simpson 1993.) In particular, writers interested in contrasting the ways women and men respectively are represented in language have pointed out the non-reciprocal meanings of apparently paired terms (e.g. Hoey 1996; Lee 1992; Miller and Swift 1989).

Texts in which 'children' are substituted by some other category of human being might seem bizarre, but are not completely unimaginable: advertisers, for example, might find ways of, and reasons to, complete the following. It may be interesting to see whether they can be made to make sense, and to identify what presuppositions are implied.

(1a)   PROTECT OTHER [ . . . ] 'RESIDENTS'? 'CITIZENS'?: DON'T MAKE THEM [ . . . ]

(2a)   CHILDREN. BUILDING SITES ARE DANGEROUS. PLEASE KEEP YOUR [ . . . ]
       'PARENTS'? AWAY.

(3a)   IMPORTANT NOTICE. PLEASE DO NOT ALLOW ADULTS/PARENTS TO [ . . . ].
       THANK YOU.

(Notice again the non-reciprocity of lexical possibilities in the child/parent : child/adult pairs.)

(4a)   NO WHEELCHAIRS
       OLD PEOPLE
       BIKES
       PETS
       ALLOWED

(5a)   NO MORE THAN TWO [ADULT CATEGORY] ALLOWED IN THE SHOP AT A
       TIME.

(6a)   ADULTS HAVE TO BE AT LEAST 43 YEARS OF AGE AND 5–6 FEET
       WITHOUT SHOES.

What social group other than children could be discriminated against as in (4a) and (5a) in contemporary Britain without flouting legislation or causing an outcry?

Notices in public places can prohibit things or practices which may be closely associated with certain groups of people, such as 'jeans' or 'muddy boots' (in a public house), or 'smoking' or 'loitering', but in none of these cases is the social group itself categorized as unacceptable. Corsaro (1997: 199–200) reports on an observation in Leach (1994) prompted by Norwegian children's objections to rules directed to them in a housing cooperative, such as 'children are not allowed to make noise in the corridors'. Leach's point is that anti-social behaviour should be understood as anti-social whoever engages in it, and that rules should proscribe it universally or not at all. In fact, however, as Qvortrup (1994) notes in relation to the legal system, children can commit 'status offences' by doing things such as 'running away from home' which would not involve the law if done by adults: 'In general terms we have laws that pertain only to adults and other laws pertaining only to children' (p. 1).

Significantly, children constitute 'the only group of citizens in the UK who can legally be hit. Current laws in the UK are founded on a concept of "reasonable chastisement" from the 19th century' (Willow and Hyder 1998: 7). However, this situation is currently under review following a decision taken by the European Court of Human Rights.

Contemporary concerns about children stress the need for adults to protect them, but this need arises partly from the world adults have created. Hood-Williams (1990: 165), for example, writes of 'the geographical restrictions on children and the long list of places where they may not or cannot go' partly because of 'the adult-centred architecture of public life'. Texts which denote both danger to and protection of children are commonplace; however, as with all critical linguistic analysis, it can be illuminating to consider the range of meaning potentials available in the language, and not to accept without question the 'angle of telling' (Simpson 1993) implied in familiar ways of speaking and writing.

This is the theme of the first part of this book, which is concerned with the ways in which children are represented in the contemporary English language. I have used a range of authentic data to explore this question, taken from a variety of sources, including short- and medium-length individual texts such as the public notices above, two radio broadcasts and half a dozen stories intended for children to read; more substantial texts such as one year's headlines from one newspaper and all the stories about one event from several; and the much larger British National Corpus. The language is analysed with reference to the range of referring expressions used for children; by looking at the word *child* and words derived from it – *children*, *childhood*, *childish*, *childlike* – in terms of collocations and syntactic patterns; and by drawing attention to other linguistic features of texts which either represent children or deploy the key words used to denote them in order to represent other things.

The first two chapters analyse the discourse of newspapers, because of the part played by the public language of the news in influencing how we conceptualize people and events. A number of studies have examined how different social groups are represented in news reporting: van Dijk (1988) discusses the representation of ethnic minorities and squatters; Clark (1992) considers representations by one newspaper of men who perpetrate violence against women, and the women themselves; Meinhof and Richardson (1994) explore representations of poverty and the poor; van Leeuwen (1996) deals with a range of social actors; and in their analysis of the media coverage of the murder of a 2-year-old by two 10-year-olds, Davis and Bourhill (1997: 29) claim that '[t]he media portrayal of children's involvement in crime, either as perpetrators or victims, is central in creating and reinforcing public perceptions of childhood'.

Journalists work under pressure to tight deadlines, and are therefore likely to use accessible and sometimes unreflective ways of representing the world, which is one reason for choosing to analyse newspapers as a source of public discourse (Simpson 1993). We cannot escape from the fact that we need linguistic resources to represent social actors, and there are no absolutely neutral, objective, value-free ways of doing this. Even the apparently disinterested label 'child' or 'children' presupposes a relation between those who are or can be denoted by it and those who are not, and in analysing some texts I found the label more ambiguous than I had anticipated, as I shall explain in Chapter 1.

The close lexical and syntactical analyses led to the identification of some recurring themes in this kind of public language used about children, which are foreshadowed by aspects of the public notices discussed above, and are used as the basis for organizing the first two chapters. The repeated expressions which connote the phenomenon of harm directed towards children provide the first theme, and those which relate to the responsibilities of adults for the care and protection of children provide the second. The representation of children as active, effective participants in the social world was found to be quite limited in these texts, and this is the third theme examined in Chapter 1.

Chapter 2 draws on the same range of data to consider the theme of growth, development and change in all children's lives. The second theme in this chapter is the representation of children as a distinct social group, often defined in relation to the more numerous adults who have so much more power to determine the nature of social relations. The third theme discussed is the idea of childhood as a persisting social phenomenon, which is sometimes related only metaphorically to the lives or actions of actual children.

Chapter 3 moves away from the public discourse of newspapers to consider both a large corpus of English language data, including a much wider range of text genres, and some other specific texts which throw a slightly different light on the issues raised in Part I. The decisions to look at specific texts and extracts in detail and also at larger corpora, and to use both computer-assisted and also more interpretive methods of analysis, are influenced by the developments in linguistic theory and method which are very well explained in Stubbs (1996). These ideas will be explored more fully in Part II.

The concerns of the book present a linguistic challenge of their own, one which has been faced by other writers seeking to question assumptions about children's place in the social and cultural world. I have come across the coinages 'childist' (Hunt 1984) and 'non-childist' (Wall 1991), as well as 'adultism' (Scraton 1997) and 'adultcentric' (Sutton-Smith 1982), but such terms are not yet well established, and it remains to be seen whether the associations they suggest, reminiscent of terms in 'feminist' linguistics, will be replicated in this field. The unorthodox vocabulary item which I introduce in this book arises from my need for a term to denote the distinctive characteristics of being a child, without invoking the cultural connotations of either 'childish' or 'childlike' (see Chapter 3). The term I need is one which can signify the *relational* nature of the state of being a child, as discussed in Chapter 2, rather than any *essential* qualities attaching to that stage in the lifespan; that is, *in relation to* non-children, children lack status, power and responsibility and are dependent. The necessarily negative nature of these relational qualities has not gone unremarked (see, for example, Archard 1993; Corsaro 1997; James 1993; Waksler 1991). Children also have needs and interests which can be distinguished from those of adults. To denote any of these distinctive characteristics of children's place in the world I shall use the term 'childly'. However, I shall also argue that belonging to the category of 'child' or 'adult' will not necessarily define or determine our social and linguistic experience.

# 1

# Children in the News (1): Threatened, Protected, Active

*The modern child has become the focus of innumerable projects that purport to safeguard it from physical, sexual and moral danger, to ensure its 'normal' development, to actively promote certain capacities of attributes such as intelligence, educability and emotional stability.*

ROSE (1989: 121)

## 1.1 Introduction

How do children feature in the news? Children are relatively powerless members of society and not in a strong position to affect the world and others in it, except at a quite local level. When they do, it may be not so much as agents of their own actions as in the role of recipient or victim of the actions of others. These claims are relatively objective facts about the way society is organized and structured, and the language used to report events of national significance involving children will obviously reflect this state of affairs. Bell's (1991) list of categories of people who are likely to be 'news actors' includes political figures, officials, celebrities and so on. It implicitly excludes children as a social group, with two main exceptions: as victims and as 'human interest figures'. Most of what counts as 'news' is not only made by adults but read by adults. Bell also points out that, although 'generally everything which is published or broadcast in mass-audience daily media is in some sense held to be suitable for the whole population to receive' (1991: 93), nevertheless it is children who constitute a segment of the mass media audience whose access to some of its texts is proscribed. These two aspects of children's roles as actors and as audience in news discourse are important in the context of exploring children in the news.

The data for this and the next chapter consist of three kinds of newspaper discourse.[1] Data Set 1 comprises all the headlines of one year's output of one national British broadsheet, *The Independent*, in which the words *child, children* or *childhood* appear. I examine headlines because 'newspapers use them to encapsulate the view of the whole report' (Clark 1992: 213). Similarly, Bell (1991) likens the headline to the abstract in oral narratives, and in fairly large numbers headlines thus provide a corpus from which to explore some patterns in the representation of children and childhood in one very public and accessible domain of language. The headlines are for all kinds of story covered by the paper, including both 'hard' news and features, as well as special topic sections (often 'Education') and letters. Although all the items are classified by the CD ROM of this corpus as 'headlines', which we might expect to make a direct impact in few words when printed above hard news, some of them are quite discursive, particularly those used to introduce feature articles. The CD ROM version of *The Independent* for 1996 stores 70,252 articles, of which 888 appear from a computerized search to contain the target word *child\**. This mechanical method of identifying relevant text for analysis is necessarily rather inexact (Soothill and Grover 1997), generating a number of false positives (words such as the name 'Childers' with no semantic or morphological connection to children, for example) and obviously not succeeding in finding any headline where child participants are only referred to as 'kids', or 'a boy', 'a nine-year-old' and so on, or are individuated by name. Therefore, a more interpretive, semantic approach was taken to identifying items for inclusion in the other data sets.

Data Set 2 includes reports in a range of national newspapers, both broadsheets and tabloids, published on 29 October 1996, when a story about a child was front page news in the British press. It is important to include texts from the whole spectrum of newspapers, including tabloids which are widely read, because these may draw on quite different discourses from the broadsheets in representing people and events (Bell 1991; Fowler 1991). Eight daily papers were examined, namely *The Independent, The Times, The Guardian, The Daily Telegraph* (all classified as 'up-market' by Jucker (1989), as reported in Bell (1991)); the *Daily Mail, The Express* ('mid-market'); the *Daily Mirror* and *The Sun* ('down-market'). The story is not typical of national news stories about children, which, as will become apparent, are overwhelmingly concerned with harm directed towards them, but it provides a context for exploring how children can sometimes be represented as social actors in their own right. The basis of the story is that a 10-year-old pupil, accused of violent and disruptive behaviour, had been taught individually by a supply teacher instead of in a class. When the school's governors decided that there were no longer sufficient funds to employ an individual teacher for the boy, teachers belonging to one of the main teaching unions threatened to strike rather than accept him back into classes, and the head teacher sent a letter to parents informing them that the school would be closed the following day as staff would not be available and he could not therefore guarantee pupils' safety. This led to the involvement of officials beyond the school, and to controversy about the respective responsibilities of head teacher, governors and local and national officials.

Data Set 3 comprises stories from two local newspapers serving the West Midlands area of England. The criteria used by local newspapers for selecting what is newsworthy are somewhat different from those of the nationals: 'geographical closeness can enhance news value' (Bell 1991: 157) and local children's exploits can therefore be newsworthy in this context. Each day's *Coventry Evening Telegraph* published during the week of Monday 4 to Saturday 9 November 1996 was examined, as was each day's *Birmingham Post* published during the week Monday 18 November to Saturday 23 November 1996. The former newspaper is of tabloid size and the latter is a broadsheet. Every item about children, as defined below, was included in the corpus, giving a total of 31 and 20 items respectively, totalling approximately 11,300 words.

The newspapers in this data set demonstrate the instability of the term 'child' at its outer limits, and in some ways this helped to define the criteria which I used to determine whether particular stories should or should not be included in this corpus. One source of ambiguity in the word *child* derives from its use in the relational sense discussed in the Introduction. Everyone is somebody's child, and continues to hold that status in relation to the person's parents throughout life, so adults may be labelled 'children', especially if their parents are famous. (An example of this is a headline in the finance pages of a national paper, about 'Kirkham children' raising funds from their shares – the reader learns from the body of the story that they are in their late twenties.)

At the younger end of the continuum which designates people as 'children' are those of up to 3 years old, sometimes referred to as 'children', but also designated as 'babies' and 'toddlers'. Such people rarely feature in any independent social action in news stories. In the newspapers I examined, very young children were newsworthy exclusively as victims or recipients of events or actions carried out by older people. Therefore the younger age limit for stories to include in the local news corpus was set at 4 years old.

At the older end of the age-group, different news stories tend to refer to people of roughly 12 or older in different ways according to their role in the story. Where the person is a victim, their childliness may be emphasized, as in a story in the *Coventry Evening Telegraph* (9.11.96) about a man convicted of sexual offences with minors. Throughout the text, his victims are referred to as 'children', and a sentence about the pornographic films he made states that some involved 'girls as young as 12 and 13' (p. 7), thus making it clear that all the 'children' in this text were at least 12 years old. In a story in the *Daily Mail* (29.10.96), with the headline '*Queen in mercy bid for drug girl*', the 'girl' referred to is 25 years old. This example, when contrasted with those which follow, suggests the possibility of a gender difference linked with classification by age: females may continue to be designated as young females by the use of the word 'girl' beyond the age where the word 'boy' would be used for males.

The childly status of people aged 12 and above may be stressed when the story encourages the reader to be impressed with an achievement because of the age of the protagonist, in sport or creative art, for example. This perspective is similar to that used when the person achieving some accomplishment is surprisingly elderly (for example: 'World's oldest motorcyclist rides into the record books', *Birmingham Post*, 19.11.96). On the other hand, in news stories where teenage protagonists are perpetrators of deviant behaviour, their childly status may be played down. Thus, one story about 14- to 16-year-olds attacking firemen refers to them not as 'children' but as 'a gang of youths' (*Coventry Evening Telegraph*, 4.11.96), while another story, about teenagers carrying out an armed robbery, reports: '. . . one of the *men* was . . . in his mid teens' (*Coventry Evening Telegraph*, 6.11.96, my emphasis).

Wishing to focus on people who do fall unequivocally into the category of 'children', therefore, I included in this data set only stories about people of roughly the age covered by primary school, so that the phase of childhood represented is from 4 to 11 years old. This is consistent with the claim made by Archard (1993: 31), that for contemporary Western cultures, which 'periodise' childhood, 'it is almost as if the child proper was that which is no longer an infant but not yet a young person'.[2]

## 1.2  Children in danger

During the period when I have been conducting the research for this book, children have repeatedly been in the news because of harm inflicted on them, usually by adults. A large number of events have been reported in recent years, both within and outside the UK, in which one or more children have featured as victims of murder, violence, including sexual assault, neglect and various other negative experiences. It has to be noted that 'negativity' is considered a key criterion of newsworthiness (Bell 1991), and there is some debate about whether the high incidence of the reporting of negative things happening to children has led to an exaggerated anxiety about threats to their safety (Scott et al. 1998). In any case, it is not entirely surprising to find that the word *child* functions as the modifier of another noun denoting a 'negative' activity in a large proportion of its 269 occurrences in Data Set 1.

The relationship between the semantic import of these linked nouns and the syntactic structures in which they are realized is not always of quite the same kind, partly because in general nouns can modify other nouns in English to signify a wide range of relationships. The corpus-based COBUILD *English Grammar* informs learners: 'The use of noun modifiers in English is very common indeed. In fact, when the context makes it clear what you mean, you can use almost any noun to modify any other noun' (COBUILD 1990:

102). This productive feature of English is a potential realized in a particular way in news texts in what Bell (1991: 189) calls the 'distinctive, monosyllabic lexicon of headline rhetoric'. Two examples from my data of sequences of several nouns are 'Beck child sex abuse duo' and 'Internet child porn sentence'.

Of collocations like these, 'child abuse' is the most common, occurring 35 times, and followed in 19 cases with other nouns: 'child abuse inquiry', 'child abuse case', 'child abuse fears', 'child abuse scandal', and so on. Added to this are 15 occurrences of 'child sex', 14 of which are followed by one or more further nouns: 'child sex claims', 'child sex abuse allegations', 'child sex inquiry hero', and 10 occurrences of 'child pornography', usually shortened to 'porn', which, again, are followed by further nouns in five cases: 'child porn ring', 'child-porn jailing'. Sometimes, but not often, there is further pre-modification, as in 'fresh child abuse report' or 'Net [i.e. Internet] child porn'.

Other noun phrases denoting harmful activity directed towards children include the following, each of which occurs once: 'child assaults', 'child snatching', 'child murders' and 'child murder scandals'. The effect of seeing these phrases in a cumulative list is disturbing. The activities reported are perpetrated on actual children, but the linguistic phrases in which 'child' modifies 'abuse', 'sex' or 'porn' denote phenomena rather than people. The structure is similar to that found in other phrases headed by 'abuse', such as 'substance abuse', 'drug abuse', 'alcohol abuse', where the abused entity is an inanimate thing rather than a person. Naming these activities in this way to some extent dehumanizes, in that it necessarily de-individualizes, the children towards whom the activity is directed (cf. Fowler 1991: 80 on 're-ification' of processes). Another type of construction names the agents who carry out these negative activities: 'child (sex) abuser(s)' (8), 'child molester' (2), 'child sex tour agent' (1) and 'child killers' (1).

'Child' is also found to precede other nouns when it is children who are carrying out or being active in a process, but often with an implication that coercion and/or suffering of some kind is involved. The two main phrases in this category are 'child labour' (8) and 'child prostitution' (4), with 'child workers' (2) and 'child slavery' (1) also included.

In some stories, the occurrence of 'child' in the headline denotes one or more specific children who make the news as victims of people or events, including 'child victim(s)' (5), 'child survivor of family murder' (1) and the postmodified 'child at risk' (1). The noun sometimes stands alone in (often ellipted) clauses with 'child' as the subject in passive clauses, as in 'child injured by flying elf' (a December headline), or as the direct object of active clauses, as in 'jail for mother who killed child with salt'. 'Child' is sometimes modified: 'a small child' (subject of the passive clause which continues 'is left to scavenge crumbs'), 'second trapped child', 'a kidnapped child'. 'Child' can also be linked with other nouns to denote both medical conditions and those who suffer from them: 'child cancer' (1), 'child fits' (1), 'liver swap child' (1), 'child haemophiliacs' (1).

This dimension of children threatened or actually harmed by people, processes or events is represented in just under half (45.35 per cent) of the occurrences of the word *child* in these headlines.

Of the three key words researched in this data set, *children* occurs most frequently in the corpus – 495 times. Because I wanted to look in greater detail at the clauses containing the word than such a large list would allow, I selected every eighth headline (see Bell 1991) to reduce the full corpus to a random sample of one hundred, in which it was found that the target word *children* occurs 63 times. As will be explained below, these 'children' are not always central to any process denoted by the headline, but in the 30 headlines naming processes in which children clearly are participants, slightly more than half (18) feature *children* as the participant on the receiving end of the process realized in the verb. This is often in the role of victim, and often in a grammatical construction where *children* is the subject of a passive clause, such as 'Somali children sold in Europe', 'children put at risk by parasite teacher agencies' and '. . . delays while dead children were identified'. Other phrases completed by *children* are: 'effect on', 'labour of', 'misery of', 'murder of', 'danger to' and 'violence against'. Together, they comprise another catalogue of various kinds of unpleasant things that children may encounter in the world.

The news story which is the basis of Data Set 2 contrasts strongly with these findings, because the child concerned is represented as more threatening than threatened, so no examples from these texts are included in this section.

In Data Set 3, the local news stories, the lexical item *child* occurs only 25 times, and in 12 of these instances it is as the kind of modifier found so frequently in the national headlines, particularly in the phrases 'child sex (abuse)' and 'child pornography'. Children (named using a variety of referring expressions) also feature as affected by disruption to normal events or procedures and as the victims of human action, as in the reports of children left 'in squalor' while their parents went on holiday, the theft of a 4-year-old's toys, and the theft of computers bought for a school by community fund-raising. They can also be the casualties of accident, illness and natural disasters, as in a plea for bone marrow donors for children and an item reporting children 'at risk' in an unsafe play area.

## 1.3   Children as beneficiaries

The obverse of the naming of practices which affect children in the negative way discussed above is the incidence of *child* linked with other nouns to make a phrase denoting children's protection and well-being. It is in this semantic sense that I intend the term 'beneficiary', although there are also in this section examples of *children* occurring as 'beneficiary' in the (related) sense in which it is used in functional grammar, to express the role of the participant in a process traditionally labelled the 'indirect object'. And it is also striking how frequently in these texts *children* is linked to a process by a preposition, functioning as part of an 'adjunct' to or 'circumstance' of the main action. Examples where this relationship is clearly negative for the child were included in the previous section; neutral or positive instances are discussed here.

The most frequent noun phrases including *child* as the modifier of a noun denoting a positive enterprise in Data Set 1, the headlines corpus, are 'child benefit' (6) and 'child care' (6), although – consistent with the principle of negativity in newsworthiness – both are sometimes modifiers of a further noun denoting a threat to the enterprise, as in 'child benefit cut' and 'child care crisis'. 'Child support' occurs five times, 'child agency' twice, and 'child welfare', 'child guidance' (in 'child guidance clinic') and 'child safety' (in 'Child Safety Week'), once each. Agents directing their efforts towards children in general are represented in the phrases 'child carers' (2) and 'child psychologist' (1). Instances like this, of *child* in phrases denoting care and protection, amount to 14.5 per cent of the total.

*Children* in the plural can also be beneficiaries of processes, as for example in this headline, in which the actor is a country personified: 'A nation takes to the streets to protect its children.' This metaphorical use of 'a nation' suggests a similarity between the smaller unit of the family, divided into the vulnerable younger generation and the protecting adults, and the meta unit of the nation, an image found again in 'Israel seeks lost children of Yemen exodus' (where *children* is the goal of the process).

In addition, I found a high proportion, common to all the data sets, of prepositional phrases ending in *children*. It is found in five of the headlines in Data Set 1 which lack finite verbs, including 'misadventure verdict *on* beach children', or the letter headed 'slowing down *for* children'. In another six, things are done 'for' and 'to' children, such as 'provide warmth and security for', 'seeks truth for', [a book which] 'will appeal to', and so on. The local news stories (Data Set 3) were tagged so that all the referring expressions for children could be identified ('pupils' and '10-year-olds', for example, as well as 'children'), and the following lines from the concordance of these expressions illustrate the pattern of prepositional phrases. The code <CN> precedes each nominal group referring to children. (Other codes tag the components of the text, such as the headline and the 'lead', or opening paragraph.)

1. for

```
80 d has so far raised more than £1 million for <CN> children in the area. Once you
81   the school's budget is effectively used for <CN> pupils up to seven, at Key
82 's good provision and effective teaching for <CN> pupils with special educational
```

```
83      <Head 1> 10p pledges are rolling in for <CN> the children </ Head 1> <Lead>
84 p to consider a national tracking system for <CN> children transferring schools.
85 o build up as many computers as possible for <CN> the children." The computer was
86 test drummer has been searching Coventry for <CN> the stars of the future to
87                        <Head 1> Tags for <CN> young offenders 'will be
```

## 2. to

```
205 a Kerr, of Tesco, hands over the computer to <CN> Alderman Harris pupils <C>
207 d 1> <Head 2> Awareness message to go out to <CN> all midlands 10-year-olds </
208   cash will be spent giving a helping hand to <CN> sick and disadvantaged
209 and a dance and drama group which is open to <CN> all children. "They're looking
210 o 1 5 are acting as "Valued Youth Tutors" to <CN> primary school youngsters. It
211 ng a "secret political agenda" to push on to <CN> youngsters. Cllr Crookes said:
212  erned that shops may be selling fireworks to <CN> minors are encouraged to call
```

## 3. with

```
231 a or hypersensitivity. "We tend to work with <CN> kids who are struggling for
232 s programme for the teenagers' sessions with <CN> younger pupils. They can get
233   difficulties and teach them how to work with <CN> their children. It will help
234   the Midlands yesterday after a holiday with <CN> the Duchess of York's
235 e: Author Andrew Davies discusses books with <CN> pupils at Stoke Primary School
236  and Nuneaton's Marion Hays will appear with <CN> young Keighley actors <C> Emma
237  Michael Brennand-Wood has been working with <CN> pupils at Milby Primary School
```

Given the arresting headlines in the national newspapers (Data Set 2) about the boy who was reported to have 'closed' his school, we might expect in the stories a catalogue of actions carried out by this 10-year-old, but this is not in fact the case: the majority of references to the boy report things done to and for him. In the composite text of the eight news reports, noun phrases denoting the boy signify most often the participant affected by the action of the clause. The verbs in these clauses mostly reflect the conventional relations between a child and the adults in the institution of the school, becoming newsworthy where this process is disturbed. So active verbs used include 'taught', 'tutor', 'took' (in the same sense), 'look after' and 'supervise', and also 'declined to teach', 'refused to teach', 'had gone back on a promise to teach', 'is refusing to accept . . . back into normal classes'. The interference with the teaching relationship which puts the child 'at the centre of the dispute' (*Daily Mail*) is further depicted in verbs such as 'expel', 'ban', 'exclude', 'refused to have . . . in their classes', 'moved to another school' (in the context of a conditional construction denoting what some of the adults involved wanted to happen). One report quotes the chairwoman of governors as saying she did not think it was 'a good idea to *criminalise* a 10-year-old boy by teaching him in isolation' (*The Guardian*, emphasis added). A large proportion of noun phrases denoting this child, moreover, are embedded in prepositional phrases, reporting the 'row', 'dispute' or 'battle' '*over*' him, and 'provision *for*' him, 'a supply teacher *for*' him, and 'money being spent *on*' him.

Matters to do with schooling and education are prominent in the local news stories analysed, 15 of which I categorized as concerned with legislation, systems or procedures, such as pupils' performance in national educational tests, and the launch of a comic as part of drugs education. Classifying the roles played by children in the stories, the largest category is as recipient(s) of something, or affected by others – for example, in the context of suggestions about changes to the primary school curriculum, a report of a celebrity's visit to a school, and an item on why children should be vaccinated. The combined totals for the passive roles of 'recipient', 'victim', 'casualty', 'witness' and 'bystander', at 46, significantly outnumber the more active roles of 'achiever' and 'perpetrator', at 17.

Another construction which represents children as beneficiaries involves the possessive -s, in phrases such as 'children's books', 'children's tv', 'a children's movie', which are found in Data Set 1. That this construction is less an indication of ownership than of an enterprise directed towards children, cultural productions for which children are the audience, is suggested by the alternative 'Books *for* children', a regular feature in *The Independent*. A similar meaning of -s applies to the phrase 'children's homes', as homes provided *for* children. 'Children's toys' is interpretable either as toys belonging *to* children or as toys produced *for* children. In context, the headline in which it occurs is about these artefacts being brought by mourners to the site of a bomb which killed 168 people in Oklahoma, 19 of them children. These toys are symbols which represent children's culture, irrespective of whether they have belonged to any specific child.

Instances in the headline sample of *children* occurring in constructions about children's culture often feature someone or something else having an effect on them. Two examples are: 'End-of-year activities send children into an adrenalin-fuelled frenzy . . .'; and, over an article about Disney: '. . . the Mouse has been keeping children happy for decades. Now at least 16 million parents want their kids protected.' There are hints in these examples of some of the tensions in 'children's culture', signalled in the second example by the resurfacing of the protection theme. Children can be 'kept happy' but also 'sent into a . . . frenzy', and what 'keeps them happy' may also be doing them harm. In this context, it is also worth noting the construction, found in the headline data, where *child* modifies nouns like 'licences' (1) or 'jails' (1), arrangements which serve to restrict children's potential as social actors.

## 1.4   Children as social actors

In much of the data considered so far, references to a 'child' or 'children' denote those affected by an event or process rather than an agent causing events to happen. There is, however, a repeated noun phrase structure in which 'child' modifies a succeeding noun to make it clear that the actor involved is a child. What seems to be operating here is something analogous to the modification with a sex category of nouns denoting typically 'gendered' occupations ('lawyer', 'nurse'), to produce 'woman prime minister' or 'male nursery teacher'. The gratuitous use of such modifiers is criticized by various writers (for example, Miller and Swift 1989), and its effect is well summarized by Simpson (1993: 172): 'The ways in which referring expressions are deployed asymmetrically to designate men and women is another index of a symbolic order in which "male" constitutes the norm and "female" a deviation from that norm.' (See also Hoey 1996.) However, having said this, it must be conceded that, given the news value of unexpectedness or novelty (Bell 1991), a person doing something which is predominantly the preserve of the opposite sex may itself constitute the newsworthiness of the item. (Simpson, 1993, discusses a headline reporting the conviction of a 'woman poacher' as one such example.)

Considering how *child* is used as the modifier of a noun denoting 'type of actor', we might say that the aspect of the 'symbolic order' of news discourse under discussion here is an assumption that 'adult' constitutes the norm and 'child' a deviation from that norm; hence, 'child shoppers' (which occurs once in Data Set 1), with the implication that 'shoppers' are normally adults.[3] There are some asymmetries in these naming practices. *Woman* (noun) seems to pair with *male* (adjective) in this kind of modification ('woman doctor'/ 'male nurse'). There is the option of *female* in the sex-category system, but no age-specific adjective to denote *child*. The two adjectives formed from *child* in English – *childish* and *childlike* – both carry connotations of the archetypical (or perhaps stereotypical) characteristics of children relative to adults, and are more analogous to *feminine* and *masculine* than to *female* and *male*. This point is explored further in Chapter 3.

There are 20 instances in Data Set 1 of *child* used as this kind of modifier, of which 13 are in the phrase 'child bride(s)'. This phrase is an indication of the fuzzy edges of the category 'child', as discussed above. In one sense, it is a contradiction in terms, since, within the laws of this country, to be a 'bride' is, by definition, to be in a category of those considered adult enough to marry (although the different ages of majority for consenting same-sex and opposite-sex acts, for marrying with and without parental consent, for voting and so on are an indication that there is no clear consensus about when one arrives at adulthood). The story associated with most of these headlines concerns a 13-year-old who married in Turkey, and of course the state-sanctioned beliefs about the age at which people leave childhood are very varied in different countries around the world – and have varied at different points in history (see Stainton Rogers and Stainton Rogers 1992). This provides further evidence that the practice of assigning people to age-related categories, and its realization in language, are not without problems.

Another example of a group of nouns where *child* modifies an occupation to newsworthy effect is 'child pilot crash plane'. The headline is about the claim that the plane which crashed was overloaded, the pilot at the time being a child. One other noun phrase of this type is worthy of attention: 'child spies' in 'call for child spies to enforce smoking law'. The construction 'call for' is an indication that these children are not yet active in the proposed role, and that whoever is making the call is unlikely to be a child, but the headline is unusual in denoting a situation in which children would have some power to affect events by their own actions (albeit actions to enforce age-related proscriptions on what members of their own social group can do!).

In Data Set 1, those instances where the word *child* stands alone to denote an active 'newsmaker' number only two – once in a clause of which *child* is the subject ('child recants abuse lies') and once in a headline about damages awarded to a teacher 'injured by child', where *child* features as the agent in a passive clause. Added to these are two instances where the headline indicates that a child has been consulted as a source of information. Each names a (different) journalist and continues: 'talks to (a) parent and child about . . .'. The topics are drugs and truancy.

The examples of *children* actively doing things in Data Set 1 are similarly limited. The two most definitive actions taken by children are represented in two of the headlines: 'children died . . .' and 'children disappeared . . .'. (The children in this latter story were later found to have drowned.) In neither case was the action voluntary and in both it resulted in death for the children concerned. There are, incidentally, no instances in the sample of an action carried out '*by* children' where 'children' is the agent of a verb in the passive voice.

One process in which children in this sample of headlines engage is to 'arrive', in the fundamental sense of 'be born'. The main topic of the headline in which this example occurs is women's working lives, with the subordinate clause 'when children arrive' serving as a temporal adjunct to the second main clause, 'they ["single women"] still make the sacrifices'. This formulation both links women conceptually with their offspring, in the juxtaposition of the two, but it also distinguishes the 'women' from the 'children', in that the former are not represented explicitly as responsible for the latter – consequently, in this particular context, children can be said autonomously to 'arrive'. In another example, 'children' occurs modified by 'adopted', making possible the ambiguity already identified as to whether the term means 'young human being' or (potentially adult) 'offspring'. The process represented is 'decide to trace their natural mothers', so although it does refer to an active mental process, making a decision, it is something that children under a certain age cannot legally do.

Children's participation in the wider cultural world is represented in a headline which announces that 'children are now as label-conscious as their parents', while another includes the similar phrase 'fashion-conscious children'. Why should such a phenomenon be newsworthy? Children are meant to be socialized into the ways of the world at large, and yet some of those ways are intrinsically unsuitable for them *as children*. Behaviour connected with sexuality is obviously a very sensitive area in relation to the childhood phase of one's biography (see, for example, Corteen and Scraton 1997; Scott et al. 1998; Stainton Rogers and Stainton Rogers 1992 esp. ch. 10), and 'fashion' is arguably concerned at least partly with the semiotics of sexuality. Children may have only limited awareness of this, perhaps, but the connections are sufficiently disturbing to generate public concern about child contestants in beauty contests, child photographic models posed in particular ways – and children taking an active interest in fashion.

Finally, *children* are actors in a story about a voluntary community Saturday school, whose headline contrasts 'white' children who 'take the day off' and 'black children' who 'are back at school today – and getting results'. This headline offers a glimpse of the obverse of the negative connotations of 'child labour', a phrase which implies both exploitation and an inappropriate deployment of children's time. We are clearly right to be disquieted by the idea of 'child labour', but as James et al. (1998) point out, the distinction between 'child labour' and 'child work' is context-dependent and often more moral than analytical. Children used to be involved in agricultural work in pre-industrial times and in a wide range of jobs in early industrial societies. It is easy in contemporary, Western commentaries on childhood to ignore or repress 'the fact that most of the world's children work' (Burman 1994: 60). If this idea, which conflicts with the stereotype of children as people who play, is offensive, might it not be the case that '[i]nstead of seeking to protect children from the awfulness of adult labour, we should make that labour less awful for everyone' (Archard 1993: 47)? The work children do is typically marginal, associated with low pay and low status (James et al. 1998). It can also be invisible and/or emotional labour, as women's work has often been (Leonard 1990). As Hood-Williams (1990: 161) puts it, '[i]t is *affectual* work. . . . Like much of the Western economy it seems that many children have shifted into the service sector.' And children may be seen as undertaking unpaid 'work' by attending school (Corsaro 1997; Qvortrup et al. 1994; Stainton Rogers and Stainton Rogers 1992). As James et al. (1998: 119) observe, '. . . what children do at school conforms to any definition of work which extends beyond paid employment'. In the school-related headline cited, the expressions 'take the day off' and 'get results' do help to suggest the 'world of work' where, for example, some companies use more productive working practices than others, so that childly status becomes less salient in this context.

Another example of this theme is found in Data Set 3, where a report about the impressive results of an OFSTED (Office for Standards in Education) inspection explicitly draws an analogy between workers' productivity in the industrial sector and teachers' work with pupils. This is the opening of a report in the *Birmingham Post* on 19 November 1996:

> There would be bonuses all round and drinks in the boardroom if a factory more than doubled the quality of its output in a year.
> So what, then, do staff and the 241 four to 11-year-olds at Birmingham's Welsh House Farm junior and infant school deserve?

Several of the local news stories which report on schools' successes and failings in inspections by OFSTED, and in standardized national tests, draw on a discourse which is also to be found in recent educational policy documents (see Sealey 1994, 1997). Children play an ambiguous role here. On the one hand, they are crucial actors in that their progress as learners, particularly in literacy and numeracy, is the focal point of measurement and has significant consequences for the institution and the adults who work in it, as well as for local government officials, national politicians, and ultimately the electorate (is the government's educational policy working?). On the other hand, it is rarely the children who are held to account for their learning – at least not in this discourse – which is why texts which draw on this representation of the schooling process can imply a rather passive role for pupils. For example, a story in the *Birmingham Post* quotes a government politician: '. . . Education Minister Mrs Cheryl Gillan said the "encouraging" results confirmed that 11-year-olds were doing better as teachers built on the first year of tests.' The role of the pupils is ambiguous in this sentence: although the children are described as 'doing better', the final clause restores 'teachers' as agents of the more active process of 'building'.

In relation to Data Set 2, as I have explained, the boy is represented in the actual stories as a less active protagonist than might be expected from headlines such as 'One boy closes a school' (*The Express*). The child's role in the relations between him and the school is represented in the following verbs of which he is the subject: 'returned to lessons', 'returned from the half-term break', 'arrived with his mother'. The dramatic significance of this in the context of the story is suggested in some accounts by reference to the fact that the chairwoman of governors went with him. *The Guardian* reported that she 'accompanied' him, but the *Daily Mirror* and *The Express* both report the criticism directed at her by a union leader for '"marching" the boy to school'. This expression warrants attention. The power struggle between the school's teachers – backed by their union – and its governors is a significant strand in the story, and the image evoked of the chair of governors 'marching' towards the school emphasizes the 'battle' metaphor which is found in these reports. (Lexical items from the eight reports which contribute to this metaphor include: 'attack', 'battle', 'confrontation', 'show-down', 'explosive situation', 'clashed', 'drafted in', 'held to ransom', 'siding with', 'last-ditch appeal', 'militancy', 'impasse', 'keep the peace'.) At the same time, the use of 'march' as a transitive verb, with the child as direct object, connotes more Shakespeare's 'whining schoolboy... creeping like snail unwillingly to school' than a powerful fellow combatant.

Of course, as the attention-catching headlines suggest, this child had presumably done *something* to warrant the news coverage. With the exception of the headlines, only one report unequivocally attributes the boy with agency in the 'crisis' which the story depicts. *The Sun* reports that he 'triggered a showdown when he turned up for lessons again yesterday and spent the day in the headmaster's office'. Even here, however, the subordinate clause modifies the suggestion that the 'showdown' was within the child's control, with the colloquial and slightly pejorative verb phrase 'turned up' equivalent to 'return' and 'attend' as the referent for his attested action.

Before the events of this day's news, however, the boy had been 'accused of attacking a teacher and wielding a baseball bat in the playground' (*Daily Mirror*). A passive construction like this is used in most versions of what he is said to have done, framed by 'accused', as here, or in a construction such as 'staff...claim...' or 'teachers...say...'. The reporting of his alleged actions, always as 'claims', is one way in which his undesirability is represented. In addition, he is sometimes labelled as having intrinsically negative characteristics. The claim that he *is* an 'unteachable bully' is usually in quotation marks, clearly distancing the report from specific protagonists' points of view. 'Unteachable' is an example of an adjective formed from a verb by means of the suffix '-able'. Bolinger (1980) suggests that this is a linguistic means of transferring responsibility from the one who does the action (in this case the teacher) to the goal of the action (in this case the pupil). With considerable sympathy for teachers (I have been one myself), I can appreciate the impulse to assign 'teachability' to pupils rather than 'ability to teach' to teachers, but I would argue that this capacity is always an emergent product of the interaction between both parties (as well as the broader context) rather than a fixed characteristic of either one.

There are perhaps two pressures on the journalist reporting such a story in relation to representing this social actor. Stylistically, it is dull to repeat either the name or a noun phrase each time this individual is referred to, so variants must be found. In addition, the use of condensed noun phrases can connote an attitude towards the person and his actions. The wide variety of referring expressions for this boy which are used across these eight reports is arguably an instance of what Fowler (1991) calls 'over-lexicalization', 'the existence of an excess of quasi-synonymous terms for entities and ideas that are a particular preoccupation or problem in the culture's discourse' (p. 85). Following a basic convention of news reporting, the first identification of the child in each report is by FN (First Name) + LN (Last Name), although some reports attach modifiers, some more emotive than others: 'FN + LN, 10' (*The Daily Telegraph*), 'pupil FN + LN' (*Daily Mail*), 'the unruly pupil FN + LN' (*The Guardian*), 'tearaway FN + LN' (*Daily Mirror*), 'ten-year-old yob FN + LN' (*The Sun*). Subsequent mentions of the boy by name use FN only, a convention which could be interpreted in several ways. The other protagonists are referred to first by the same convention (FN + LN), and thereafter by Title + LN. The use of FN alone can carry connotations of familiarity or even solidarity, but, given the conventions of English address terms, it is difficult to imagine an alternative in this case: LN alone would imply disrespect and perhaps also suggest adult status, while Title + LN would suggest a degree of respect that would probably appear ironic in the circumstances. (Child members of the royal family and aristocracy, as an 'elite' group, are an exception to the convention that children are not afforded titles.) The most neutral referring expression is 'the boy', and near synonyms are 'the youngster' and 'the lad'. Other noun phrases include: 'a disruptive 10-year-old boy', 'an unruly 10-year-old boy', 'a disruptive pupil', 'rebel FN', 'twice-expelled FN'.

Some of the reports quote not only the staff who claim he has these negative qualities, but also the chair of governors who is reported as claiming to 'speak up' for children. She is quoted as saying, 'The lad has done magnificently' (*The Guardian*) and alluding to 'his improved behavioural record' (*The Daily Telegraph*) which are unusual instances of his being represented as having taken an active part in the events, and as being something other than a fixed quantity. Many of the other referring expressions imply a static significance for two attributes: being anti-social and being 10 years old.

Local newspapers provide more scope for children to be active agents than do the stories valued by national news media. This is usually in a limited way – they are no more involved in local government than in national politics, but the news value of 'relevance' ('effect on the audience's own lives', Bell 1991) can encompass more localized events, while 'personalization' (ibid.) creates an opening for the kind of 'human interest' stories that are to be found among the texts in Data Set 3. Here children are represented as taking a wider range of roles in processes of various kinds, and featuring more frequently as achievers than as perpetrators of misconduct.

Children do feature in the local news stories as wrong-doers of various kinds, but it should be pointed out that the expressions that label them as such are all found in only four of the 51 stories I analysed. One of these, comparatively lengthy at over 500 words, concerns a suggestion that young offenders should wear electronic tags, and both the offending and the youth of those who would be affected are foregrounded in the story, whose lead sentence is:

A Government plan which could see offenders as young as ten wearing electronic tags yesterday prompted a warning from penal reform campaigners that juveniles would view them as 'trophies'.

(*Birmingham Post*, 22.11.96)

The construction 'offenders as young as ten' is a means of conveying the significance of the ages at which children are 'these days' found to be engaged in activities which are expected to be done only by adults, or at least older 'young people'. The expression also illustrates the point that even the apparently neutral classification of social actors by chronological age represents an 'angle of telling'. Being 10 has different salience depending on the context: to be 'as young as ten' and 'already' have a criminal past is one thing; to be 'as old as ten' (unattested) and 'still' unable to read has a different social significance. It is in this text that other expressions are used to denote young offenders, including 'juveniles'[4] and 'miscreants'.

Another story, about measures to reduce truancy, deploys the referring expressions 'truants' and 'stay-aways'. The idea that attendance at school is compulsory is so familiar to us that it is not necessarily obvious how the very term 'truancy' implies a conflict of interest between what some children might want and what adults want for them.[5] At one level, this subversion of adult priorities is a prototypical childly activity, denoted by a wide range of local dialect terms useful for anti-authoritarian activity (Opie and Opie 1959). One of these, 'wagging', is alluded to in the article. Another formulation, however, presents 'truancy' as a phenomenon (contrasted with 'attendance'), a process carried out by 'stay-aways', who 'are harming the education of other youngsters as well as their own'. In this text, these wrong-doers are surrounded by a number of perspectival expressions: 'chase', 'warn', 'targeting', 'on their tails', 'problems'.

'Problem primary children' feature in another text about 'rehabilitation', while the final source of more negative terms for children is in a seasonal story about the dangers of irresponsible actions with fireworks. One reference to children in this story suggests an image of unruly groups, 'gangs of children'. While members of 'gangs' may use the term positively ('Do you want to be in my gang?'), its use to denote social groups in news discourse is predominantly pejorative. The other referring term here is 'pranksters', suggesting an anti-social activity which is perhaps not too serious. One sentence in this report implies, unusually, a role for children in decision-making and acting responsibly: 'Police say there have been no reports of injuries so far but children, as well as the people who sell the fireworks, had to realize the dangers.'

There is a set of terms for children who, normatively, are too young to be involved in adult activities, which is complementary to the terms for wrong-doers. The two expressions found in these texts which fall into this category are 'minors' and 'under-age children', relating in these instances to the sale of fireworks and to sexual abuse, but other contexts are possible: alcohol consumption, watching certain films, smoking, driving and so on.

The referring expressions for children who feature in these stories because of their achievements or involvement in a performance sometimes relate in specific terms to what they have done to make the news. Phrases include 'drummer boys – and girls' and 'the winners', and three expressions which highlight the participants' youth: 'young helpers', 'young Keighley actors FN + LN, FN + LN' and 'the stars of the future', a phrase which illustrates 'the socialisation paradigm' (Scott et al. 1998: 694), 'in which children as future adults, rather than the lives of children in the present, is the main issue'.

Many of the names are included in captions to the pictures which accompany the text of the story. I was struck in these texts by the way in which many of the non-negative items about children do include pictures of them, usually identified precisely in the caption by FN + LN and often ages as well. This practice is consistent with a function assumed by local newspapers of alluding to, and perhaps helping to construct, the idea of a local community which includes readers in its membership and is of interest to them as content. Children can feature as part of 'human interest' in this context in the not unreasonable assumption that many readers know at first hand the locations, schools and, sometimes, the families included in stories. Naming expressions are often reduced to FN only, which enhances the sense of familiarity between text and reader, recalling the kind of community in which residents know the local children by name and watch out for them, collectively.

In this context, children are reported to have done such things as raising funds for charity and achieving outstanding academic results (a different focus from the accountability of inspection results, one concerned more with a specific child as an individual). Another story explicitly includes a declaration that children's achievements should be publicized. In the context of a report about a primary school where a remembrance day service had been organized:

> A school spokesman said: '. . . In view of the adverse publicity schoolchildren often receive, we would like to try to redress this.
>
> 'We want people to know of the sensitive and understanding way our nine-and 10-year-olds have tackled the subject of Remembrance Day, and their concepts of war and its effects.'
>
> (*Coventry Evening Telegraph* 4.11.96)

Thus children can sometimes – if rarely – be seen to feature as a resource for local news stories by dint of their positive role in the community, not only in their capacity as citizens of the future but also as current social actors.

## 1.5  Summary and conclusions

This chapter has introduced a number of themes about the representation of children in language, taking as its data three kinds of newspaper texts: headlines in one 'up-market' newspaper, national coverage of a specific story which is linked with more general concerns about unruly children, and a number of stories in local newspapers in which children are depicted in more varied ways. Although newspapers are texts – and commodities – with their own specific values and priorities, they draw on and reflect patterns found in discourses associated with other spheres of social life, such as the legal and education systems, for example, and they are therefore a useful starting point for exploring the representations in language of various social groups. It was found that the selection of stories for analysis raised questions about who is and who is not included in the category 'child' in contemporary (English) English, and, as the focus of the book as a whole is children in middle childhood, this chapter and the next concentrate on language about children of roughly 4 to 11 years of age.

The first theme discussed was 'children in danger', which was explored at different linguistic levels. In compact noun phrases it was found that *child* frequently functions as a modifier of *abuse* and other words denoting harm, while *children* are frequently victims, denoted syntactically as the object (or goal) of negative processes.

It was found that, whether the processes denoted are harmful or beneficial, *child* and *children* often occupy similar positions in the phrase and clause: *child abuse* can be compared with *child care*, and *risk to children* with *books for children*. Thus discussion of the second theme of this chapter, children as 'beneficiaries', revealed a pattern of children again depicted in comparatively passive roles.

The third theme considered in this chapter was children being active in the social world, and it was recognized that representations of children in this role are bound to be limited, particularly in national newspapers. It emerged that in the story featuring a 10-year-old 'closing' his school, it was in fact predominantly the actions of adults that were represented as having significant effects on events. Children do sometimes feature as wrong-doers in these texts, and there are some expressions particularly associated with child-perpetrated offences, such as 'truancy' and 'pranks'. It was also found, however, that in the local news stories in particular children may be depicted as sources of 'positive news'. In this respect, children can have a symbolic significance, representing hope and optimism, and it is the cultural *idea* of the child that is the focus of the next chapter.

## Notes

1. I recognize the importance of other semiotic systems in the construction of meanings in texts, especially newspapers, but as my focus in this book is specifically on *linguistic* issues, I have not attempted to explore the significance in the texts of visual images, layout, typography, etc.

2. Because 'child language' is so often taken to refer to the period of initial acquisition and development, with an emphasis on the first five years of life, it is important to make it clear here that this aspect of 'child language' is not the main, nor even a very significant, concern of the present volume.

3. It is interesting that the noun *child* used in this way does not take a plural morpheme, and is thus more analogous to 'lady doctors' than to 'women priests'. This is a subtle distinction but perhaps the singular form connotes more the generic category than the actual people in this position.

4. At the time of writing, reforms to some of the terms used in the justice system are being introduced, so that 'child' is likely, eventually, to replace 'minor' and 'infant' in legal discourse.

5. In January 1999, the abduction of two primary school pupils coincided with the announcement of new government guidelines on truancy. These contained a recommendation that parents should be contacted by schools whenever children fail to arrive. As Goldson (1997: 27) observes '. . . children are objects for both care and control and what society does *to* them is profoundly confused with what society does *for* them'.

# 2

# Children in the News (2): The Idea of the Child

*... children, like adults, live in present, concretely historical, and open-ended time ... Children's interactions are not preparation for life; they are life itself.*

(THORNE 1993: 3)

## 2.1 Introduction

One of the most sensational news events in the UK in recent years was the abduction and murder by two 10-year-old boys of a 2-year-old, James Bulger. The fact that not only the victim but also the perpetrators were children provoked extensive comment and debate in the media. There was detailed press and television coverage first of the incident, then of the trial and subsequently of further legal proceedings. In addition, several books were published which sought to explore the issues raised by the case. Morrison (1997), for example, explores in some detail what kind of conception of childhood allows us to make sense of the brutalizing of innocence personified in the 2-year-old victim and, simultaneously, of the capacity of 10-year-old children to commit murder. A recurring theme is the ways in which children are both the same as and different from adults: in their capacities for strongly felt emotions – anger, love, fear; in their sexuality; and in their ability to understand their experience and the consequences of their actions.

This chapter is concerned with the various conceptions of 'the child', and with how these are represented discursively in the same data sets of newspaper texts that were discussed in Chapter 1, together with editorial and opinion columns published in the same newspapers as Data Set 2 on the day of the threatened school closure; I refer to these as Data Set 2a. In this chapter, I focus first on representations of the rapid change, growth and development which characterize the childhood phase of life.

What, if anything, unites the 2-year-old with the 10-year-old? One response is to recognize that children can be thought of as a unitary social group if they are understood *in relation to adults*. So this chapter will also consider point of view, and the way texts which are the product of inter- actions between adults, as producers and as readers, necessarily make use of relations – and distinctions – between adults and children. Children can be perceived as a social presence, an abiding group in the world, despite the equally inescapable fact that every adult was once a child and yet is a child no longer. This leads to a consideration of the symbolic significance of this phase and the way 'childhood' is deployed metaphorically.

## 2.2    Growth, development and change

As was illustrated in Chapter 1, the most fundamental action that children are said to take is to 'arrive', although they have no choice about this. Follow- ing birth, the period of infancy is associated with vulnerability and the need for protection, as has been noted, and yet adult responsibility, paradoxically, involves supporting children as they gradually relinquish their dependency. The identification of any given individual with the particular social group denoted by the word 'children' (except metaphorically, nostalgically or rela- tionally, of which more below) is thus inevitably only temporary. James (1993: 106) expresses this well, highlighting the child's own perspective:

> . . . the changing face of childhood for children . . . means that in a West- ern culture such as Britain, children should act and behave as children in the same moment as they must also learn to leave their childish ways behind them. Similarly, constructions of childhood, oriented towards the past (through nostalgia and sentiment) coexist with those focused on the future (through processes of socialisation and biological maturation) to make the present of childhood a precarious and unstable context.

Children's precise ages are often included in references to them in my data, as are a high proportion of temporal expressions generally, and the links which James notes between 'socialisation and biological maturation' are particularly relevant in the context of schooling. In Data Set 3, 'pupils' is one of the most frequent referring expressions for children, occurring 41 times. In keeping with the discourse of measurement in education men- tioned in Chapter 1, 'pupils' is sometimes modified with specifics: 'pupils in the first five school years', 'primary school pupils', 'pupils of all ages', 'pupils up to seven' and so on. This discourse is often concerned both with 'stand- ards' of expectation of accomplishment, in relation to time – what the child of 7, for example, should know and be able to do, if taught correctly – and also with appropriateness – what is and is not fitting for the 'primary school pupil', in terms of access to knowledge about drugs, sex or politics. For instance, opposing points of view about a proposal to include political education in the curriculum are attributed to two councillors in a story in the *Coventry Evening Telegraph* (5.11.96) with one quoted as saying 'I think you cannot discuss politics early enough. It's based on how people live their lives' while another 'said he did not see how younger children could effectively be taught about politics'.

This preoccupation with ages and stages illustrates Scott et al.'s (1998: 692) claim that 'developmental perspectives remain prominent in everyday thinking as well as in professional and public discourse'. They cite as illustration guidelines issued by the NSPCC on what children can or should be expected to manage on their own at various ages – a practice which obscures differentials in individual children's own experiences.

Texts in the different data sets imply different degrees of agency for children in their own socialization. In Chapter 1 I presented some examples of phrases denoting 'children's culture', as a distinct enterprise, but the culture at large is also theirs to inherit. This looking forward to membership of adult culture is exemplified by a headline in Data Set 1, prompted by a film about teenage sex, which poses the question, 'if parents face the facts and discuss them, does it equip children to make good decisions, or merely to make mistakes?'. A presupposition here is that the parents will initiate the 'discussion', being the people who are in possession of 'the facts'. There are two things which children as social actors can 'make': 'good decisions' and 'mistakes' – both possibilities implicitly projected into the future by the verb 'equip' followed by the infinitive, encapsulating a notion which could be seen as the essence of socialization.

These concerns also feature in Data Set 2a, the editorial and opinion columns in the newspapers which report the threatened school closure. Some of these draw a figurative parallel between moral growth and physical maturation, spiritual 'food' without which children's 'development' is stunted. This is quite explicit in *The Times* editorial: 'It is as wrong to withhold traditional wisdom from the young as it is to withhold any other form of nourishment.' Children are located discursively in a longer time frame than that of their personal biographies. On the one hand, retrospectively, 'traditional wisdom' stretches back into history. Other expressions include 'traditional attitudes . . . the bedrock of decent behaviour' (Shephard, *The Sun*), where the metaphor is of time embodied in the landscape; 'gone are the days' of simple physical punishment. On the other hand is the perspective which looks towards the future, the notion that childhood should be a preparation for later experience: 'preparing young people for adult life' (Shephard, *The Sun*); 'a stake in their joint future' (Daley, *The Daily Telegraph*); 'today's children . . . the coming world' (*The Times*).

In the next chapter I shall consider how children's perspectives are represented in literature written for them, including some commentary from various children's authors, and their reflections on the distinction between adults' and children's responses to messages intended to socialize. It is a children's author who writes, in an informal article about her attitude to her work, that children:

> ... sense at once when we want them to do something because it suits *us*. It's sad to think how much at our mercy children are: ninety per cent of their time we are organizing them and guiding them and making them do things for utilitarian reasons – and then, the remaining ten per cent, likely as not, we are concocting pretexts for getting rid of them.

(Aiken 1977: 176)

She continues provocatively: 'So much of education consists of having inexplicable things done at one for obscure reasons. . . .' Making a similar point, but in the context of an academic review of research perspectives on children's lives, Qvortrup (1994: 8) points out that institutions such as schools are

> [t]ypically . . . analysed from the point of view of [their] socializing or educative capacities or functions as caretakers: do they actually meet the requirements for the schooling of children, or: are we placing our children in secure surroundings when leaving them at schools, kindergartens etc?.

Furthermore, '[i]f schools were to be seen as society's courtesy towards children, we would be at pains to explain why schooling is obligatory' (p. 10).

This potential disjuncture between what adults, or the culture at large, value and wish to hand down to children, and the image of what children may prefer if they are to be 'attracted' towards these things is found in some of the headlines in Data Set 1, including a report on museums, which, it is claimed, 'are in danger of becoming too like theme parks in their attempts to attract children'.

In various ways, then, these examples acknowledge that there is more than one perspective on the world, and it seems possible that another cultural preoccupation, alongside fears for children's safety, is the fear that they may be out of control, improperly socialized. There is a line of argument which can resolve the potential contradiction between children-in-danger and children-as-danger, and this is the belief that if the values of the 'adult world' are themselves corrupt, and if children grow up 'too quickly', the badness of adults will be incorporated into the 'world' of children, who will thus themselves be bad. The obvious conclusion is that adults must therefore take a general moral stand for the good, and this theme runs throughout many of the editorials in Data Set 2a. Expressions denoting this basic relationship between adults and children include: 'inculcate attitudes', 'maintaining discipline', 'how those values could be instilled in kids' hearts and minds', 'preparing young people for adult life', 'passing on a proper frame-work of values', 'nurtured and developed', 'constant, concerned supervision'.

Corsaro (1997) discusses the way in which commentators both deplore outrages committed on child victims, especially middle-class children, and are yet inclined at times to 'blame the victim'. He uses as an example debates in the USA about welfare reforms and the effects on teenage mothers (admittedly an older age-group than is my concern here). He links this double standard to a trend he identifies in American politics, away from communal responsibility and towards individual accountability. Thus, rather than exam-ine the complex and cumulative effects of political and economic strategies on job opportunities and each generation's capacities for self-determination and escape from poverty, it is easier to cite one simple, voluntaristic cause – feckless adolescent self-indulgence. This idea can be set alongside Fowler's (1991) claim that newspapers, particularly the popular press, often personal-ize stories so as to link abstract or complex phenomena with specific human beings. He presumes that the functions of this 'personalization': ' . . . are to promote straightforward feelings of identification, empathy or disapproval; [and] to effect a metonymic simplification of complex historical and institu-tional processes . . .' (p. 15). Davis and Bourhill (1997) also identify, in their discussion of media coverage of the Bulger murder, a tendency to portray 'childhood evil as the enemy within the child' (p. 48).

The depiction of the 10-year-old schoolboy as representative of a more general threat to social order could be read in this light. These ideas, about children in general and the points of view from which they are represented, lead into the next section – children as a social presence.

## 2.3   Children as a social presence

Although newspapers are not explicitly proscribed reading for children, they have many features which presume an adult reader, in the sense that Fair-clough (1989: 49) suggests that all 'mass discourse has built into it a subject position for an ideal subject, and actual viewers or listeners or readers have to negotiate a relationship with the ideal subject'. Another critical linguist (Fowler 1991), no doubt unwittingly, exemplifies the implicit assumption that readers are adult in his discussion of this very issue of newspapers' role in constructing a consensus, positioning readers as of like mind and with shared interests. Among such (falsely) consensual assumptions he includes these: 'everyone can buy shares, choose their children's schools or health care . . .' (p. 50). This example echoes that presented by Simpson (1993), who draws attention to the gender bias in Brian Walden's claims about what 'most people' want: 'a good job, a nice wife, pleasant children, friends and a bit of fun' (p. 159). Both writers expose the androcentrism in statements about 'people' (for which read 'men'), but neither is struck by the implicit exclusion of children: 'everyone' and 'most people' can relate to their 'wives' *and* their 'children' only if they are not members of either of those categories themselves.

In the discussion of notices in public places in the Introduction, I drew attention to texts whose 'ideal reader' is a parent of young children, and several of the headlines in Data Set 1 include this presupposition in the noun phrase 'your child'. These are often above feature articles with concerns such as 'Tired of not getting any sleep because your child is always crying?', or about what to do with 'your child's money' (which, of course, presupposes not only that you, the reader, have a child, but also that this child has money, and that you, the parent, want a good return for it on behalf of your child, will decide about this on behalf of your child, and so on). The most explicit such presuppositions are inherent in the phrase 'your child', which occurs 11 times, and 'your child's' (2). There are also two occurrences of 'my child' and one of 'their child'. As the example 'What is wrong with my child?' illustrates, the perspective from which the reader is encouraged to consider (in this instance) the question of disability is – quite understandably – that of the parent rather than the child. The expressions 'their children' and 'our children', and to a lesser extent 'your children', are also frequently found. These possessives both position the reader as adult, as suggested above, and make use of a construction which can be used to signify ownership. Of course children can routinely speak of 'our mother' and 'my brother', so any such implication is reciprocal. However, without wishing to over-stress its implications, I am reminded of the formulation, criticized by feminist writers, which names women in news stories primarily through their relation-ship to a man, as 'Mr X's wife/girlfriend/mistress', rather than as 'Ms Y' in her own right. The children who 'belong to' celebrities, although not them-selves 'elite' social actors, can make the news by their very existence: three mentions in this data set of the singer Madonna's child (before it was born) fall into this category. In Data Set 3, a number of referring expressions are used for two other celebrity children: 'the Duchess of York's daughters', 'little princesses' and 'Princesses Beatrice and Eugenie', an example of the children of 'elite' social actors being newsworthy – and individuated – be-cause of their relationship to their parents.

Apart from some exceptions like these, children are able to occupy fewer social roles than adults. A single adult individual can be, among other things, a doctor, a wife, an employee, a higher-rate tax-payer, English, British, a vegetarian, a mother, a motorist and so on. Some of these classifications are involuntaristic: we have no say about when and where we will be born, nor into what kind of family; but certain things are much more likely than others to follow from our location in one kind of social group rather than another. The hypothetical occupational profile sketched out here is more likely to belong to an individual born into a family able to support academic success, both financially and culturally, although this is not inevitable. The classifications are also relational: doctors stand in relation to patients, wives to husbands, mothers to sons and daughters, higher-rate to lower-rate tax-payers, and so on. Other social groups to which people belong are partly a matter of personal choice, although what seem on the surface to be purely individual decisions may in practice be constrained by factors beyond our control. Being a vegetarian is easier to accomplish at a time when many people taking that decision create a market for meat-free products in shops and dishes on menus, for example. Becoming a doctor was barely possible for women in the last century, when sex discrimination was overt and institutionally sanctioned. How do these general claims about people's membership of social groups relate to children?

As I have said, relational classifications are fundamental to the category *child* itself, in terms of both age-status and kinship, with no lexical means of distinguishing between them. Children's social standing is ambiguous, given the crucial role of employment in differentiating groups in socio-economic terms. Since children receive no remuneration for their school labour (Qvortrup 1994), they '. . . are accounted for in terms of their parents' economic situation . . . in accordance with criteria that do not characterize their own life conditions' (p. 16). (The changing patterns of employment and changing conception of 'the breadwinner' make this classification even of adults a thorny problem for sociologists and policy-makers.) Nevertheless, children born into poverty will inevitably experience all the negative consequences of poverty.

In respect of some social categories, children are both included and excluded. Some of the headlines from Data Set 1 represent nations as claiming ownership of 'their children': 'A nation takes to the streets to protect its children'; 'as a nation, we seem to have lost confidence in our ability to teach, protect or set an example to our children'. This linguistic move denotes children as *owned by* nations, in which case they cannot simultaneously be members of the nation, owning themselves, but must be separate from it, there to be owned.

Thus children are sometimes excluded from the group which implicitly constitutes Us, the community of readers who share the values and perspective of the newspaper we read. One of the ways we all make sense of the world is by classifying our experience of it, and several writers have described the 'schemas' and 'scripts' which we employ to place both new experiences and new texts within an existing mental framework: the alternative would be an impossibly laborious 'starting from scratch' throughout every day. In terms of social issues in the news, such pre-existing frameworks often include notions of in-groups, an Us to which we as readers feel we belong, people with whom we identify, contrasted with out-groups, a Them, a group against which We, the included readers, contrast our values and behaviour. (This is not a mechanistic process, oppositional readings are possible, and reader-identifications are not entirely predictable. All these issues will be addressed further in Chapter 5.)

In relation to my theme of children in news discourse, two such contrastive groupings are particularly relevant in relation to the texts which comprise Data Sets 2 and 2a. One pair is obviously children as opposed to adults; the other pair opposes the socially responsible with the irresponsible, the latter group ranging from the feckless to the incorrigible criminal.

The distinctiveness of childly status is highlighted in the texts concerned with the school closure incident, and with the teaching of morality in schools. For example, the boy 'at the centre' of the story is depicted as childly in referring expressions such as 'little terror' (caption to picture in *The Sun*), and 'tearaway'. Although perhaps associated more with adolescents, this noun is strongly suggestive of young people and their tendency to break with existing traditions, conventions and rules. In the editorial in *The Sun*, he is described as 'one unruly 10-year-old', and the application of the adjective 'unruly' contains the idea that children are usually 'ruled', so it is still a childly thing to be '*unruly*'. The *Daily Mirror* editorial states that he is *not* 'just a cheeky young lad', all the lexical words in this noun phrase connoting childliness. The implicit proposition is that there are children – 'lads' – who are prone to being 'cheeky', but that this individual crosses a line into behaviour which is beyond childly norms. Scott et al. (1998: 697) have suggested that, for the media, 'one way of dealing with the unruly child, with the spectre of the demonic child, is to declare that child not a child'. This boy is referred to as 'a little thug' at the end of the *Daily Mirror* editorial, and a 'thug' is rarely a child, although 'little' achieves a link between serious misdemeanour and being a child; 'little' can also be used pejoratively of adults to metaphorically diminish their status.[1]

The other conceptual opposition, which cuts across that between children and adults, divides Us from Them as groups of rule-and-law-abiders rather than rule/law-disregarders. The 10-year-old in the news stories is represented as belonging to both out-groups, children and the 'unruly', a 'rebel'. Several of the texts in this group deploy inclusive 'we' expressions which shore up consensus and suggest ways in which the children of out-groups can be saved from 'mak[ing] the mistakes that their own parents made' (Daley, *The Daily Telegraph*). Shephard (a government minister at the time) in *The Sun* obviously has a political interest in depicting a united society, and uses several expressions consistent with it: 'the whole nation has been rocked by a recent spate of tragedies' (which uses personification of an abstract entity); 'shocked us all', 'our schools', 'all children', 'agreed by society', 'the kind of society we all want to live in'. Daley in *The Daily Telegraph* also writes about 'the state school system as a whole' and invokes 'the public's wishes'. Children, or the implicitly homogeneous group 'the young' (*The Times*), can be kept within this protected 'Us', with the vigilance described. Or they may, if not reined in, go to the bad. The metaphorical 'line' between the two groups is alluded to in *The Sun*; children were once physically punished if they 'stepped out of line'. In the *Daily Mirror*, the teachers are depicted as holding a line 'against violent pupils' – they 'insist', 'are determined' and 'are desperate'. Shephard (clearly not standing on quite the same line as striking teachers), says 'we must take a stand for the kind of society we all want to live in', while *The Times* asserts, again using a territorial, spatial metaphor, that 'power comes from a strong moral hinterland'. Children, so the argument goes, may be either included within this cordon, or positioned beyond it. According to *The Sun*, '. . . fine words won't make a scrap of difference to rowdy or violent pupils'. In depicting such an out-group from among schoolchildren, this newspaper is being consistent with a pattern in its representation of social conflict, noted by other researchers (Clark 1992; Fowler 1991), which isolates and to varying extents demonizes certain people. Daley's view is more optimistic: children who 'do not live in traditional families', attending schools 'serving the sink council estates of which we hear so much' can, with moral training, be liberated, if we (society in general) were to return to the 'belief that the purpose of education was to free children from the disadvantages of their backgrounds'. As Scott et al. (1998: 697) point out, '[i]t is interesting to note that childhood is the only form of social subordination equated with a state of freedom'.

Again, extrapolating from the discourse represented in these particular texts, children can be members of either the in-group, Us, or the out-group, Them, but these are options for the future. At present, with notable exceptions such as news-making trouble-makers, they are in the childly group of not-adults, not-Us, represented for the most part as having little capacity for agency in either direction.[2]

A further way in which children can be represented as a social presence is consistent with their role as the beneficiaries of protection, services and facilities, which I discussed in Chapter 1. In this capacity, children may be depicted as a group about which things are and should be done: hence the prepositional phrases identified in Section 1.3. Newspapers, and everyday discussions, routinely classify people into such groups – 'the poor', 'the sick', 'the elderly', 'the unemployed', 'immigrants' and so on – which are depicted in this way, as in need of social and political services and attention, and this may be done with varying degrees of benignity, anxiety or hostility. Fowler (1991) discusses how even news reports which aim to be critical of inadequate attention for a particular group are constrained by the available discursive resources. Hence a story he reviews about whether waiting lists for National Health Service treatment were unacceptably long. Fowler's point is that even the journalist intending to expose the suffering of the patients represented the issue in terms which depersonalized patients and reproduced the practice of privileging the voices of those in authority – in this case doctors and politicians. In Data Set 2, where almost all the actions which comprise the story as reported are taken by adults, many of these events are constituted by the speech acts of significant actors (cf. Bell 1991; Fowler 1991). In the social world of 'institutional facts' (Searle 1995), the news is often statements indicating the decisions of politicians, for example, or of 'captains of industry'; here it is those responsible for educational processes. Clearly the 'voices' heard in this story are not those of children (emphasis added in all examples which follow):

1. There is a verbal claim about the boy's conduct: 'a boy they [his teachers] *accuse* of being "an unteachable bully"' (*The Daily Telegraph*).
2. The teachers' position is represented via a verbal act: '*threatened* to strike' (*The Independent*), '*refused* to teach' (*Daily Mirror*), '*say* they will stop work' (*The Daily Telegraph*).
3. The governors' conclusion that funds for individual tuition are exhausted is another verbal claim: 'governors *say* the budget can no longer stand the £600-a-week cost' (*The Daily Telegraph*), '*announced* their intention to withdraw the funding' (*The Express*).
4. The actual closure of the school is communicated by the head teacher in a letter: '*telling* parents that teachers were walking out . . .' (*Daily Mirror*), also represented orally: 'headmaster [FN + LN] *announced* that he was shutting . . .' (*Daily Mail*).
5. Reports of the negotiations between involved parties – the boy's mother, governors, union officials, local authority officials – use quotatives and vocabulary denoting verbal processes: 'said', 'claimed', 'urged', 'proposed', 'suggestion'. Also, the then secretary of state is reported as having '*called on* the county council to intervene' (*The Guardian*).

In contrast, although hardly surprisingly, the child himself is not reported as having anything to say. Presumably, even if he did, its illocutionary force would not be as significant as that of the pronouncements made by the much more powerful actors whose words are reported, since, as a child, he does not possess credentials as an 'authoritative source' (Bell 1991: 191). A similar pattern is found in Data Set 3, although local newspapers are more likely than the nationals to report the perspectives of less powerful groups. In Data Set 3, although children may be depicted as agents of both mental and verbal processes, their thoughts and words are represented only indirectly. Examples include: '[the] head teacher at the school . . . said: "The children are absolutely sickened by this theft. . . ."'; 'Cllr Edwards said . . . "I can remember going round all the primary schools when I was Lord Mayor and kids asking me if I was the king. . . ."'; 'Heidi's mother said her daughter thoroughly enjoyed her five-day stay . . .'.

Another feature of the discourse which encodes the practice of homogenizing less powerful groups, according to Fowler, is 'impersonality of style' and the use of nominal expressions. In his health service example, '[p]eople and their medical predicaments are encoded in the highly abstract words "case", "wait", "matter" and "list"' (p. 128). The individuals involved are also 'subsumed in an aggregate of people' (p. 129). I was struck in my own Data Set 3 by the high number of quantifying expressions associated with children in the plural, which both illustrates Bell's (1991: 158) claim about the news value of 'facticity' – 'hard news thrives [on] . . . locations, names, sums of money, numbers of all kinds' – and also intensifies the effect of representing children as a group, a 'social presence', regardless of the individuality which, by contrast, typically characterizes the doings of 'elite' social actors. These are some examples:

> 'at least 12 children a year'; 'just 22 per cent of Welsh House Farm's pupils'; 'About 250 youngsters aged from four to 11'; 'Some 340,000 Midlands youngsters'; 'About 40 youngsters'; '58 per cent of 11-year-olds'; '8 per cent of the city's children'; 'a substantial number of children'; 'A lot of children'; 'a small handful of children'; 'all midlands 10-year-olds'; 'Around eight out of ten seven-year-olds'; 'large numbers of young offenders'; 'more than 80 per cent of children with dyslexia'; 'More than 200,000 children in England'; 'thousands of young Britons'; 'up to ten times more children'.

Children can thus be represented as a social group through the use of referring expressions containing measurements and other statistics. Another formulation, found fairly frequently in Data Set 1, is the use of 'the child' as a generic, as in 'Give me the child', a saying attributed to the Jesuits and quoted in a headline over a story about banks seeking to attract young customers. There is a not dissimilar allusion in the headline above a letter: 'Loving parents spare the child.' Despite the apparent specificity conferred by the definite article, the intended meaning is not one individual child, but one child invoked to stand for all. A slightly weaker version of this strategy for naming those who occupy the social category 'child' occurs when the noun is preceded by the indefinite article. Two examples are 'parents' evenings offer little insight into how a child is progressing' and 'is it ever right to expose a child to the media?'. In some cases, the object of interest is something associated with the generic child by possessive -s, as in 'a child's reading ability', 'a child's self-esteem'.

The presupposition is that there are qualities associated with being 'a child' which are relevant to all children. This may indeed be the case, but the further one moves from specific individuals in the representation of issues involving social groups, the more likely it is that referring expressions such as 'the child' will function generically, and will carry metaphorical or metonymic connotations. Thus there are various instances in Data Set 1 of the word *child* which are related less to actual children than to the idea of childhood itself. The phrase 'child's play', for example, occurs nine times in various contexts. This is such a common collocation in English that it has a dictionary entry of its own. Chambers English Dictionary (1988) defines it as 'something very easy to do'. Implicit in the phrase is the adult-as-norm idea: 'child's play' is something which is easy relative to what adults normally do. Also embodied in the phrase is the association of children with play: adults do work and serious things, while children 'play', by definition. I shall return to this theme in Chapter 6.

In these headlines, the 'child's play' referred to includes various sports undertaken by adults, a feature about concern over a boy playing with dolls, and a further twist is given to the connotations of the phrase by using it in a context where, rather than adults doing something which 'even' children could do, it actually is a child who is tackling something considered challenging: 'netsurfing'. This example is in conflict with the conventional expectation that one learns the ways of the world as a child, from adults. When the ways of the world, as represented by computer technology, for instance, change so quickly, there is the possibility that this pattern will be disrupted. So now, as in this instance, 'child's play' can begin to have a slightly different connotation. Corsaro (1997) points out that there are other situations where children do not necessarily follow behind adults in acquiring expertise, considering migrant families as an example. While the parental generation might be far from home and unfamiliar with the surrounding culture, to the children this *is* home – and of course a 'foreign' language for the parent may present much less of a challenge to the children. (See also Ervin-Tripp 1986.)

A blurring of the boundaries between children and adults is evident in the phrase 'the child within', which occurs twice in Data Set 1, and is another familiar collocation, an allusion to the notion that people carry with them at least part of their childhood identities into their adult lives. This idea is also continued in the use of *child* in naming phrases referring to adult newsmakers. Four of these modify 'child' with 'wild', a rhyming phrase used to refer to various celebrities. Perhaps the connotations draw on a contrast between 'tame' children, with the childlike qualities of obedience, docility, respect for adults – who will reproduce the cultural order – and the 'wild children' who rebel and make their own way, bringing about changes in the cultural order. This fundamental contrast between the two archetypes of the child – angel and devil, paragon and monster, inheritor and destroyer – has often been identified in 'discourses of childhood'.

One phrase from Data Set 1 which refers to the generic state of 'childhood' is 'the Nineties child', illustrating the presupposition that the experience of being a child is differentiated partly by when it occurs, in historical time. Likewise, 'children' can 'belong' not only to nations and families as discussed above, but also to times and ideologies. Data Set 1 contains a reference to 'Stalin's children', for example, and another headline reports 'Israel seeks lost children of Yemen exodus'. Here, it is not clear whether the 'children' are literally all not-adults, or whether the intended meaning is that to be the 'child' of a place or a set of ideas is to have these as one's heritage, throughout life. Of the key words investigated in these texts, *childhood*, in particular, seems to carry this metaphorical potential.

## 2.4  The idea of childhood

In the next chapter I shall discuss some findings relating to words for and about children in the language, with reference to the British National Corpus, a database of authentic texts in the English language large enough to identify some linguistic patterns as fairly robust across different kinds of discourse. For comparison with data in the present chapter I investigated the word *childhood* in the BNC to see which words were most likely to be found immediately preceding and immediately following it (most likely, that is, when their overall frequency in the language is taken into account). The results provide a context for presenting the data from the news texts.

It emerges that *childhood* can be deployed, rather as *child* can, as the modifier of another noun, to mean 'something which happens at the stage of life when people are children', particularly something to do with (ill) health; thus the following words are all found with a significantly high frequency immediately after *childhood*: *leukaemia, immunization, cancer(s), morbidity, mortality, illnesses, diseases, disorder*. This finding is consistent with one pattern in Data Set 1, where in seven instances *childhood*, which occurs a total of 39 times in the news headline data, marks a bounded phase in the generic human lifespan: 'childhood epilepsy', 'childhood tumours', for example.

In relation to the collocates immediately preceding *childhood* in the BNC, there are two patterns which suggest that people's childhoods are entities which can be thought of as belonging to them. Five of the words found in this position denote a quality of childhood, which is either neutral or evaluative: *unhappy, deprived, lonely, happy* and *normal* (there is also *common*, but this may be found when *childhood* precedes a second noun, such as *illnesses*), while seven words are possessives (*my, his, her, our, your, their* and also *own*).

Another seven words in this position have some temporal significance, hinting at a slightly different version of the connection already noted between childhood and time: instead of a focus on growth and change, there is the implication of childhood as enduring, available to be taken up and regarded, like an old photograph. The words in this group are: *earliest, early, since, during, throughout, from* and *later*. Words immediately following *childhood* include, in addition to the illness-related group, *memory(ies), fantasies* and *dream(s)*.[3] This latter group evokes the ephemeral qualities of childhood, retrospection and nostalgia, and, in Data Set 1, many of the headlines in which *childhood* occurs are also related in some way to time. Twelve instances of *childhood* occur in clauses which denote explicitly a retrospective theme, and which include one or more of the following words: 'recall(s)', 'remember(s)', 'reminiscent', 'memory(ies)', 'memoir', 'recollection'. In this data set, as in the BNC, *childhood*, which sometimes takes a determiner such as 'a', 'your', 'their', is often represented as a thing which has an existence independent of the person of whose biography it is a part: one headline speaks metaphorically of 'buying back' childhood. 'Childhood' can have a location in space as well as in time: 'a Zimbabwean childhood', 'a Shankill childhood', 'a Glasgow childhood', and, combining both dimensions, there is a reference to 'a cindery path out of childhood'.

A further 16 instances, despite lacking lexical items such as those mentioned above, nevertheless include a strong implication of retrospection. 'Childhood' can be depicted as an entity in time – 'dark age of childhood' – and as a place viewed from a distance. This is sometimes achieved by the use of locative expressions: 'notes *from* childhood', 'tales *from* a Yorkshire childhood', 'patterns set *in* childhood'. (This applies to 'path *out of* childhood' too.)

*Childhood* is personified as a cultural entity in the claim about a puppeteer whose work 'changed the face of childhood'. There is deviation from the dominant present tense of the newspaper headline in this and several other examples: 'My childhood: His *was* a family where . . .'; '. . . our childhood friend. Whatever *happened* to . . .'. These examples illustrate the fact that a simplified notion of a linear progression from childhood to adulthood, the apparently commonsense time sequence which was the theme of Section 2.1, is sometimes inadequate. I want to suggest that in thinking in general about how children, language and the social world are linked, it is helpful to differentiate between three kinds of timescale. The first timescale is the personal biography we all experience, which includes the stage in our lives when each of us is a child. As we live from day to day, our experience contributes to 'the development of the self as a linked series of evolutionary transitions, or transformations in identity and personality at various significant junctures in the lives of individuals' (Layder 1997: 47). The second timescale accounts for the continuing presence in society of people grouped in the social category of 'children', ever present, regardless of which individuals belong in the category at any one moment. Corsaro (1997: 30) makes a similar distinction between these two timescales: '. . . while childhood is a temporary period for children, it is a permanent structural category in society'. There were children in the world before any of us was born, and there will be children as a social category long after our own adult lives are over. My third timescale recognizes the changing cultural idea of 'childhood', and the fact that the nature of this category, its boundaries, the expectations people have of it and its members will shift over time, to have different connotations and to be mobilized in different ways at different points in history. The idea of different temporalities in the social world will be explored further in Chapter 5.

## 2.5    Summary and conclusions

This chapter has approached the news texts introduced in the previous one from a different perspective, exploring the way children and childhood are represented as cultural phenomena.

What childhood is deemed to be is not fixed and stable across history and cultures, and commentators have drawn out the links between 'the rise of science and modernity', concerns with 'the comparison, regulation and control of groups and societies', and 'the development of tools of mental measurement, classification of abilities and the establishment of norms' (Burman 1994: 10–11). In the texts under discussion in this chapter, a preoccupation with the specifics of children's ages and stages of development was identified in the first section, which considered how growth and change are particularly characteristic of the childhood phase of the lifespan. This section also located the anxieties about '. . . children (as particular cherished beings) and childhood (as a cherished state of being)' both represented as 'at risk' (Scott et al. 1998: 691) in the context of language used to depict the historical and cultural resources of society as children's legacy, itself potentially 'at risk' from unsupervised children.

The second section explored the way most of the texts under discussion imply an adult as an ideal reader, often a parent, and I drew parallels with the assumptions identified by other writers about the 'normal' status of the male reader and the 'marked' status of the female. It was observed that children both form a social category, contrasted with adults, and also belong to other categories, often by association with the adults who head family units. Dichotomies between groups deemed to constitute Us and Them are useful for appealing to shared values, and children can sometimes be represented as belonging, to a nation, for example, while at others they are depicted as outside a notional boundary; this was noted in respect of 'unruly' children, who pose both a present and a future threat to moral order.

Children's status as a social group about whom things need to be done was identified in the absence from the texts analysed of their own voices, speaking on their own behalf. Also contributing to this effect was a high incidence of statistics and measurements associated with items concerned with children. Finally in this section, the use of *child* in a more generic sense was discussed, illustrating the blurring of boundaries between adulthood and childhood, a topic which will be explored further in relation to speech styles in Part III.

The third section of the chapter demonstrated the symbolic significance of *childhood*, and the potential which this concept has to become reified, a 'thing' which adults continue to possess 'within' themselves, and a social structure which endures irrespective of its specific membership.

Having identified the themes which emerge from analysis of specific texts and types of texts – namely, newspaper stories – in the next chapter I shall consider their relevance in the language more generally, as well as explore some texts which provide contrasting data.

## Notes

1. It is probably worth pointing out here that there are undoubtedly ways in which this particular child's sex influences the language used to name him and his actions. The term 'thug', for example, is available to denote a miscreant boy but would seem marked in quite a different way if applied to a girl accused of the same kinds of actions. However, I have not come across an equivalent story involving a girl (which may be significant in itself), and many of the gender issues relevant to child language are explored by other writers. One of these, Thorne (1993), although primarily interested in gendered patterns in children's interactions, also notes that '[t]he "protected" status of children (which, from another vantage point, constitutes a pattern of legal, economic, and political subordination) cuts across gender and mutes male privilege' (p. 172). From my own perspective, which is the analysis of discursive representations of children as a social category, I shall not give extensive prominence to issues of gender except where they seem particularly relevant or important in explaining the findings.
2. For further commentary on children represented as the agents of moral decline, see Scraton (1997).
3. James et al. (1998) identify 'the unconscious child' as one of five 'pre-sociological' versions of 'the child', in a model which links Freudian notions of the unconscious with 'the child within' – present but 'dispossessed of intentionality and agency' (p. 21).

# 3

# Children in the English Language

*By searching out frequent collocations, we can glimpse the recurrent wordings which circulate in the social world, and glimpse how linguistic categories become social categories.*

(STUBBS 1996: 194)

## 3.1  Introduction

The previous two chapters have mainly considered newspapers as a source of data to illuminate how the English language in England represents children and the state of childhood, and have explored some characteristics of newspapers as particular types of media, whose function is likely to have a bearing on these representations. This chapter aims to widen the exploration from those texts to look at language patterns in some other specific texts but also to draw some general conclusions about how the language as a whole influences our perceptions of children.

The analyses presented so far have problematized any commonsense definition of the main naming expressions for children and the state of childhood. This chapter will explore the networks of connections between some of the lexical items that have emerged as significant in the texts discussed in Chapters 1 and 2. The main data for these investigations are to be found in the British National Corpus, but I shall also look at a charity advertisement, some radio discussions and some fiction written for children, in order to extend the range of 'real language' considered.

## 3.2  Collocations in the British National Corpus

The British National Corpus comprises 100 million words, structured with the aim of constituting 'a microcosm of current British English in its entirety' (Aston and Burnard 1998: 29). The principal method used in the present analysis is to explore collocations. Characteristic collocations, notes

Stubbs (1996: 172), '. . . show the associations and connotations [words] have, and therefore the assumptions which they embody'. Corpus studies allow us to discover facts about the language from that point of view. Thus, as we shall see, the word *childish* is predominantly found in the company of words with negative connotations, such as *ill-mannered* and *irresponsible*. Once we begin to notice these linkages, our attention is drawn to the seemingly very well-established patterns of co-selection which lead to speakers and writers repeatedly producing several words together as units of meaning, as though there are such well-worn paths in the landscapes of discourse that language use which strays from them is marked in some way. (*Spoilt* + *brat(s)* turns out to be one such unit.) These networks of connections in the language can constrain the ways in which we think about groups of people. As Stubbs (1996: 169) puts it:

> The study of recurrent wordings is . . . of central importance in the study of language and ideology, and can provide empirical evidence of how the culture is expressed in lexical patterns. The cultural assumptions connoted by such patterns, especially when they are repeated and become habits, are an important component of socialization.

With these ideas in mind, I investigated some of the key words relevant to this study of children and social identity.

### 3.2.1   Collocates of *child* and *children*

The newspaper headlines discussed in Chapters 1 and 2 demonstrated that *child* often occurs as a modifier of another noun to denote a process directed towards children, such as 'child care' and 'child abuse'. I sought to discover whether this pattern permeates the language – as represented by the BNC – and is not simply a feature of news texts. The query was posed so as to rank the results by their 'mutual information value'. This '. . . compares the frequency of co-occurrence of two words in a given span with their predicted frequency of co-occurrence, i.e. that which would be expected were these each randomly distributed in the corpus' (Aston and Burnard 1998: 83–4). In other words, we need to distinguish between words which are likely to score highly as collocates of lots of words, because they occur very frequently in the language anyway, and those which are found distinctively in the company of the target word, regardless of their individual frequencies. The 10 nouns which occur most frequently immediately after *child* in the corpus, as ranked by their mutual information value, are all of the type which denote processes directed towards children, or the people responsible for those processes, with the single exception of the word which comes seventh in this list, *prodigies*. (In the phrase 'child prodigies', *child* classifies the kind of actor denoted.) The list of the 10 nouns with the highest mutual information value comprises: *molester, molesters, minding, molestation, rearing, minders, prodigies, abuse, abduction, abusers.* This list illustrates again the now familiar pattern of harm directed towards children, and the perpetrators of that harm, as one key cluster of collocations, balanced in part by the processes – and the people responsible for them – of caring for children: *minding, rearing, minders.* One important aspect of this method should be stressed here. The searches reported in this section always start from words denoting children, but words like *child* are much more common in English than the word *molester*, for example. Therefore, there is considerably more evidence that a 'molester' is 'someone who molests children' than that a 'child' is 'someone who is molested'! (Berglund, pers. comm.)

A similar pattern emerges if a wider horizon is set, of three words on either side of *child.* Again if only nouns are included in the result, it emerges that the ten most common collocates, ranked by overall frequency, are, in this order: *care, abuse, mother, benefit, family, protection, parent, development, welfare* and *school.* Once again *child* collocates with (institutional?) processes of nurturing (*care, benefit, protection, welfare*), with a familial context (*mother, family, parent*), with processes of growth (*development*) and with the context of *school.*

The same query ranked by mutual information values gives slightly different results. There are some anomalies, as are often thrown up by words with a low overall frequency. Thus, for example, the French word *ventre*, which only occurs 25 times in the whole corpus, achieves a high mutual information value because on seven occasions it occurs in the −3 to +3 horizon with *child*; these occurrences are in the context of only two texts, both using a specialized discourse, concerned with the legal status of an unborn child 'en ventre sa mère'. Similarly, *mongol* features in tenth place, occurring only 35 times in the corpus in total, of which six occurrences collocate with *child*, in only three texts.

Otherwise, lemmas of *molest* again occupy three of the top four places in the list, suggesting that, despite its low overall frequency (*molester* occurs only 13 times in the whole BNC, *molesters* only 12 and *molestation* only 22) it is a word which is very closely associated with *child*.[1] The item *abuse* occurs much more frequently in the BNC – 3338 times – and achieves the ninth highest mutual information score with *child* because it is a collocate in 579 of these instances, occurring across 150 texts. It thus seems safe to conclude that the lexical pattern of nominal groups in which *child* modifies a harmful process or person, in the sense of denoting a target of that harm, is not confined to news texts but is a feature of the language at large.

In some ways, the word *children* behaves rather differently. It is a feature of English that the kind of modifying structure discussed above requires the singular form of the noun, so constructions such as 'children minder' or 'children abuse' would be highly unlikely. However, if we examine how both *child* and *children* are themselves typically modified, by discovering which adjectives, again ranked by mutual information score, are most frequently found immediately preceding both of these words, there is a striking overlap. The first 12 items in the list of adjectives preceding *child* are, in this order: *unborn, autistic, spoilt, new-born, hyperactive, stillborn, handicapped, illegitimate, dyslexic, spoiled, abused* and *youngest*. The same query in respect of *children* throws up some anomalies, with some very infrequent words scoring very highly, including the somewhat specialized phrase *non-maori* in second place because it is a collocate of *children* in 14 of its 29 occurrences in the BNC, all in one text.

In order to concentrate on more familiar items, the list was modified to omit those adjectives which occur fewer than 40 times in the whole BNC. Adjectives which collocate frequently with *children* are then shown to include: *autistic, pre-school, dyslexic, abused, handicapped, orphaned, malnourished, grown-up* and *unborn*. One of the preoccupations suggested by these lists is the classification of some members of the group as implicitly in need of special attention, either because of an inherent deviation from the norm (*autistic, dyslexic, handicapped, hyperactive*) or as a result of events (*abused, orphaned, malnourished*). Other collocations highlight the developmental stages of childhood: *new-born, pre-school, grown-up, unborn*.

This kind of corpus analysis makes it easier to discover which words collocate frequently with *children* than to identify the most frequent syntactical role of *the children* in clauses. It is not easy, for example, to know whether *the children* is more frequently the agent or the goal of the clause, if a large corpus has not been tagged in this way. However, it is possible to investigate '[t]he collocation of a word with a particular grammatical class of words [, which] has been termed *colligation*' (Aston and Burnard 1998: 14). Given the frequency of prepositions before *children* in the news texts analysed, a similar investigation was undertaken with the BNC. Consistent with the earlier findings, it emerged that prepositions are found in this position far more often than any other word class. Words tagged as prepositions rank highest at 1943 instances, followed by *of* (traditionally classed as a preposition in most grammars, but recently identified as worthy of reclassification, see Sinclair, 1991, and below) at 982. The next two classes in this ranking are conjunctions and infinitive forms of the verb, with the considerably lower scores of 415 and 387 respectively.

This finding may be typical of a particular syntactical arrangement, and not peculiar to the social group *the children*, but the hypothesis that there may be a tendency for 'children' to feature as 'circumstantial' to and beneficiaries of processes, as suggested in Chapter 1, is lent support by the high frequency of the same three prepositions identified there: in the BNC there are 476 instances of *for the children* in 314 texts; 317 instances of *to the children* in 193 texts; and 314 instances of *with the children* in 213 texts. By contrast, the phrase *by the children*, in which children are potentially represented as agents, occurs only 93 times in 79 texts.

Another investigation I carried out generates some interesting findings about the construction *children's*, which further undermines the notion, also introduced in Chapter 1, that -'*s* is always 'possessive'. *Children's* occurs 4474 times in the BNC, in 1097 texts. The ten nouns which score most highly by mutual information value in the construction 'children's + noun' in the BNC are *playgrounds, playground, imaginations, hearings, toys, schooling, homes, panel, hospice* and *bureau*.

To investigate occurrences of *children's* from a more semantic point of view, I looked at a random sample of 100 sentences containing *children's*, restricted to one per text. Since some of these sentences contained the item more than once, I had 107 instances to analyse. I was interested to see what children can actually be said to own, and I grouped the noun phrases modified by *children's* into some general categories, excepting three which I found unclassifiable. Of these categories, the largest (28) contains terms for facilities, places or organizations provided by adults for the education and welfare of children, including 'children's charities', 'children's classes', 'children's home(s)', 'children's hospital(s)' and so on. A further 15 are cultural artefacts – or their producers – again made by adults but aimed at children: 'children's adventure story', 'children's books', 'children's playing blocks', 'children's publisher' and the like. Recreational (as opposed to education and welfare) facilities aimed at children are named in 12 instances: 'Children's farmyard', 'children's party(ies)', 'children's playground(s)'. A further group of 13 includes material artefacts used, but not necessarily literally owned, by children, such as 'children's clothes/clothing', 'children's dress', 'children's foodstuffs'. Together these categories comprise 68 of the items analysed.

Another category I identified is that of the corporeal attributes which each of us can be said to 'own' involuntarily, and in this group of 10 I included 'children's': 'feet', 'hair', 'heads', 'voices' and 'warm squirming bodies'; also 'children's health' and 'children's leukaemia'. There is also in my sample a single instance of the involuntarily 'owned' family member, in 'children's fathers'. The preoccupation in discourse about children with another involuntary attribute they are said to 'possess' – namely, change, growth and development – is reflected in a category containing eight items such as 'children's development', 'children's formulative [*sic*] years', 'children's progress'.

Two kinds of 'possession' of *children's* also found in the data are abstract qualities of a mental or emotional kind, and actions carried out by children. The first group comprises nine items, including 'children's': 'abiding memory', 'innocence', 'natural curiosity', 'learning', 'self confidence'; and the second, six items, includes 'children's': 'achievement', 'doings', 'play', 'game'.

This brings us finally to the instances where *children's* functions as a modifier of an actual, material possession belonging to children, and in this category there are only two items: 'children's savings' and 'children's ticket', although I am not entirely sure that the latter belongs in this group, since it is perhaps a facility aimed at children – or those financially responsible for them.

Based on this sample of evidence about the construction *children's* then, children are said to 'own' their body parts and attributes such as innocence and curiosity as well as their actions and achievements. However, a much larger proportion within this sample of the things which are named as being 'children's' are directed *to* and provided *for* them, rather than chosen and owned *by* children themselves.

These investigations were prompted by the findings which emerged from the other methods of discourse analysis used on both shorter and longer texts in previous chapters. They are by no means exhaustive of the ways in which *child* and *children* might be investigated by means of corpus studies. Two fascinating areas suggest themselves, quite apart from many other detailed studies which could be undertaken using the BNC or other large corpora. One line of inquiry not addressed here concerns diachronic variation: How do contemporary uses of these words suggest different cultural preoccupations from those we might find in texts from earlier in the twentieth century, or from texts much older than these? Another possibility would be to compare English with other languages in terms of the findings presented here. Is a cultural preoccupation with harm directed towards children, for example, as is suggested by these linguistic data, inevitable and universal, or is it thrown up by specific political and economic circumstances, and by particular cultural perspectives? I can speculate about the answers to such questions, but unfortunately any empirical evidence about such contrasts is outside the scope of this study.

## 3.2.2   *Childish* and *childlike*

As mentioned in the Introduction, I had felt the need even before starting this corpus investigation to find a more 'neutral' adjective than those conventionally in use: the weight of cultural connotations associated with describing an utterance or an interest as 'childish' or 'childlike' had led me to resurrect the archaic 'childly' (Sealey 1999a). The inappropriateness of *childish* and *childlike* for denoting children's own experience and behaviour is partly a product of the adult-as-norm phenomenon discussed in the previous chapters. Rather as the word *effeminate* is used to describe someone who is not a woman behaving as if he were (in terms of the perceived conventions of 'feminine' behaviour), *childish* and *childlike* are usually used of non-children acting as children are perceived to do. Intuition suggests that the two words map on to the two dominant stereotypes of what such behaviour is like: selfish and unrestrained in the case of *childish*, naive and innocent in the case of *childlike*.

For the empirical investigation of these ideas, I discovered that there are 1230 different adjectives which collocate with *childish* in a horizon of −3 to

+3 in the BNC. The mutual information scores reveal that most of the first 50 adjectives listed in this category collocate with *childish* only once; minor exceptions include *stupid*, with eight occurrences as a collocate, and *immature* and *irresponsible* both with three. Since these quantitative findings are therefore of doubtful significance, I decided to look at a sub-sample of the collocations in more detail. Restricting the occurrences to one per text generates a sample of 318 occurrences of *childish*. The following discussion concerns not which individual words are found most frequently in the company of *childish*, but rather the semantic patterns in the wide range of words which collocate with *childish*, and it does not therefore rely on quantitative statistics.

Like most adjectives, *childish* is susceptible to gradation. From my BNC examples it is clear that one can be 'very childish', 'so childish', 'totally childish', 'purely childish', and in context these descriptions usually signify an implicitly undesirable quality: 'don't be *so* childish!'; 'that's *nothing short of* childish', for example. The undesirability of being childish is also signalled by hedges associated with its use in context: 'of uncertain temper and *rather* childish'; 'as though such enthusiasm were *a bit* childish'. Seven instances of *childish* in this sub-sample are in inverted commas, or scare-quotes, another way in which authors distance themselves from commitment to a word: 'the "childish" Spartan way of taking decisions'; 'adults may indulge in "childish" behaviour'.

*Childish* often occurs as one item in a list. (For example: 'the sort of ignorant, absurd and childish platitudes that . . .'; 'I know it was silly, stupid and childish, but . . .'.) Although, as I have noted, the other items in such lists are not so frequent as to show up in a quantitative analysis, there is nevertheless a semantic pattern in the adjectives which tend to surround *childish*. Among these are words denoting absence of intellect or judgement, including 'stupid', 'simple', 'amateurish' and 'silly'. The anti-social characteristics of those described as childish, including its self-centred dimension, are denoted by collocates such as 'dangerous', 'reckless', 'destructive', 'irresponsible', 'unfair', 'churlish', 'ill-mannered', 'petulant' and 'selfish'. Other negative collocates include: 'dull', 'absurd', 'arbitrary', 'banal', 'emotionally unstable', 'soppy', 'unrealistic', 'pathetic', 'ill-placed' and 'disjointed'. The people, qualities and things (i.e. the nouns) which are modified by *childish* suggest a similar lack of self-restraint to that revealed by its adjectival collocates: 'crudity', 'defiance', 'impetuosity', 'ill-temper', 'misdemeanours', 'petulance', 'rage', 'vanity', 'venom', 'whim' and 'whine'.

There is more ambiguity about some of the other nouns which are modified by *childish*; eight of the occurrences in this sample are 'behaviour', four are 'way(s)', three 'attitude(s)' and three 'occupation(s)', all of which are not inherently evaluative. The indulgent tolerance of *mis*behaviour is suggested by *childish* as a modifier of 'antics', 'mischief', 'prank(s)' and 'tricks'. These collocates highlight some of the other connotations of being 'childish' – namely, a freedom from restraint which is not wholly undesirable – implied likewise in the collocates 'amusement', 'nonsense', 'delight', 'ecstasies', 'enthusiasm', 'excitement', 'game(s)', 'glee', 'jape' and 'joke'. The positive qualities of childish inexperience are evoked by its modification of 'anticipation', 'candour', 'charm', 'curiosity', 'fancy', 'fantasy(ies)', 'imagination', 'fascination' and 'innocence'. Yet this characteristic may also be disconcerting: *childish* also occurs in this sample as a modifier of both 'fear' and 'bewilderment'.

When we say, then, that a person, or that person's behaviour, is 'childish', we call up a range of connotations. Many of these are negatively evaluated, but there is still room for the distinctive characteristics of being like a child to include fun and freedom. For some of the other positive associations with childliness, English also provides the alternative adjective *childlike*. *Childlike* occurs 137 times in 113 texts, and I analysed these from a similar perspective, not quantitatively in terms of high-frequency collocates, but more qualitatively, grouping the collocates found in semantic terms.

The hedging noted with some uses of *childish* is even more pronounced with *childlike*, which is qualified by 'almost' in 12 of the 137 instances. 'Very childlike', by contrast, occurs only once, and there are no instances of 'so childlike'. *Childlike* sometimes occurs as one among a list of several adjectives, which may be negatively oriented – for example, 'tragic', 'silly', 'tired', 'stilted' and 'regressive'. It also collocates with neutral, physically descriptive adjectives such as 'light blue' (of eyes), 'pink' (of a face), 'white' (of a party frock) and 'thin' (of a voice). A similar meaning inheres in constructions found in this corpus where *childlike* modifies a physical characteristic denoted by nouns such as 'eyes', 'face', 'form' (i.e. body), 'hand', 'mouth', 'physiology', 'planes' (of a face) and 'voice', and also physical products of the hand and eye: 'drawing', 'handwriting', 'writing'.

The other main semantic field of *childlike* seems to be in the affective domain, where undisguised emotions are positively orientated. Collocations with other adjectives include 'loving', 'passionate' and 'tender', while the nouns it modifies which illustrate this dimension include 'affection', 'happiness', 'longing', 'pleasure', 'pride', 'serenity', 'simplicity', 'squeal of delight' and 'whoop of delight'. The last two again evoke the physical, expressive qualities which seem to attend this word. If expressions of uninhibited emotion are typical of childliness, a closely related shade in the spectrum of its meaning is its association with an unspoilt state. *Childlike* is found to collocate with the adjective 'innocent', and again the nouns which it modifies strengthen this link; they include: 'awe', 'frankness', 'freshness', 'gaiety', 'innocence' (and 'state of innocence'), 'trust', 'vulnerability' and 'wonder'.

There are two other adjectives which are commonly used to denote attributes of human beings younger than adults: *infantile* and *juvenile*. To a much greater extent than *childish* and *childlike*, these adjectives have the potential to denote people (and issues pertaining to them) who actually belong to the non-adult age-group, as well as being used figuratively of people – or behaviour – likened to children.

*Infantile* is an infrequent word in the BNC as a whole, which means that quantitative information about it is of limited significance. The two nouns which most frequently follow it (using mutual information values) denote medical conditions. The next two are *masturbation* and *sexuality*: phenomena which are presumably unmarked among adults but qualified when associated with children. The fifth-ranked noun in this position is *dependency*.

The most highly scoring noun immediately following *juvenile* in the BNC, ranked by mutual information, is *labour-market*, but as this collocation occurs eight times in a single text any significance for general discourse contexts is limited. *Juvenile* has connotations of the legal system, and lemmas of a term associated with law-breaking, *delinquent*, are three of the four most frequently occurring nouns following this adjective. Others among the 12 highest scoring nouns in this position include: *offenders*, *crime*, *courts* and *justice*, and also *liaison* and *bureau*. The other nouns in this list include *diabetes* and *mortality*, both of which allude to concerns about children as a defined subgroup of the population.

### 3.2.3   What are children like?

I have demonstrated that many of the adjectives which collocate frequently with *child* and *children* denote physical or age-related characteristics, or classify children in terms of health or education. (A composite list from those adjectives identified earlier would include *unborn*, *autistic*, *spoilt*, *new-born*, *hyperactive*, *stillborn*, *handicapped*, *illegitimate*, *dyslexic*, *spoiled*, *abused*, *youngest*, *pre-school*, *orphaned*, *malnourished* and *grown-up*.) These highly scoring modifiers once again reflect the involuntary nature of many of the categories to which children are often said to belong. However, it is possible to look beyond these involuntary characteristics. I decided to thin semantically the 100 adjectives which collocate with *children* most frequently by mutual information values in the BNC in order to identify those which denote attributes associated with agency and choice and those which denote qualities of character.

The concepts underpinning these categories – agency and personal characteristics – raise an ambiguity about children and responsibility which is a recurring theme in this book. When the adjective *naughty* is used to describe children, it denotes a characteristic of them and their behaviour, and implies a degree of choice on the part of the 'naughty' actor; but what about the semantically close item *spoilt*? *Spoilt* is used of inanimate objects which have suffered due to the action of animate beings, usually humans, and spoilt foodstuffs, flowers or paintings are not thought to be responsible for their condition. When *spoilt* is applied to people it is usually to children – although an adult may be said to be behaving *like* a spoilt child – and it carries within it the implicit notion that children who behave badly may *not* be responsible if their anti-social actions are considered to be the result of poor parenting. Thus the items found by selecting from the list of highly scoring modifiers for *children* those associated with voluntary behaviour and with personal characteristics cannot easily be separated into two distinct groups, and will be considered together.

The list of adjectives of this type is short, comprising (ranked in the following order by mutual information score): *spoilt, disturbed, delinquent, recalcitrant, naughty, disruptive, innocent*. The first two items display in their morphology the implication that an action has been carried out by which the children stand affect*ed*, but the same is not true of the others in this list.

I was interested in the other phenomena and entities in the social world which are associated with these adjectives, as a means of inferring what we are likening children to when we say they are 'naughty', 'disruptive' or 'innocent'. Such a line of inquiry is analogous to the more familiar comparisons between words routinely used to speak of women and men respectively. It has been established, for example, that, while '[t]he numbers of occurrences of "women" and "men" in the corpus [i.e.the BNC] are very similar, . . . there are clear differences in their collocates, men being more rarely beautiful and women more rarely handsome' (Aston and Burnard 1998: 83). (On some other contrasts in COBUILD-based dictionary entries referring to women and to men, see Hoey 1996.) Other writers have noted, in analyses of specific texts representing minority groups, the use of terms with non-human associations to refer to both people and processes (Sykes 1985; van Dijk 1988; van Leeuwen 1996). The purpose of the current investigation is to identify what other kinds of entities are described using those adjectives that frequently describe children.

*Spoilt* precedes only three nouns five times or more in the BNC (*brat, child* and *children*), which suggests that it is indeed only human beings belonging to this category who are routinely said to be 'spoilt'. Nouns which are immediately preceded by *disturbed* include physical processes and things (*sleep*, and, metonymically, *nights*, also *ground* and *area*) and people and their actions (*children, patients, state, behaviour, motor function*). An antagonism between young people as a group and an adult norm is implicit in the collocations of *delinquent*, which typically modifies both groups of people and their activities. Thus the highest-scoring nouns modified by *delinquent* (using mutual information scores) are *subculture(s), girls, youth, behaviour, boys, values, activities* and *children*.

The stereotype of children as a challenge to institutional norms is further reinforced by considering the collocates of both *recalcitrant* and *disruptive*. The number of occurrences of the former is low (168 in total) and it occurs as a collocate only two or three times with each of the 14 nouns generating high mutual information values, except *children*, with which it collocates in this position six times. The other nouns denote animals (*mule, dog*), people in institutionally related positions, including the workplace (*strikers, unions, manager, labour*), and other social systems (*defendant, authorities, members [of society/of the community]*). Thus a child or children, like other individuals, when said to be 'recalcitrant' are linked with non-conformity to a social or institutional process of some kind. *Disruptive* has similar connotations, collocating in higher raw numbers than *recalcitrant* with *pupils, behaviour, influence, effect(s), potential, force* and *children*. Children in their institutionally relational role as pupils can 'disrupt' the smooth running of an institution much as workers, in what is perhaps a similar relational grouping, can 'disrupt' production, each by not conforming to the norms of their respective institutions.

The cultural connotations of *naughty* – another term frequently applied to children – are of a rather different kind. Dispreferred behaviour can be of different degrees of seriousness, and 'naughty' behaviour, like 'pranks' and 'mischief', is implicitly more tolerated than those infringements of acceptable norms implied in other words already discussed. *Naughty* occurs more frequently in the BNC than the items already considered, and a list of nine nouns, which immediately follow it on five occasions or more, ranks highest (by mutual information value), three which denote people: *schoolboy, boy* and *boys*. Three other nouns denoting people feature in fifth, sixth and seventh place in this list: *girl, child* and *children*. In fourth, eighth and ninth places are nouns which do not denote people: *bits, words* and *things*. Described as 'naughty', then, are young human beings, or those behaving like them, and there is a connotation of negatively evaluated behaviour, but in terms of self-indulgence rather than wickedness. The concordance of *naughty* in context includes references to food which is enjoyable rather than healthy, and allusions to sexual behaviour: 'naughty lunches', 'naughty pictures', 'naughty lady', 'naughty nineties', 'a naughty seaside postcard'. It is the case with *naughty*, rather as with *childish*, that one does not literally have to be a 'boy' to be referred to as one. Pleasurable, self-indulgent behaviour which infringes tiresome moral rules may be 'naughty': the indulgence granted to children – if they are considered not fully capable of, or responsible for, moral choices – links their behaviour to those activities of adults which are likely to be labelled 'naughty'.[2]

Unlike the modifiers discussed so far in this section, *innocent* occurs over 2500 times in the BNC overall, generating a much longer list of nouns which it precedes on five occasions or more. Of the first 30 of these, 10 are non-evaluative nouns denoting people, including *person, people, man, men, child, children, girl, girls, woman, women*. A further small group denotes people described as 'innocent' in relation to a (presumably negative or harmful) process: *bystander(s), civilians, victims, party(ies)* (and, in two and three legal texts respectively, *sub-purchaser* and *purchaser*). Aspects of communication can be 'innocent': *looks, remarks, expression, smiles, face, explanation*, as can some experiences: *fun* and *pleasure*. The cluster of connotations in this term which collocates strongly with children, then, would appear to be the passivity of one caught up in a negative event, as well as the appearance and experience of involvement in positive processes.

Various collocations of words connected with children have been identified in the preceding discussion. These can be seen to cluster around a number of themes, including perhaps three meta-themes:

(i)   *Physical existence*
      the passage through the life-span (birth, health, growth)
      physical attributes (parts of the body)

(ii)  *Involuntary status*
      as potential victim of intentional harm
      affected by unintentional processes
      as beneficiary of care, services, goods

(iii) *Distinctive qualities of the child stage of the lifespan*
      innocence, inexperience, enthusiasm
      deviance, wilfulness

## 3.3   The patterns realized in texts

### 3.3.1   Contemporary childhood discussed on the radio

If there are contours in the contemporary English language which condition its users to draw on themes like this in various discursive contexts, we would expect to encounter examples in specific texts. Some such examples from newspaper reports have been discussed in the previous chapters. A slightly different context is provided by two radio programmes in which childhood was the focal topic. One was a national phone-in discussion occasioned by the recent arrest of five 9- and 10-year old boys in connection with the alleged rape of a classmate at a primary school. (The case subsequently went to court and the boys were acquitted.) A number of the contributions to this discussion about child crime draw on the discursive themes identified above. For example, children are described as in need of resources which adults should provide:

'. . . young children do need guidance between what is right and what is wrong . . .'

'. . . too many of these children lack care and attention and time, which is what children need . . .'

'. . . because I think children require two parents, need quite definitely to be shown what is right and what is wrong from an early age . . .'

'. . . children need to be taught from an early age as to what society will accept as correct and appropriate behaviour . . .'

'. . . these children who are clearly more difficult, need more support, need more attention . . .'.

Note how many of the active clauses here include 'children' as subject of verbs such as 'need', 'require' and 'lack'.

Children are represented as subject to harm from adults:

'. . . I think children are more abused in our society than abusing . . .'

'. . . the general public are more aware over the years; you know, the talk of child abuse . . .'

Children are also said to have distinctive needs and occupations appropriate to their stage in the lifespan:

'. . . children need to be able to play . . .'

'. . . children have **always** come home from school, picked up some crisps and then gone out and then played // what I would hate to do is for us to go back to a society which suddenly starts condemning what is normal childhood behaviour . . .'

Some contributions encompass several of these themes at once:

'. . . I mean they grow up in a moral vacuum / it's not their fault // nevertheless, they haven't had attention, they haven't had love, they haven't had discipline, a structured life, fun, you know the whole gamut of what a child should have . . .'.

The second radio programme also took a topical theme, that of children's play, considering the facilities available in contemporary communities, and also attitudes towards children's unsupervised behaviour. Similar concerns, and similar patterns of ways of expressing them, are found in this discussion too. Concerns about responsibility, permission and, in particular, the distinctive nature of childhood are found in the following extracts from contributions, the first two from members of the public and the others from 'experts' in the studio:

'. . . the problem is / is that people who are adults don't care about other children / they won't keep an eye on them // they don't feel it's their responsibility to say hey don't do this do something else . . .'

'. . . if they [parents] would take responsibility for what they did then I won't mind but they / these kids out here have no discipline whatsoever . . .'

'. . . working in such a way that you allow children to be children in a genuine sense and it seems to me that what's really required is to bend the stick, to allow kids free time for free play, allow them to get into trouble . . .'

'. . . the key issue is to treat children like children to allow them to be children . . .'

'. . . one of the features of our contemporary culture is that we have effectively plundered childhood // we have denied children childhood and it's not the children who have abandoned it / it's in a sense our adult culture has taken it away . . .'

Partly, of course, because of the topic, with its focus on children and play, these contributions highlight what is distinctive about children, contrasting children as a group with adults, and 'contemporary culture' in general. They exemplify the idea of core, and implicitly essential, attributes of childhood, alongside a concern that these are being eroded. If these characteristics are essential to childhood, of course, they could not be taken away from children. Unless that is, it is proposed that children can cease to have them, but then lose their status as 'proper' children experiencing a 'proper' childhood.[3]

### 3.3.2 Several themes mobilized in a single text

The final text to be discussed in this section is an advertisement published by the charity Oxfam and aimed at raising support for 'a tough EU code of conduct on arms sales' (see Fig. 3.1). The image, caption and accompanying text are powerful and disturbing. The overall theme is support for 'Oxfam's **Cut Conflict** Campaign', arguing for a reduction in small arms as an important contribution to reducing the number of casualties of violent conflict around the world. Significant sections of the text deal with global economics and international politics, and as such they seem remote from the stereotypical concerns of children. However, part of the impact of the advertisement is the interweaving of just these themes with the sombre and initially adult-oriented subject matter.

The first words are the formulaic opening of a child's letter to 'Santa'. This is a tradition invented by adults expressly for children: a magical and benevolent old man who provides gifts to children and is addressed in large numbers of letters every year. The tradition gives rise to some issues about which there are differences of opinion. It has led to a rite of passage within childhood associated with the realization that it is a fiction, and some people thus see the myth as a rather manipulative deception of children. Others believe that myths about Father Christmas or the tooth fairy are appropriate, and as acceptable as other stories told to children to protect them from some of life's realities (comforting versions of morality and justice, sanitized explanations of where babies come from, and so on). Meanwhile, the Santa

Dear Santa,
Please don't send me
a gun this Christmas.

**SOME OF OUR CHILDREN WILL GET TOY GUNS THIS CHRISTMAS.**
Many Third World children will get real ones. AK47s and M16s. Kids as young as ten will be forced to use them. To kill.

Child soldiers are a sad fact of modern warfare. From Angola to Sri Lanka, children are press-ganged to fight, kill and die with the adults. In brutal initiations new recruits are often drugged, beaten and raped, and then made to kill loved ones or execute prisoners. Even butcher other children.

Their innocence is damned.

In the last ten years, in Africa especially, Oxfam has seen a big increase in the use of child soldiers. Guns are cheap ($10 for an AK47 in Liberia) and easy to use (an M16 can be stripped down and reassembled by a child of ten). And young men raised on violence are quick to train the next generation of boys – and girls.

In a world where 90 per cent of war casualties are caused by small arms, child soldiers are increasingly pulling the trigger. But something can be done, and you can help.

In two weeks the UK assumes the Presidency of the European Union. This is your chance – to join us in calling for a tough EU code of conduct on arms sales. One with teeth. One without loopholes. One that opens arms sales to public scrutiny before the guns are exported.

Oxfam is part of a growing movement for controls on arms sales. To cut the flow of guns to repressive regimes hooked on heavy military spending. Will you join the campaign to stop small arms falling into small hands?

By Christmas we want 10,000 people to say they care, to get the politicians to listen. At this time of giving, please give a damn. Be one of the first to call our 24-hour number. If you don't take action, who will? Santa?

Please ring now. Thank you.

**0345 10 11 10**
www.oxfam.org.uk/campaign/cutconflict/

PHOTOGRAPH: DEAN CHAPMAN/PANOS

 OXFAM

Oxfam's **Cut Conflict** Campaign
Oxfam is a Registered charity no. 202918. Oxfam UK and Ireland is a member of Oxfam International

Fig 3.1

myth has been incorporated into commercial practices, so that the same children who are encouraged to participate in a tradition of make-believe by writing to Santa with requests are also – often indirectly – consumers in a lucrative industry. If 'Santa' is not to disappoint children, their parents are encouraged to buy them the toys and games which are heavily advertised and promoted in various media.[4] These large-scale economic relationships mean that choices about what are 'suitable' or 'appropriate' cultural artefacts for children to play with are not entirely within the control of individual parents or children (Kline 1993; Seiter 1993). Many goods manufactured and marketed as children's toys are (usually miniaturized) replicas of people, animals and things found in the 'real', adult world. Children's play is often an enactment of the things adults do: making buildings (out of blocks), feeding and caring for babies (dolls), driving (toy) cars and, of course, acting out armed conflict with toy versions of guns, swords, bows and arrows, uniforms, armour and so on.

This replication in play of adult actions represents the overlap between childhood and adult culture, but it also represents what the difference is supposed to be. The introduction to the main text of the Oxfam advertisement highlights the contrast: 'Some of our children will get toy guns this Christmas,' it reads, 'Many Third World children will get real ones.' Two contrasts are drawn in these parallel sentences, between 'our' children and 'Third World' children, and between toy guns [supplied by Santa] and real ones. The implication is that the important contrast is between an authentic childhood, undisturbed by violent conflict, and a childhood destroyed by involvement in activities which are inherently repulsive and even more so when they involve children (cf. James et al. 1998: 141). Hence the bald statement: 'Their innocence is damned.' Thus the caption representing a letter to Santa highlights the commonality of childliness. Although it modifies the conventional request 'Please send me . . .' by inserting 'don't', it reminds the reader that children in general are positioned as supplicants in relation to the adults (including 'Santa') who determine so much of what happens in their lives. A final persuasive question asks the reader, 'If you don't take action, who will? Santa?', using first a rhetorical question and then an ironic one to underscore the responsibility which adults have to use their greater power and knowledge of the world's realities to help rather than harm children.

A further rhetorical effect is the inclusion of a number of items associated with violence and war in sentences in which children are the themes of the main clause. Although the coercion involved is clear, in that many of the sentences are in the passive – 'kids . . . will be forced to . . .'; 'children are press-ganged to . . .'; 'new recruits are . . . made to . . .' – it is children who remain the focus of this part of the text. Its force derives in part from this thematic foregrounding, along with lexis associated with horrific human interactions: 'kill', 'drugged', 'beaten', 'raped', 'butcher'.

As the text moves into an account of the overall context, children become less central as theme, but the concept of children as resources in wars undertaken by adults is introduced in such phrases as 'a big increase in the use of child soldiers'.

The physical reality of children's limited age is invoked in parts of the text: 'kids as young as ten'; 'an M16 can be stripped down and reassembled by a child of ten'; 'the campaign to stop small arms falling into small hands'.

An advertisement such as this obviously has to negotiate a series of sensitive issues. Although shocking, it draws together many of the themes about childhood which have been discussed in this book so far, combining references to the responsibility of adults to protect and nurture children with a recognition that children are not an entirely separate section of society, and also implying that what is not desirable for children, in this instance, may also be undesirable for human society as a whole.

## 3.4   An alternative perspective: children's literature

The linguistic trends which I have identified so far, in specific texts of various kinds and in a large heterogeneous corpus, emphasize particular cultural preoccupations in respect of children and childhood. The language data examined has contributed to a homogenized representation of children as a group, albeit a group with both positive and negative characteristics. To some extent, this finding is an inevitable product of the research methods used. The words, phrases and clause structures highlighted by searching for instances of *child*, *childish* or *children*, for example, are not those which individuate and distinguish members of the group, but rather those which are likely to represent the group as a whole. However, some of the texts analysed have focused on individuals, including deviants from the notional norm, and even these examples have illustrated a pattern of children as archetypical representatives of particular human qualities and characteristics in contrast to others.

Representations of 'otherness' in fiction have been explored by researchers in cultural and linguistic studies who have identified ways in which, for example, women or minority groups are represented as demonstrating particular characteristics *in relation to* the 'core' characteristics of the white male whose gaze has often been taken as the unmarked vantage point from which 'others' are viewed (see, for example, Donald and Rattansi 1992; Gilbert and Gubar 1979; Said 1978). The parallel in the present study is the way the point of view of the adult writer or speaker is likely to be dominant, unmarked, a 'norm'. The construction and reproduction of such discursive representations are neither simple nor inevitable, however – an issue that will be explored further in Chapter 5.

In contrast with what has gone before, the final section of this chapter will use as data just a few examples of an extensive genre of written texts in which the trends identified above are not evident, and indeed are in many ways reversed; namely, fiction written for child readers. Although by far the majority of texts *for* children are written *by* adults, the intended readership has a significant influence on how children and adults respectively are portrayed and represented discursively. Some commentators have drawn attention to the part played by children's fiction in reproducing the same kinds of power relations between adults and children as those already discussed (see Hollindale 1992; Knowles and Malmkjaer 1996; Stephens 1992; Wall 1991, for example), as much in contemporary stories involving social realism as in the cautionary tales written in the last century overtly intended to shape moral values. My present concern, however, is less with this aspect of children's fiction and its potential ideological role than with the linguistic means by which a childly perspective on the world can be constructed.

In order to select just a few texts from this impossibly extensive and diverse category, I applied some basic criteria and then simply took six books at random from among those which satisfied them. Because of this book's focus on middle childhood, the texts chosen were aimed at, and often about, children in roughly the junior school age-group (or 'Key Stage 2'). Because this book is largely about children and language in England today, the texts were relatively contemporary and popular in English schools and libraries at the time of writing. Surveys of teachers' recommendations and practice (e.g. Raban et al. 1994; White and Karavis 1994), as well as the awards for children's literature such as the Guardian Children's Fiction Award, the Carnegie Medal and the Whitbread Children's Novel award help to identify some of the most respected and widely-read authors for children, and I selected books by some from among this group.

Many writers of fiction for children are uneasy with a hard distinction between children's and adult fiction: 'After all, children live in the world with the rest of us, they aren't a separate race. I'm a bit uneasy about this cult of treating children as creatures utterly divorced from adult life' (Aiken 1977: 172). Several children's authors explain the key differences between children's and adult fiction in terms of specific aspects of form, but insist that children's literature, while necessarily more 'simple and transparent', nevertheless makes 'a fully serious adult statement, as a good novel of any kind does' (Paton Walsh 1977: 193). Paton Walsh explains how some of the conventions of children's stories, such as settings in distant places or times, or the inclusion of humanized non-human characters, represent solutions to the 'simplicity-significance problem': children are included in fiction which acknowledges the realities of the human condition, but protected from some of the immediate relevance to actual lives like their own by various distancing devices.

Whether the central character is a recognizable human child from the present day, a child experiencing the events of some previous era, or a humanized toy or small mammal, a distinctive characteristic of texts for child readers is the narrative point of view: these texts are likely to include protagonists with whom the child reader can identify or empathize.

As an initial illustration, here are the opening sentences from two of the novels I selected, *Crummy Mummy and Me* and *George Speaks*:

> I don't think my mum's fit to be a parent, really I don't. Every morning it's the same, every single morning. I'm standing by the front door with my coat on, ready to go. School starts at nine and it's already eight-forty or even later, and she's not ready. She's not even nearly ready. Sometimes she isn't even dressed.
>
> (Fine 1988: 1)

> Laura's baby brother George was four weeks old when it happened. Laura, who was seven, had very much wanted a brother or sister for a long time. It would be so nice to have someone to play with, she thought. But when George was born, she wasn't so sure.
>
> (King-Smith 1988: 5)

Fine's story, written in the first person, exemplifies an internal narratorial viewpoint, that of a child who expresses, with a strong modality, definite views about her mother and by implication about her world in general. The routine depicted (evoked by 'every', 'every single', 'sometimes' and the simple present tense) is the child's routine; the obligation, to attend school on time, is a child's obligation, and thus the childly orientation is established from the outset.

This is not only true of first-person narratives, however. King-Smith's novel is in the third person – it is not Laura who recounts the action, but the stance is what Simpson (1993) describes as 'co-operative'. In other words, the narrator's perspective is congruent with that of the central character. Thus in the opening lines of the King-Smith extract are a number of 'verba sentiendi' – words denoting thoughts, feelings and perceptions. King-Smith tells the reader what Laura 'very much *wanted*', what, for her, would be 'so nice', and that she then became less 'sure'. This text continues to represent the action and the other characters in ways sympathetic to the child's point of view. The author describes Laura observing the reactions of others – adults – to the new baby, but represents her (contrasting) perceptions through a formulation expressive of Laura's viewpoint: 'How could anyone with a round red face and a squashy nose and little tiny eyes all sunken in fat be called beautiful?' (p. 6).

A third variation is provided by extracts from a novel by Roald Dahl, who has been described as 'a friendly adult story-teller who knows how to entertain children while at the same time keeping them in their place' (Knowles and Malmkjaer 1996: 133). In *James and the Giant Peach*, the adult author distances himself somewhat from the central child character by simultaneously offering more than one perspective on events. When James's parents are eaten by an escaped rhinoceros, he notes that this is '... a rather nasty experience for two such gentle parents,' continuing, '[b]ut in the long run it was far nastier for James than it was for them.... all at once he found himself alone and frightened in a vast unfriendly world' (Dahl 1990: 7). James is presented throughout as a character whose knowledge of the world is limited compared to that of the implied child reader, so author and reader can collude in sympathizing with James's harsh treatment and deprivation. Emphasis has been added in the following extract, from the concluding episode, to highlight this:

> Soon, there was a trail of children a mile long chasing after the peach as it proceeded slowly up Fifth Avenue.... And *to James, who had never dreamed that* there could be so many children as this in the world, it was the most marvellous thing that had ever happened.
>
> (p. 133)

The contrast between these texts and others discussed in previous sections is rather like that brought about by altering the depth of field in a camera's lens. What was central and foregrounded in newspaper reports or legal texts (social expectations of parents, for example) becomes backgrounded or peripheral in texts addressed to children. The adult characters introduced in these texts are denoted in relation to the children – 'my mum', 'James' parents' – while the younger children too serve as reference points for the main perspective – 'my baby sister', 'Laura's baby brother George'. That children are the focus of the narrative is also taken for granted in *A Chance Child*, which partly concerns the working conditions of children at the time of the Industrial Revolution. Thus when two of the central characters (all of whom are children) come across a forge and its machinery, the reader is told: 'The two boys stared at that also. But there were no children working here, only sturdy men' (Paton Walsh 1978: 51). When one of these boys hears another child crying, the expectations that have become normalized for him are implicit: 'Creep sat and listened. He was waiting for the adult to come and deal out blows and curses' (ibid.: 31). In this formulation, it is 'the adult' who remains anonymous, occupying a generic role in relation to the crying child, with whom the reader is invited to empathize, along with the child protagonist.[5]

The stylistic means by which this childly point of view is constructed as normal rather than deviant include not only this kind of deixis but also the narratorial orientation to the fictional landscape. In *A Chance Child*, another central character, Christopher, who is from the present day, is directed to the library, which he is told (by an adult) is 'by the Butter Cross in the town centre'. The author leads the reader along with Christopher as he sets out to find it: 'Christopher had never, as it happened, been to the Butter Cross in his life.' The implication of 'as it happened' is that there is nothing remarkable in this inexperience, despite his teacher's casual assumption that he would know the place. The passage continues:

> He knew his way to the shop on the corner, where he bought bubblegum and crisps and Vimto when he had money to spend. He knew his way through the council estate, across the great shadows of giant tower blocks, where his friends had addresses all of block and floor numbers . . .
>
> (Paton Walsh 1978: 116)

Once again, although the narrative stance is third person, the reader meets landmarks in terms of their significance for the child Christopher, whose knowledge and perceptions are presented as valid and authentic. The sinister and relatively unfamiliar nature of the 'giant' tower blocks with their 'great' shadows is partly due to their size *in relation* to a person of a child's height.

One of the themes identified in previous sections, of children's physical growth, and other aspects of their experience of development and change, is represented in some of these texts from a childly point of view. Knowles and Malmkjaer (1996: 54) point out that '[d]ifferentiation in literature for children often takes the form of an exaggeration of the difference in size between different groups'. *George Speaks* plays with the idea of Laura's brother being developmentally a baby in every respect except his remarkable capacity to speak fluently and knowledgeably, including helping her with her school work. Much of the humour derives from the contrast between his size and physical abilities and his oral style:

> He waved his little arms and kicked his pudgy legs in the air.
> 'Talking's a piece of cake,' he said. 'Trouble is, I haven't learned to control my body very well yet. In fact, I'm afraid we'll have to postpone the rest of this conversation until another time.'
>
> (King-Smith 1988: 11)

The relative ages of a brother and sister in *A Chance Child* are important for a challenge they face together, where being small can be an advantage, but one outweighed by inexperience:

> She was very small, not very good at looking; she kept going back to search the same places again. The boy was better, though he scratched his face and hands crawling over and under things. He was older – just beginning to grow long and gangling.
>
> (Paton Walsh 1978: 20)

A variation in the representation of this preoccupation in *James and the Giant Peach* is the child's encounters with creatures and other everyday phenomena of unpredictable sizes. James not only finds the world, after the death of his parents, 'vast and unfriendly', but he also meets insects as large as dogs:

> Every one of these 'creatures' was at least as big as James himself, and in the strange greenish light that shone down from somewhere in the ceiling, they were absolutely terrifying to behold.

> (Dahl 1990: 38)

This fantasy theme is familiar from, for example, *Alice in Wonderland*, *The Borrowers* and *The Shrinking of Treehorn*, illustrating that measurement of size in children's fiction can be in relation to childly rather than adult norms, including rapid and unsettling changes.

The central character in *Crummy Mummy and Me* often quotes the words of other (adult) characters, including those which express their perceptions of her. Here, she attributes to her step-father, 'Crusher', an acknowledgement of both her physical size and her maturity: 'Crusher spun me round and round in his arms. (I knew he was ecstatic. Usually he says I'm far too big for that now, and I'll put his back out)' (Fine 1988: 42).

If children are represented in these texts as viewing the world from a different perspective than adults do, the difference may be to the children's advantage. Some of the qualities identified earlier as typical of children are given a more positive spin. Thus baby George warns his sister Laura that, unlike her, their parents may find it hard to accept his abilities: '". . . it would have been too much of a shock for grown-ups. They don't have the imagination"' (King-Smith 1988: 29), and, '"That's the trouble with grown-ups – something out of the ordinary happens and they panic. Children are so much more sensible"' (ibid.: 37). Where lack of access to the resources available to adults (including 'know-how') constitutes a barrier to a desired goal, a child can still be depicted as having legitimate interests: 'Nick knew now exactly what he wanted to do, but he had no idea at all how he was going to do it' (Morpurgo 1987: 26).

In addition, children are permitted in texts like these to have a range of qualities and personalities. There are many children's books in which a group of children find themselves having adventures away from adults altogether, in the convention identified by Stephens (1992) as 'time out'. (Examples include Blyton's *Famous Five* stories, Ransome's *Swallows and Amazons* and its sequels, Lewis's *Narnia* books, and many others.) In these contexts, the salience of being a child *in relation to adults* is much reduced, and each child character has a distinctive personality. This may not give the author as much scope as an adult cast, which can include longer, more diverse personal histories and responses to experience, but there is still room for heterogeneity. In the texts I selected, child characters (or the authors who represent their experience) are able to reflect on and compare their own and their peers' ways of being, and to demonstrate that there are different versions of childly experience:

> She wasn't inviting Leonie Shanks; Leonie Shanks was just a show-off. Pavindra Patel wasn't bad, but she was never allowed to go anywhere even when she was invited. Jackie-Lee Gibbs was OK; she'd invite Jackie. . . . Soozie was as nutty as a fruit cake. Sophie quite liked her . . .
>
> (Ure 1987: 9)

> I can cope pretty well with most things. But it is good to have someone on your side when you feel really stumped.
>
> (Fine 1988: 96)

> No one else in her class knew all their tables right up to twelve times, like she did.
>
> (King-Smith 1988: 72)

> He was one of those bragging brutish boys who could hit harder, run faster and shout louder than anyone else.
>
> (Morpurgo 1987: 12)

> Ben Morrison was one of the Zombies: the Zombies liked to talk of people doing things that were violent.
>    Sophie didn't really believe in vampires . . .
>
> (Ure 1987: 23)

Although these comparisons and distinctions between different child characters may not be particularly subtle, they do encourage the reader to see each one as an individual rather than as a mere representative of childliness. Such differentiation also makes it possible for the central character to have more status or power than others in the story. Much of the action in *A Chance Child* concerns children helping each other, while *Conker* is about a boy who is moved to save a dog which is being badly treated: '. . . the dog began to whine and whimper and yelp. It was a cry for help which Nick could not ignore' . . . 'The dog followed him to the end of his chain. "I'll be back," he said. "I promise I will"' (Morpurgo 1987: 21, 26). As I shall suggest in Chapter 6, children in middle childhood are rarely able to relate to others as superordinates, but younger siblings and pets can be spoken to from this position. Minna, in *Crummy Mummy and Me*, explicitly appreciates that her step-father treats her justly: ' "He doesn't take advantage of the fact that he's grown-up and I'm not . . ." ' (Fine 1988: 37), and she herself is portrayed as protective towards her baby sister, while James, in *The Giant Peach*, gains an equal status with the giant insects.

Indeed in both Fine's story and *George Speaks*, there are explicit adult–child role reversals, used primarily for comic effect, but with a potentially more serious interpretation. In the former, Minna sees herself as having to take some responsibility for 'Crummy Dummy', the baby, claiming that her mother '. . . ought to run the house a bit better, and dress Crummy Dummy up in nicer clothes (and stop everybody calling her that – her name is Miranda!)' (Fine 1988: 18). In King-Smith's book, baby George chooses Laura to reveal his secret to (that he can talk), deploring the adult characters' use of baby language:

> . . . talk about making noises – that's all some of them do. They bend over me with silly grins on their faces, and then they come out with a load of rubbish. 'Who's booful den?' 'Who's a gorgeous Georgeous Porgeous?' 'Diddums wassums Granny's ickle treasure?' It's an insult to the English language.
>
> (King-Smith 1988: 9–10)

These limited examples taken from this genre of writing provide a contrast with the data presented earlier and demonstrate that both kinds of tendency – to homogenize children as a group and to represent them as diverse individuals – coexist in the language. From this consideration of texts for children, and reflections from some of their authors, there also emerges another kind of representation of children, as readers. Several authors make a point, like this observation by Trease (1977: 148):

> . . . the writer is left with one obvious and inescapable difference between child and adult readers: the former have not lived so long, and in the nature of things they cannot have built up the same mental and emotional capital of background knowledge and first-hand experience.

The matter of adults' responsibility towards child readers who are necessarily impressionable is often mentioned by those who write for them, alongside an unwillingness to see children as lesser simply because they are younger:

> . . . the emotional range [of children's fiction] ought to be the same, if not greater; children's emotions are just as powerful as those of adults, and more compressed, since children have less means of expressing themselves, and less capacity for self-analysis.
>
> (Aiken 1977: 179)

Men and women and children have always known happiness, felt terror, been angry, felt irritable, known despair... Children are not less intelligent than grown-ups. The problem is that they *know* less.

(Burton 1977: 162–4)

Of course, these authors are not themselves members of the group 'children', and there is always some element of 'socialization' in texts by adults for children, but, like all polysemic texts, these are capable of various readings.

A final word to this section is provided by Anne Fine, who returns us to a consideration of the connotations of 'childish'-ness:

'Children are not childish,' she says. 'I'm not childish, I never was childish, I never will be childish, I hate childish people and I can't stand childish children. I don't write childish books. I write books for children, which is a completely different thing.'

(Newnham 1997: 28)

## 3.5  Summary and conclusions

This chapter has provided some different approaches to analysing the ways in which children are represented in contemporary English, taking evidence firstly from a large corpus, and secondly from discussions and a charity advertisement, all of which are concerned with problems around children and childhood. The third source of data was fiction written for children, which provides contrasting evidence about how children and their experience can be represented.

The analysis of collocations in a large corpus illuminates certain kinds of patternings in language in ways which close analyses of individual texts cannot do. The particular methods used in this chapter have shown how certain words seem to be 'attracted' to the words used to denote children, and to co-occur frequently with them. It emerges once more that children feature frequently as targets of harm and as beneficiaries of care in noun phrases, while patterns of colligation demonstrate that *children* is often the noun in a prepositional phrase; similarly *children's* is often followed by a noun which denotes not what they voluntarily 'possess' so much as the name of a product produced *for* them. Patterns of usage of descriptive words for children and childly qualities clearly illustrate the two paradigms of the archetypical child: the demon and the angel.

The radio discussions highlighted these ideas too, and also underlined the way in which the stage of childhood often becomes a significant idea because of contrasts with the longer, more powerful phase of adulthood, and the charity advertisement made use of these contrasts in startling and provocative ways, to appeal to readers to support both children and policies to reduce violent conflict.

Finally, the chapter presented some examples of fiction written for children. The need to appeal primarily to a child audience leads to a childly point of view having a *de facto* authenticity in all the texts discussed here, in spite of the range of ways in which authors handle narratorial voice. Various devices for constructing a childly perspective were considered, including a reversal in the norm for representing relationships: adults can be presented as a more homogeneous group, contrasted with children who can be more fully drawn and differentiated. Quotations from some of the authors who write for children demonstrate that many of them see the enterprise as having much in common with producing adult fiction, except for their awareness that children, by definition, cannot have experienced as much as adult readers must have done, and that this does lead to modifications in ways of writing.

Although this chapter has attempted to draw comparisons between synchronic textual data, there is obviously potential for a diachronic perspective – although that would be a different study. Nevertheless, it is worth noting, in conclusion, that none of the findings presented here is likely to be universal and enduring for all time. The meta-literature on children's literature includes reflections on its changing social and cultural role. Until relatively recently, of course, the idea of a separate genre of children's fiction had no currency at all (Kline 1993; Postman 1985), and several writers point out that some of the great myths, legends and folktales of the past, including those revered as part of a classical education, would be likely to feature on a children's list if accepted for publication today (Avery 1989; Paton Walsh 1977). The idea of narrative as an essential organizing enterprise in which everyone engages, and of stories which embody many layers of insight, links texts of many kinds, including some at least of the texts written primarily for children: 'As has often been remarked, no first-class children's book has ever failed to hold countless adult admirers' (Trease 1977: 150).

These ideas begin to bridge some of the dichotomies between the textual and linguistic representations of children and others. One kind of universality which can be identified in relation to children and adults is the human condition, and this idea, among others, will be explored more fully in Part II.

## Notes

1. This collocation is not restricted to newspapers and television news scripts. Some of the citations are from popular magazines and fiction, including reported speech.

2.  In a recent survey carried out by the National Children's Bureau and Save the Children (Willow and Hyder 1998), the child respondents often reported that it was 'being naughty' which led to 'being smacked'. 'Being naughty', the children said, would sometimes be 'hitting people', but a 'smack' is a particular type of 'hitting' – done *by* adults *to* children. There are probably other subtle distinctions between words for similar actions carried out by adults and children respectively, but they will not necessarily be revealed by corpus analysis of this kind. For an investigation of *play* from this perspective, see Chapter 6.

3.  This circular argument is reminiscent of essentialist arguments about sex and gender: if women/men demonstrate that they can be and do non-gender-typical things, they risk being designated not a *'real* woman/man' by those for whom maintenance of the category is preferable to change.

4.  For a discussion of the relationship between toys, especially the Christmas gift, and children's economic status in the family, see Hood-Williams (1990). It is also perhaps significant that the letter to Santa is used as a research tool by market researchers (Kline 1993).

5.  Knowles and Malmkjaer (1996: 217) comment on another Dahl novel, *The BFG*, in which the central – child – character is subject to rules 'imposed by the referents for "they"', who never enter the story in person. Likewise, the character of Alice in Lewis Carroll's novels is distanced from adults by the device of 'making her refer to them with the third-person plural pronouns *them, their* and *they*' (ibid.: 227).

# Perspectives on Children, Language and the Social World

# Introduction to **Part II**

*... there is nothing particularly mysterious about children or childhood. Children are human beings, not only 'human becomings', they have not only needs, a fact which is recognized, they have also interests, that may or may not be compatible with interests of other social groups or categories, and they are exposed to societal forces like other groups, layers, and classes.*

(QVORTRUP 1994: 18)

Part I of this book has identified some of the patterns to be found in the ways children are routinely described. In this second part of the book, I aim to draw out more explicitly what I see as the connections between children, language and society. Chapter 4 deals primarily with how research has illuminated particular kinds of links between children and language, and Chapter 5 adopts a more theoretical approach to exploring the links between language and the social world.

In Chapter 4 I argue that research into children and language conceptualizes the connections between them in some particular ways, for reasons which are not difficult to identify. The following quotations exemplify three different priorities to be found in the literature which reports research into children and language.

> The crux of the argument is that complex language is universal because *children actually reinvent it*, generation after generation – not because they are taught, not because they are generally smart, not because it is useful to them, but because they just can't help it.
>
> (Pinker 1994: 32, original emphasis)

> Taking all the available evidence together, then, we can state the situation as follows. Children learn language because they are predisposed to do so. How they set about the task is largely determined by the way they are: seekers after meaning who try to find the underlying principles that will account for the patterns that they recognize in their experiences.
>
> (Wells 1986: 43)

> No matter how uncouth schoolchildren may outwardly appear, they remain tradition's warmest friends. Like the savage, they are respecters, even venerators, of custom; and in their self-contained community their basic lore and language seems scarcely to alter from generation to generation.
>
> (Opie and Opie 1959: 22)

These three summarizing quotations demonstrate that it is not only newspaper texts which provide evidence of an 'angle of telling' in the language used to denote children and what they do. Academic discourse contains its presuppositions, its traditions, its habitual ways of representing the objects of its authors' inquiry: the present volume, of course, is no exception. Although some recent work has addressed the discourses found in academic writing about children and childhood (e.g. Stainton Rogers and Stainton Rogers 1992), there is little *linguistic* analysis of this topic. However, different ways of researching, and writing about, aspects of the relationship between children and language do manifest themselves in somewhat contrasting styles, and the short extracts quoted are representative of some of these.

Steven Pinker is an American cognitive scientist who explores in his best-selling book a wide range of issues about the nature of human language. His work exemplifies a powerful tradition in the study of children and language which knits together knowledge about language as a universal human resource with knowledge about the human organism and its ability to process language in its components and as a whole. The particular claim quoted here foregrounds *language*, acknowledging the part played by children in its reproduction, but representing this in a fairly deterministic way, as though children's role is to be the instrument through which language, the central focus, is to be transmitted and preserved down through the generations.

Gordon Wells's study in Bristol, England, had an applied dimension, highlighting the implications for teachers of what the project found: the subtitle of his influential volume *The Meaning-Makers* is 'children learning language and using language to learn'. Like Pinker, Wells acknowledges the importance of observing children in order to understand language, but, as this extract illustrates, his concern is partly with how their learning is accomplished, in diverse social contexts. In this quotation, Wells foregrounds children rather than language, and their active drive to seek – and make – meanings, to engage with their experience and be active participants in their social world. Even accepting Pinker's claim that no one teaches children their first language, in a formal sense, there is nevertheless considerable concern among educationalists about children's differential performance in schools, the significance of their language in this, and the ways in which language teaching is and should be carried out.

A considerably older classic text about children and language is that from which the third extract is taken. The British folklorists Iona and Peter Opie were not very much concerned with the nature of language as a system, or the composition of the human brain. Their interest was more in how the oral tradition is maintained around the country (and in some cases around the world), and their work involves two perspectives on children in this process. One is the things children do, as children, and their beliefs, social codes and so on, so that there is some concern in this research with stages in children's development, as there is in research into both acquisition and pedagogy. The second perspective is the part played by children in preserving certain rituals, customs and beliefs on behalf of the community as a whole.

From each of these three vantage points some familiar themes can once again be seen emerging: children as very much a part of the social world in general, and yet, in other ways, separate from it; the expectation that children will grow, change, develop, learning as they do so; and children as preservers of a cultural resource, looking back to tradition, and yet entrusted with its maintenance for the future. Once again, I shall use a thematic approach in Chapter 4 to explore these three main ways in which links between children and language have been researched and written about.

Chapter 5 addresses some questions which are central to sociolinguistics, about the nature of the relationships between people and the many varieties of language which are associated with belonging to the different categories into which they are grouped – by virtue of where they live, how old they are, what sex they are and so on. These questions require a view on what language is, what society is and what choices are open to individuals about their social identifications. Such issues have been considered by scholars working in a wide range of disciplines, including philosophy, sociology, social anthropology, psychology and, of course, linguistics. Sociolinguistic researchers themselves have approached the question of the relationships between individuals, society and language from several different perspectives. Some have been concerned to shed light on the nature of language as a system and the processes of linguistic change; others have been more centrally interested in the role of discourses in the maintenance and change of social institutions; others still have focused on how and why individuals make particular decisions about their linguistic allegiances and self-representations. All of these issues may be relevant in discussions of children, language and the social world.

I have already noted, in Part I and in the discussion above, the strong tendency to view the relationship between children and language from a developmental perspective, seeking to determine the route by which children become users of the adult language. A similar implicit 'adultism' has been identified within sociology: as Alanen (1994: 27) claims, whereas 'adults are readily understood by their actions, relevances and experiences, . . . the same does not apply to children'. Contributors to the sociology of childhood point out that as children live out their day-to-day experience, they may not be particularly concerned with being in a process of development towards something else. Alanen (1994: 28) continues:

> There is no reason to argue against childhood's being a stage in individual development and a period of preparation for adult life and, therefore, a condition of relative vulnerability. But participation in the sense of being and acting in society does not begin first when a defined age limit or degree of adultness has been reached.

How might this recognition be acknowledged in descriptions of children's *linguistic* behaviour? The idea of 'communicative competence' (Hymes 1972) will be discussed in Chapter 4. For children, to be communicatively competent means knowing not only how to use the linguistic resources available in the culture, but how to indicate as one deploys them that one can abide by the norms of behaviour acceptable from a child in relation to one's interlocutors, be they younger children, older family members, other adults in authority and so on. Likewise, the recognition within sociolinguistics of 'age-grading', or linguistic conduct appropriate to the period one occupies within the lifespan (Coupland and Nussbaum 1993; Romaine 1984), also indicates that children are required to be competent social actors *as children*, as well as preparing to be more comprehensively competent members of society when they 'grow up'.

In Part III I shall consider talk involving children and adults, to explore both commonalities and differences. However, the fact that children are human beings and social actors, with immediate as well as potential needs and interests, is stressed here because it is important to bear this in mind in the discussion in Chapter 5 about individuals, groups and social structures, and the relationships between these and language. If the theories presented there have any validity in general, then unless – contra Qvortrup – we are to hive children off into some not-quite-human, non-social category, these theories should also be applicable to insights into children's language and language about children.

# 4

## Perspectives on Researching Children and Language

*What the present age knows all about is what it is to be at the stage of and in the state of childhood.*

(ARCHARD 1993: 30)

## 4.1  Introduction

In this chapter, I shall consider three broad categories of research about children and language: children's language acquisition and development; language in children's learning; and language in children's culture. Treatment of all of these will necessarily be brief, in the light of the space available, and cannot do full justice to any one of the areas, given the extensive literature in each. I am also aware that there is an emphasis on the British context, which is consistent with other data analysed in the book, although extensive reference is made to research from elsewhere, particularly the United States of America and Australia.

What follows, then, makes no claim to be a comprehensive overview, but will highlight salient contrasts between some of the main approaches to research which explores the relationships between children, language and the social world. Where it seems illuminating to do so, I shall comment on the discourse features of texts cited, but any such commentary is selective and not intended as equivalent to the linguistic analyses of texts in Part I.

## 4.2  Children's language acquisition and development

### 4.2.1  A psycholinguistic emphasis

For some writers, research about children's language is synonymous with research into children's language acquisition. *The Handbook of Child Language* (Fletcher and MacWhinney 1995), in Blackwell's series of state-of-the-art handbooks in linguistics, opens with the sentence, 'The study of child language *acquisition* is alive and well' (p. 2, emphasis added), thus proclaiming the authors' interpretation of what is often meant by the study of 'child language'. This text provides us with a useful overview of those approaches to child language research which concentrate particularly on the detail of the early stages of acquisition, and which link this knowledge with the nature of language itself. The logic of this connection is obvious: if we can find out more about the sequences in which young children gain command of the components of their native language, we can understand better what those components actually are.

Research into acquisition sheds light on the human brain and the cognitive processes involved in understanding and producing communication with other human beings. Comparative research into the acquisition of different languages generates data about what human languages have in common, continuing the paradigm-shifting work of Chomsky which proposed both an innate mechanism for language acquisition in human beings and the idea of a universal grammar underlying all human languages. It is also easy to see why work with 'disordered' children is important in this kind of child language research: comparisons between subjects for whom linguistic processing does not work smoothly, and those for whom it does, throw into relief components of what is involved.

Although the growth in acquisition studies is particularly associated with the late 1960s and the 1970s, an interest in how children learn language is common to many parents, and is not, of course, an exclusively twentieth-century preoccupation. Diaries have been kept by some scholars to record their children's progress in learning to talk, certainly in the nineteenth century, while:

> [c]hild language study has exercised its fascination on rulers and scholars alike for over 2,000 years, especially in relation to such questions as the origins and growth of language. . . . Many felt that the study of linguistic development in the child (language *ontogenesis*) would provide clues about the linguistic development of the human race (language *phylogenesis*).
>
> (Crystal 1987a: 228)

This idea, which is still under discussion, again points to the link between the stages children go through to learn language and the nature of language itself.

The diary method, where parents attempted to record in writing the early sounds and utterances of their children, has been largely superseded by audio and video recordings, and other technological developments have had a major impact on this kind of child language research. The kinds of questions which interest those working in this field require substantial quantities of data, since many of their lines of inquiry seek to explore generalizable propositions. Computers make possible both new kinds of analysis and the simulation in machines of the processes suspected to be going on within the human organism. It is worth quoting at greater length from the introduction to the *Handbook of Child Language*, because it gives us a concise summary of some of the priorities current in this kind of research:

> While maintaining the hard-won methods and insights developed over the last 30 years, language acquisition researchers continue to explore the implications of new models, techniques, and data from linguistics, psychology, cognitive neuroscience, artificial intelligence, philosophy, and socialization theory. The thirst of language acquisition researchers for new data and new data analysis procedures has been further whetted by developments in computer technology and data storage. The store of crosslinguistic samples and transcript comparisons continues to grow month to month, as does the richness of theory, observation, and experimentation with both normal and disordered children.
>
> (Fletcher and MacWhinney 1995: 2)

Several points about this extract are worthy of note in the context of a comparison between different approaches to links between children and language. One point is the priority given to empirically observable data, and to large quantities of data, mainly for the reason cited earlier – that, in the tradition of positivist scientific inquiry, researchers from this tradition tend to propose hypotheses susceptible to testing and measurement, from which to generate generalizations. (See Bloom 1993 for an explicit statement of this position.) Secondly, projects such as the development of computer simulations of language processing in the human organism imply a need for experimentation, which, as the extract makes clear, is an important aspect of this research. However, some developmental psychologists are sceptical of computer modelling of language acquisition:

> We can see the culmination of this failure to theorise the social, and the abstraction of the 'individual' as the unit of analysis, in the way computer programs are regarded as being capable of modelling thought processes. Here we have a dramatic illustration of psychology's models of the individual, rational, isolated and disembodied.
>
> (Burman 1994: 45)

A pattern common to many discussions of initial acquisition is – quite understandably – the division of both language and children into gradations: language in terms of its elements and children in terms of their ages. A typical pattern is to describe acquisition in relation first to sounds, then to words and then to grammar, with discourse organization and social context perhaps featuring after all these. Similarly, such texts routinely begin with early sound-making in babyhood and track accomplishments chronologically throughout the first years of life. The second part of Fletcher and MacWhinney (1995) exemplifies this pattern, as does a useful introduction to both linguistics and language development (Lee 1986), which is organized into pairs of chapters in the same way. (See also, for further examples, Bancroft 1996; Crystal 1987b; de Villiers and de Villiers 1979; Whitehead 1990.)

Although this is an obvious organizing device for material in this field, I draw attention to it because it may exert an influence on the way we think about children and language, precisely because it is so common. It is not inevitable, however. Garvey (1984), for example, is ordered thematically rather than chronologically, and Cook-Gumperz (1986) puts forward a convincing argument for backgrounding grammatical units in the analysis of child language, and 'plac[ing] the analytic emphasis clearly on discourse as the relevant unit of speech' (p. 51). Developmental psychology has recently been subject to some severe criticism (Archard 1993; Burman 1994; James et al. 1998; Stainton Rogers and Stainton Rogers 1992), particularly in relation to its association with the model of a developmental path which is individual, predictable, universal, and natural rather than social. Given the textual data presented in Part I, which illustrates the different timescales involved in naming and representing childhood, I am obviously sceptical of strictly linear views of development. As I shall show in Chapter 7, adults do not abandon childly discourse as they leave the 'territory' of childhood, and other data presented in Part III will illustrate that being a child is not a totally defining characteristic in all dialogues involving children.

In reviewing several of the articles in Fletcher and MacWhinney (1995), I noticed some features which contribute to its characteristic discursive style. I present some of them here, although there are obviously many other (possibly contrasting) discourse features which would be identified in a thorough analysis. A number of nominalizations and noun phrases highlight a concentration on the phenomenon of *language acquisition* (itself a nominalization), rather than on *children talking*, and on staged changes over time, rather than on experience as children live it. These include: 'onset of word comprehension', 'early child utterances', 'critical developmental transitions', 'maturational milestones', 'onset of grammar', 'start state', 'earlier lexical stage'. Also noticeable are quantifying, measuring and normative expressions, such as 'global measures like MLU [mean length of utterance]', 'parental growth rate', 'communicative development inventories', 'normal range'. And the image of children as the sites where processes occur is evoked by locative expressions, such as 'the development of grammar in children', 'grammatical development in the talk of young children', and so on.

Finally, in relation to canonical child language acquisition research, it is striking that so much of the work is concentrated in the early years of life.

The extensive CHILDES database (Child Language Data Exchange System) is heavily weighted in favour of data from the under-5's, and many other research articles and books about 'child language' assume the early stages. This is obviously because so much that is interesting occurs at this stage in the lifespan, and change can be observed at such a rapid rate. Furthermore, children in the age-group which is my interest in this book – i.e. the post-infancy, pre-adolescent stage of life – have far less still to 'acquire' in respect of the basic elements of language in the form of sounds, words and syntactic structures, although of course children continue to develop in all these areas as maturation continues.

## 4.2.2  A social emphasis

Psycholinguists are not the only researchers to find interest in the links between language as a system and children's language development. Complementary to the perspective which investigates the details of grammatical units and the processing of language in the human brain are studies and theories concerned with language as a social semiotic (Halliday 1978) and with the 'meaning-seeking' motivation for children to engage in communicative interaction with those around them (see Wells 1986). The emphasis of writers in this functional tradition is less on the progress of the individual and the internal organization of this progress, and more on the accomplishment of intersubjective ends. Language is 'progressively learned', rather than 'acquired', or '. . . obtained with maturation, like teeth or hair' (Butt 1989: 66). Halliday's observations of his son Nigel's language development include a claim about the functions of language even at the protolanguage stage, of which he says: 'The ability to mean is important to Nigel because it is functional. He is creating language for a purpose, to do something with it' (Halliday 1989: 6). Halliday (despite the difficulties attached to ascribing intention to children's vocalizations) explains the two functions that appear very early: the pragmatic function and the mathetic, or reflective, learning function. He then states:

> Nigel is using his ability to create meanings as a way of projecting himself on to the environment, expressing his concern with it – what's in it for him, so to speak – and so beginning systematically to explore it . . .
> . . . Every human language is a potential for meaning in these two ways: it is a resource for doing with, and it is a resource for thinking with. This is the most important single fact about human language . . .
>
> (p. 7)

An effect of this kind of discourse is to lead the reader's gaze away from statistics, neural networks and the component elements of the linguistic system and into the social world (the 'domains', if you like, of 'situated activity' and 'social settings'; Layder 1997 and Chapter 5 below). In the first sentence of this quotation, particularly, I am struck by the agency and capacities attributed to Nigel: 'using his ability', 'projecting himself', 'expressing his concern', 'beginning to explore'. (Recall similarly Wells's 'seekers after meaning', 'meaning makers'.) Instead of the child as a conduit *for* language, language is a resource *for* the child.

The integration of the linguistic with the social is also associated with Hymes's concept of communicative competence. Hymes is troubled by Chomsky's ideal speaker–hearer: 'The controlling image is of an abstract, isolated individual, almost an unmotivated cognitive mechanism, not, except incidentally, a person in a social world' (Hymes 1972: 272). Child language researchers seeking to involve themselves in 'ethnographies of speaking' situate their investigations in families and communities, taking account of the ways children learn from those around them not only the rules of grammar and a referring vocabulary but also conventions of how things are interactionally achieved, and how appropriate linguistic and social behaviour depend on who is speaking, who is being addressed, the topic, social setting and so on. Alternatively, some investigators seek to find out what children of different ages know about the interpersonal dimensions of language by means of elicitation experiments, role play, simulations and so on.

Research of this more socially oriented kind includes functional analyses of early child conversations (e.g. Butt 1989; Painter 1984, 1989), studies of development of the various pragmatic aspects of language (e.g. collections such as Ervin-Tripp and Mitchell-Kernan 1977; Ochs and Schieffelin 1979; Saville-Troike 1989); studies comparing the socially oriented dimensions of language development across cultures and between different age-groups (e.g. Andersen 1990; Ochs and Schieffelin 1983; Schieffelin and Ochs 1986); studies of children's acquisition of several languages in social contexts (for an overview see Mayor 1996); the development of conversational competence in children (e.g. McTear 1985). A slightly different approach to the social dimensions of language used by children is found in Romaine (1984), who is particularly interested in sociolinguistic variables. She is concerned with language change over time, as well as changes in children's sociolinguistic competence, and stresses that '[a]ttempts to trace rules, either diachronically or developmentally in terms of the changes in formal manifestation they have undergone, without regard for their communicative function are fundamentally misguided' (p. 81). For Romaine too, then, language as system and speaker as language-user need to be located in social settings and differentiated interactions, and she makes similar points about the significance of attitudes in respect of bilingual development (Romaine 1995).

Many of these studies, and others with a similar focus, will be discussed further in later chapters. Before leaving this section, however, I want to draw attention to the fact that, even where a more social perspective is adopted in the research, there is still a tendency to highlight younger children (and sometimes adolescents) rather than those in middle childhood[1] (although it is not so marked as in the psycholinguistic acquisition studies), and a concomitant tendency to preserve an age-graded taxonomic approach.

Aware as I am that the three main sections in this chapter are slightly artificial divisions of the research which links children and language, with many potential areas of overlap, I shall turn now to the second of my broad themes, language in children's learning.

## 4.3   Language in children's learning

Language is clearly the main means by which children gain access to the knowledge available to human society as a whole, and to the values and beliefs of the community or society in which they live. It is thus a conduit for learning a great deal of what they need to know, and what others think they need to know. This is true in the intimate arena of the family and its force is all the more apparent in the institutionalized setting of the school. No wonder that there is a substantial research enterprise concerned with language, children and learning. Given my concern with middle childhood, I shall concentrate here on the primary school years and on research which illuminates the connections between language and pedagogy.

### 4.3.1   Home and school language

> The Elementary School might exert a more permanently humanising influence on its products if it were not for the mistake of some teachers in treating English as ... a mere ... subject ... [T]hey have to fight against the powerful influence of evil habits of speech contracted in home and street. The teachers' struggle is thus not with ignorance but with a perverted power ... the lesson in English is not merely one occasion for the inculcation of knowledge, it is an initiation into the corporate life of man.
>
> (Board of Education 1921 'The Newbolt Report': 57–60)

An abiding preoccupation of some of those concerned about children, language and schooling is the discrepancy between the way children use language at home and the language to be found in schools. I cannot resist drawing out some of the stylistic features of the voicing of this preoccupation, in the above extract, by the committee whose duty was '... to inquire into the position occupied by English (Language and Literature) in the educational system, and to advise how its study may best be promoted in schools of all types ...'. The idea I have noted before – that in some representations children are less than full members of the human race – is quite explicit in the claim that they are 'products' that need to be 'humanized', and in the association of what they bring to school with 'a perverted power'. Not until correct values have been 'inculcated' is their 'initiation' into the composite human race ('the corporate life of man') accomplished. Although teachers are represented as having the duty to 'exert influence', the image evoked by the pugilistic metaphors used is of moral but weak human protagonists in a titanic struggle with a non-human other. Turn your back for a minute and this beast – an evil, inarticulate monster-child – will grow too powerful for your influence.

Although the way these sentiments are expressed may seem very dated, I have argued elsewhere (Sealey 1994, 1996) that there is a continuity, if not among academic researchers then among policy-makers and some public commentators, in claims of a causal association between letting children do – and speak – as they will, and a national moral decline.

In terms of research since that of the Newbolt Committee, the burgeoning interest in authentic spoken language in the second half of the twentieth century, and developments in the means of recording and analysing it, have contributed to the perceived discrepancies between children's 'home language' and 'school language' receiving serious attention. One strand of research, linked closely to educational policy, addresses an alleged 'deficit' in the language of some children. The originally American idea of 'Compensatory Education' sought to 'enrich' the language of 'deprived' children, and similar ideas were adopted in the UK. Originally, a psycholinguistic perspective was dominant, and research considered the effectiveness of different remedial approaches to improve individual children's attainment. The following extract is taken from a report on a study which used specific communicative 'techniques' with groups of young children, who were 'matched' (by age, sex and IQ scores) with a control group. The researchers introduce their rationale in these terms:

> An eclectic approach to the teaching of language is usual in most preschool programs for disadvantaged children. Since their language deficiencies are extensive, it is hoped that the presentation of a massive array of possibly fruitful techniques is bound to lead to learning. In contrast, the present authors . . . have presented the hypothesis that the deprived child's verbal weakness is so overwhelming that it blinds one to his more subtle but basic deficiency. This deficiency is the lack of a symbolic system for thinking.
>
> (Blank and Solomon 1972: 178)

These claims remind one of the belief, sometimes reported in primary school staffrooms, that certain groups of children 'have no language' (see Hughes and Cousins 1988 and Zentella 1998 for some examples). The terms in which it is expressed are much less fashionable now in the research community, if not in the press, although there is clearly continuity with abiding concerns to improve the educational life chances of less successful children in schools. Referring expressions such as 'disadvantaged children' are likely now to be considered less acceptable, and the phrases reminiscent of physical degeneracy – 'weakness', 'deficiency', 'lack' – carry an implication of victim-blaming. Such perspectives in 'deficit' theories of under-achievement have been high-lighted and rejected by several subsequent researchers (see below).

The terminology of disadvantage and deprivation is problematic. Dif-ferential distribution of and access to resources makes a real difference to people's lives, and we need ways of expressing this material fact. One effect of labelling children as 'disadvantaged', however, notwithstanding the improvement it represents on 'evil' or 'corrupt', is that the problem may become conceptually located in the victim. The term can be used to stand metonymically for a whole range of complex influences and effects, reduced at worst to a euphemism for children who are difficult to teach. The pos-sibility of change for an individual may be underestimated, and the hetero-geneity of people assigned the group label may be masked. (See Sykes 1985 for similar conclusions about the represention of 'young blacks' as a disadvantaged group.) In the 1960s and 1970s the term 'disadvantaged children' was unexceptional. However, researchers with a more sociological perspective on linguistic issues placed greater emphasis on social context in accounting for and suggesting measures to apply to the linguistic diversity associated with different speech communities. For example, Labov (1972: 208) expressed profound concern about the assumptions and methods of the educational psychologists associated with Operation Headstart:

> The essential fallacy of the verbal deprivation theory lies in tracing the educational failure of the child to his personal deficiencies. At present, these deficiencies are said to be caused by his home environment. It is traditional to explain a child's failure in school by his inadequacy; but when failure reaches such massive proportions, it seems to us necessary to look at the social and cultural obstacles to learning, and the inability of the school to adjust to the social situation.

Despite significant differences between Labov's position and that of Bernstein, the latter was also critical of the idea of compensatory education, writing in remarkably similar terms in 1970:

> The concept 'compensatory education' serves to direct attention away from the internal organization and the educational context of the school, and focus our attention upon the families and children. . . . the school has to 'compensate' for the something which is missing in the family, and the children are looked at as deficit systems. . . . Once the problem is seen even implicitly in this way, then it becomes appropriate to coin the terms

'cultural deprivation', 'linguistic deprivation', etc. And then these labels do their own sad work.

(Bernstein 1970: 112)

As a sociologist, Bernstein was interested in the effects of more macro social structures on the life-chances of different groups, but his writing on restricted and elaborated codes was interpreted by many as though these were equivalent to differently evaluated linguistic varieties. His contribution, debated and refined over three decades, and specifically his exploration of the specific characteristics of pedagogic discourse and its role in access to learning, continues to be influential. Rather than conceptualizing language as monolithic, and learners as either 'advantaged' or 'deprived', many researchers in language and education in the 1970s and 1980s sought to draw attention to the full range of sociolinguistic factors involved in speakers' repertoires, acknowledging the potential breadth of form, functions and contexts of use of the language(s) found in different communities and contexts. Thus Hymes, for example, stresses the interaction between speakers, language functions and people's affective stances towards language varieties: 'What must be known is the attitude towards the [linguistic] differences,' he writes, 'the functional role assigned to them, the use made of them. Only on the basis of such a functionally motivated description can comparable cases be established and valid theory developed' (1972: 289).

A number of research projects sought to identify more precisely the nature of differences between the language used at home and the language used at school, and some of these, including the work of Shirley Brice Heath, for example, will be discussed in the next section, on the family and socialization. Both the formal characteristics of varieties (such as, for example, dialectal variations, or Bernstein's distinction between person-oriented and position-oriented exchanges) and the functional purposes for language used in the home and at school (the negotiation of interpersonal relationships in contrast to the acquisition of formal knowledge) were identified. Researchers in various countries set out to find empirical evidence about language use at home and at school. In Britain, Tizard and Hughes (1984), for example, found fewer significant differences between working-class and middle-class families' conversations with their children than differences between the richness and variety of talk at home compared with the more limited dialogues in the nursery. Willes (1983), who studied the transition from 'children into pupils', drew attention to the contrast between adults' expectations of children's talk in classrooms and at home. The Bristol Study 'Language at home and at school' (Wells 1986) was a longitudinal study of the acquisition of language by children from a range of social circumstances. The research compared the children's language experience in the environments of the home and the classroom. These findings also undermined stereotyped assumptions of differences in children's language experience at home which were conventionally associated with social class, but supported the need to recognize that success in school requires familiarity with particular kinds of linguistic experience.

The acknowledgement of pedagogic discourse as worthy of study in its own right leads us to consider how children's talk in classrooms has been explored by researchers.

## 4.3.2   Talking to learn

> No child should be expected to cast off the language and culture of the home as he crosses the school threshold, nor to live and act as though school and home represent two totally separate and different cultures which have to be kept firmly apart. The curriculum should reflect many elements of that part of his life which a child lives outside school.
>
> (Department of Education and Science 1975
> 'The Bullock Report': para 20.5: 286)

> *Speaking and Listening*
> The objectives of this attainment target are to ensure that standards of spoken English are raised, that pupils communicate effectively and that they become confident and articulate users of standard English, and that greater emphasis is given to listening skills. . . .
>
> Council contends that this emphasis on communicating fluently and confidently and on speaking in standard English is essential if standards of spoken English in this country are to be raised.
>
> (Department for Education and the
> Welsh Office 1993, para 6.1–6.2: 3)

There are several contrasts in these short extracts from two texts published almost 20 years apart. The Bullock Report of 1975 reflects a recognition of the undesirability of a separation between home and school language, whereas the proposed revisions to the English National Curriculum in 1993 (they were not in fact implemented in quite this form) insists that schools' role, once again, is to overcome falling standards in the population as whole. Bullock's (male) 'child' is represented as an individual unit, while the National Curriculum proposals feature 'pupils' en masse. Bullock's child, although syntactically the object of 'expectations' (of teachers and policy-makers) is nevertheless a social being with a life of his own, located in his home and his school. The National Curriculum foregrounds composite 'standards' – 'standards of spoken English in this country' – and locates processes within 'pupils': 'listening skills', 'communicating fluently', 'speaking in standard English'. Children's role as the collective repositories of language resurfaces in this kind of discourse, in contrast to the 'child-centred' individualism of much educational discourse of the 1960s and 1970s, epitomized in the Plowden Report:

At the heart of the educational process lies the child. No advances in policy, no acquisitions of new equipment have their desired effect unless they are in harmony with the nature of the child, unless they are fundamentally acceptable to him.

(Central Advisory Council for Education
(England) 1967: Ch. 2, para 9: 7)

One important way in which recognition of the role of language in learning was reinforced in the UK in the light of the Bullock recommendations was in the concept of 'language across the curriculum'. Teachers at both primary and secondary level were encouraged to accept that their disciplinary subjects, the areas of study with which they were most concerned, were all mediated through language, giving them opportunities to teach language throughout the school day. Awareness of pedagogic discourse includes awareness that there are particular ways of talking about particular subjects, and that these may not be self-evident to pupils. However, there is something of a paradox in the individualistic versions of 'the child' with 'his' essential nature confronting a curriculum when so much recognition has been afforded to the role of dialogue in learning. Bruner draws attention to this when he reflects on his own research perspectives:

My model of the child . . . was very much in the tradition of the solo child mastering the world by representing it to himself in his own terms. . . . I have come increasingly to recognize that most learning in most settings is a communal activity, a sharing of the culture.

(Bruner 1983: 127)

This insight has been given extensive development by a large number of researchers in schools. Jones (1988) provides a summary of reports and research from 1963 to 1986, all of which emphasize the importance of talk in learning. The quotations he cites illustrate the tension, suggested above, between the value of talk for the learner and the utility of an articulate school population (and eventual workforce) for the state. Two examples may suffice to demonstrate this:

One of the major functions of language that concerns teachers is its use for learning: for trying to put new ideas into words, for testing out one's thinking on other people, for fitting together new ideas with old ones . . . which all needs to be done to bring about new understanding.

(National Association for the Teaching of English 1976,
quoted in Jones 1988)

The primacy of the spoken word in human intercourse cannot be too strongly emphasised. Important though the written word is, most communication takes place in speech; and those who do not listen with attention and cannot speak with clarity, articulateness and confidence are at a disadvantage in almost every aspect of their personal, social and working lives.

(Department of Education and Science 1982,
quoted in Jones 1988)

The first quotation, from NATE, a teachers' association, implies as agents of the processes 'trying out', 'testing out', 'fitting together' both teachers and pupils. People putting language to use and recognizing its 'functions' are also suggested, and the goal is 'new understanding'. The second quotation, by contrast, from a government department, foregrounds 'the spoken word' rather than its speakers. The first sentence and a half are concerned entirely, despite the adjective 'human', with relations between aspects of language: 'spoken word', 'intercourse', 'written word', 'communication', 'speech'. The speakers of the language do not appear until the second half of the extract, where they are surrounded by negatives 'do not', 'cannot', 'disadvantage'. The inclusiveness of the first extract contrasts with the discrimination in the second between those who can and do (use speech effectively) and those who cannot or do not. It is perhaps this difference in emphasis – between learners' and 'Society's' perspectives – which accounts for the frustration among politicians with education researchers who explore the role of talk in learning rather than finding a recipe for schooling articulate pupils who listen 'properly' to instructions (cf. Barnes 1988).

From the 1970s onwards, then, there was a growing recognition of a role for spoken language – if not consensus about priorities or methods. (See Wilkinson 1990 for an overview.) Classrooms proved to be sites for research by linguists into discourse in general (e.g. Sinclair and Coulthard 1975), and educationalists explored classroom talk, often in secondary schools (e.g. Barnes et al. 1971), although the ORACLE project considered patterns of exchange in primary school lessons (Galton et al. 1980).

Among the research that has looked in detail at children's talk as a medium for learning in primary classrooms are the action research projects stimulated by the National Oracy Project and the classroom language research carried out by Mercer, Edwards and Maybin. In the light of points made above, it is not surprising if tensions persist in priorities for finding out about children's language for learning (see Maclure 1988). Classroom research is often felt to require an explicitly applied dimension, and practitioners may justifiably have been confused about whether they should look to research to tell them how to improve children's spoken language skills, or whether it could tell them how talk could be used more productively in learning (Mercer et al. 1988).

In England, the National Oracy Project was established in 1987 by the School Curriculum Development Committee and administered from 1989 by the National Curriculum Council. The project encouraged teachers to explore for themselves the value of talk in children's learning, and the National Curriculum subsequently institutionalized spoken language as a legitimate curriculum area by making 'Speaking and Listening' the first of the 'attainment targets' in the programmes of study for English. One outcome of the attention to oracy in the late 1980s and 1990s was to make available in published form collections of articles, many of which include transcripts of children talking as part of learning, with commentaries exploring the linguistic processes at work (e.g. Maclure et al. 1988; Norman 1992). The LINC (Language in the National Curriculum) project's action research with teachers also contributed to such reports (e.g. Bain et al. 1992; Carter 1990; Haynes 1991).

Integrated into all this evidence of children's language for learning, however, is further evidence that 'oracy' is not an abstract quantity which can be measured in some finite way. (See Anderson and Hilton 1997; Sealey 1997 for critiques of the official talk curriculum and its associated assessment arrangements.) Children's classroom talk is always contextualized, and the institutional setting constrains certain aspects of what children can and will say, while raising the status of particular kinds of talk (Adger 1998; Merritt 1998). Furthermore, several researchers have drawn attention to the significance of gender on children's language use and achievements at school. The challenge facing children whose first language is not English, in the light of the monolingual policy of the English school system, makes a significant difference to the experience of different groups of children, while the mismatches between the culture and values of homes and schools also affects success in aspects of school-based talk.

Classroom research (for example, Chang and Wells 1988; Edwards and Mercer 1987; McCreedy 1998; Mercer 1995; Phillips 1985, 1988) also demonstrates that talk which is successfully deployed in learning has quite specific characteristics, and not all classroom discussions are helpful for children to 'construct', with their teachers, the shared knowledge which is the aim of the enterprise. Furthermore, research such as that by Maybin (1994) and Schegel (1998) draws attention to the role of informal talk and collaboration in children's meaning-making even in the classroom setting. This dialogic component of children's talk does not fit very readily with the individualism of either psychological accounts of development or assessment arrangements which insist on measuring the progress of individual pupils.

Despite recent classroom research, several authors writing in the 1990s point out how little research evidence there is about primary age children's spoken language (e.g. Brooks 1992; Hoyle and Adger 1998; Maybin 1994). Even in that area of the lives of 5- to 11-year-olds where there is so much incentive for educationalists and linguists to find out about spoken language

– namely, the school context – there is still a relative dearth of knowledge as to the full range of children's linguistic and social accomplishments in their spontaneous talk.

### 4.3.3  Language and literacy

I include a brief section on research about children and language which concerns literacy because within children's experience of education it is given such enormous priority, and could not therefore be entirely overlooked. However, this book as a whole is concerned with children's talk in interactions with others, and the representations of them and their actions in public discourse, rather than with their encounters with literacy.

I shall therefore do no more than point out that research which is concerned with children, language and education has contributed a vast amount to what we know about children's acquisition of literacy, although, again, the political context and changing priorities mean that there continues to be extensive controversy about educational practice, particularly in teaching children to read. Some of the tensions already identified continue to dog the debate. Sketched as extremes, the questions might include: Is literacy part of 'socialization', 'initiation' of the next generation into the values laid down by respected authors? Or is it a liberating tool through which children find new values for themselves? When they read, are they passively receiving meanings, or actively making meanings in a dialogue with the text, which denies fixity? Is literacy a set of skills, mastery of a hierarchy of elements, or a process, mastery of a complex of ideas? Associated with these competing perspectives on literacy, of course (or compromises between them), are equally contrasting perspectives on children (or 'the child'). Again, developmentalism is prominent in literacy research: What can children of each age and stage be expected to read, and to write? Research on oracy draws attention to some of the distinctions and links between spoken and written language in pupils' careers, particularly the need for familiarity with the genres used in written texts and the idea of 'literate thinking' (Chang and Wells 1988).

At this point I shall turn away from the school to consider in somewhat more detail the third theme in research concerned with children and language, that of 'childhood culture'.

## 4.4  Language in childhood culture

This section is concerned with research about children and language which focuses on the role of language in children's lives, rather than its development in their earliest years, or the use to which it is put for pedagogical purposes. This classification is, of course, artificial: acquisition/development continues after the age of 4 and takes place in a range of contexts, including school; school-based talk is reworked in family conversations; interactions with friends may involve role-playing both parent-and-child dialogues and school scenes, and so on. However, the different emphases and presuppositions in research under my three main headings make the classification broadly sustainable for the purposes of this chapter.

## 4.4.1   The family and socialization

Links between the previous section and the current one are evident in research which takes a socialization perspective on children and language. A number of studies have been carried out in families and communities to explore how different 'ways with words' (Heath 1983) lead to different values, norms and likelihoods of school success for the children, while other researchers have identified commonalities in the crucial role of language in socialization, even if the ways it is used for this purpose are not identical across cultures (Saville-Troike 1989; Schieffelin and Ochs 1986). The following three extracts from different researchers exemplify both similarities and differences.

1.   ... factors involved in preparing children for school-oriented, mainstream success are deeper than differences in formal structures of language, amount of parent–child interaction, and the like. The language socialization process in all its complexity is more powerful than such single-factor explanations in accounting for academic success.

(Heath 1983: 344)

In this summary of one of the findings from her detailed ethnographic study, Heath reminds us of the links between home and school expectations, and children's experience of language. The focus here, though, is on how children are learning from their early experience, about what is valued within their communities, and how, 'in all its complexity', their experience of language socialization has implications for their later experiences.

2.   Socialization through language is ubiquitous. In verbal interactions with parents, siblings, teachers, and peers, and through observing media such as television, children are exposed to and absorb many of the important values and beliefs of their communities. We have also described ... instances in which children are explicitly taught how to use language appropriately.

(Ely and Gleason 1995: 270)

This summary of the language socialization process (focused particularly on 'the common experience of English-speaking children in the Western world', p. 251) stresses how children learn values and beliefs through language, in the early years within the family, and more explicitly throughout formal schooling.

> 3. In all societies members want to get their intentions across to children ... a prerequisite for the transmission of cultural orientations from one generation to the next.

> (Ochs and Schieffelin 1995: 76)

Similarly, this third quotation reports the universality of language socialization (as a process, that is, despite specific variations).

The ideas expressed in these extracts, although the perspectives adopted are slightly different, share a rather transmissive representation of 'who is doing what to whom'. That is, in the first sentence of Extract 1, the agents of the processes are 'factors' and, ellipted but recoverable from the context, 'parents' or 'the family', while 'children' are the goal. The agent of the second sentence is 'the language socialization process', a nominalization which masks the participants, although implicit in such a concept is adults acting upon children. A similar syntactic arrangement is found in the first sentence of Extract 2, whose second and third sentences have children as the goal of 'are exposed to' and 'are explicitly taught', and agent only of the non-transactive process 'absorb'. Extract 3 has children as beneficiaries of 'get intentions across to', and a similar kind of nominalizing to 'socialization' in 'transmission', but agency is again obviously intended to be from adult to child. It is also striking in Extract 3 that 'societies' members' cannot logically include 'children', given the way the one group is represented as standing in relation to the other, providing another instance of children as both inside and outside the community as a whole (see Chapter 2 above).

The research findings from this perspective are illuminating, particularly in revealing the differentiation of roles available to children, and these ideas will be revisited in subsequent chapters. One relevant insight here is that conventional beliefs about young children's ability to participate in family conversations, and their rights to do so, vary considerably in different communities across the world (Ochs and Schieffelin 1995). Similarly, researchers from different traditions bring different views about children and language to their investigations. Some emphasize the passing on of values from the older to the younger generation, while others give greater recognition to children's own reasons for what they say and do, which may conflict with those of adults. Again, many of the studies concentrate on earlier childhood, with older children seen as junior care-givers, contributing to the socialization of younger siblings.

Some research perspectives represent children as having their own role in the socialization process, and even in socializing others. Furthermore, as the study of children as social beings has developed, and discourse analysis likewise, possibilities have increased 'for clarifying the processes by which language as speaking practice becomes a critical force in its own right (as opposed to just a medium for transmission of social cultural information)' (Cook-Gumperz and Corsaro 1986: 7).

In Extract 4, Halliday, typically, depicts the child as the agent of the learning process, where he emphasizes the inextricability of language and culture:

> 4.   A child is learning a semiotic system, the culture, and simultaneously
>      he is learning the means of learning it – a second semiotic system, the
>      language, which is the intermediary in which the first one is encoded.
>
>                                                        (Halliday 1975: 122)

Butt (1989: 68) develops this claim even further when he writes '. . . culture and language are two terms on a continuum of saying – a gradient of processes of meaning'. In this view, learning language *is* learning culture, so that 'socialization' cannot so easily be conceptualized as a discrete process involving only children: using language is using culture, throughout life and across the community. Children, in this view, are participants in, and members of, their communities, from Day 1, as it were. The implications of this view for children as social actors will be discussed further in Section 4.4.3.

## 4.4.2   The peer group and 'childhood lore'

Another influential perspective on children's language as a cultural phenomenon is that associated with a secret 'lore' exclusive to children in roughly the primary school years. If I mention to inquirers that I am conducting research into the informal talk of children in this age-group, I sometimes have to explain that I am not replicating the Opies' study; it is as though, just as 'child language research' is often equated with early acquisition, research about the language of middle childhood must inevitably concern singing games, rhymes and rituals.

The enterprise which researches children's lore provides an important contrast with the 'socialization' ideas discussed above, in that, rather than emphasizing children's initiation into ways of using language which are valued by the society as a whole, it posits a disjuncture between this society and childhood. The idea of a separate society of children is made particularly explicit in the following extract from *The lore and language of schoolchildren*:

> . . . the folklorist and anthropologist can, without travelling a mile from his
> door, examine a thriving unselfconscious culture (the word 'culture' is used

here deliberately) which is as unnoticed by the sophisticated world, and quite as little affected by it, as is the culture of some dwindling aboriginal tribe living out its helpless existence in the hinterland of a native reserve. ... As Douglas Newton has pointed out: 'The world-wide fraternity of children is the greatest of savage tribes, and the only one which shows no sign of dying out.'

(Opie and Opie 1959: 22)

The gaze of the researcher upon the unwitting group is clearly indicated in this formulation. There is a homogeneity about children, as distinguished from adults, which cuts across the distinctions noted in the socialization research discussed above between adults *and* children in different societies. The imbalance of cultural resources possessed by children and adults respectively is also evident in this extract: the adult 'world' is 'sophisticated' and its members are in a superior position, from which they can 'examine' childhood. Children, in contrast, are 'unselfconscious' (unknowing?), and, according to the analogy, 'helpless', in thrall to others (situated on their 'reserve'), 'dwindling' and remote (in a 'hinterland'). Yet, in terms reminiscent of the Newbolt extract quoted above, they are simultaneously assertive ('savage'), large in numbers ('greatest') and robust ('no sign of dying out'). This perspective is not unique to this study, as the following quotation illustrates:

The culture of childhood shares many of the attributes of primitive culture. It is handed down by word of mouth, it includes many rituals and magical formulas whose original meanings have been lost, it is hidebound and resistant to alien influences and to change.

(Stone and Church 1968: 370, quoted in
Fine and Sandstrom 1988)

The representation of the Child as curiosity, and as Other, of which these passages are examples, is reinforced by the range of referring expressions for children found throughout the Opies' text; many of these represent a literary style which is much less common today in reporting research. Some examples include: 'the fun-loving but father-fearing specimen' (p. 8), 'the grammar-school type of child' (p. 113), 'the ogre child' (p. 115), 'a London urchin' (p. 162), 'the brat himself' (p. 207), 'every lout on the street corner' (p. 136), 'a hoyden' (p. 309), 'the veriest gutter-snipe' (p. 375), 'a smug hussy, aged 11' (p. 415), 'a group of small, round-faced toughs' (p. 38), 'precocious little keelies' (p. 111), 'the little gutter queens' (p. 283), 'the motley band of urchins' (p. 284).

These often pejorative expressions suggest a distance between the writers and their subjects, which is consistent with the claims about childhood as a primitive phase in the lifespan. These recall Crystal's (1987a) observations cited earlier about childhood symbolizing pre-civilization – a claim made explicit by a more recent writer on children's culture:

> Anyone who has spent time around children and observed them carefully, or really remembers what it was like to be a child, knows that childhood is also a separate culture, with its own rituals, beliefs, games, customs, and its own, largely oral literature. Childhood, in this sense, is a primitive society – or rather, several primitive societies, one leading into the other. Ontogeny recapitulates phylogeny; the development of the individual parallels the development of the race.
>
> (Lurie 1990: 194)

This kind of perspective is manifest in the Opies' account in its presentation of childhood as a (reassuringly) constant state of credulous innocence tinged with connections to non-human life-forms. Evidence for this perspective can be found throughout the book: 'the slavish uniformity of their slang lore' (p. 35); the schoolchild's code is said to be 'of barbarian simplicity' (p. 141); 'childhood is on nodding terms with the supernatural' (p. 142) (cf. the account in Schieffelin 1983 of the Kalulis' belief that babies vocalize as they do because they are in communication with spirits); children have 'a primeval urge' to disguise themselves (p. 292). The fact that the origins of many of the rituals and sayings presented as current among children are traceable to *adult* uses of language in earlier times (with reference to accounts of adult exchanges in Shakespeare, Pepys and Swift, for example) is cited as evidence not of permeable boundaries between adult and child language uses, but of the constancy and persistence of childly (i.e. in this context, primitive) beliefs and values in the face of progress and development over the years in 'the adult world'.

Obviously this particular text, cited because of its foundational position in research on children's lore, is seen now at some historical distance, and some of the assumptions about both social class and the nature of childhood are noticeably of their own time. However, the association of middle childhood with entry not only into the life of the community beyond the family, but also into a bounded realm of pre-adolescent culture, is still found in research about children and language, as the quotation from Lurie illustrates.

From a developmental perspective, this period in the lifespan is seen as a time for establishing a limited degree of independence from the caregivers whose influence is so dominant in infancy. Secrecy and privacy in ritual games and exchanges contribute to this goal. The Opies point out that children often think they have invented rhymes, puns or nicknames which are actually centuries old, and parents are reminded of their own childhoods when their children seek to shock with taboo language as they did themselves. All of this stresses the continuities and similarities in the state of childhood, and an apparent, and perhaps comforting, predictability of each individual's path through it.

On the other hand, it is possible to see children less as somewhat mistakenly reinventing things the adult community has graduated away from, and more as creative agents of their own childhoods. The subculture of middle childhood might find a use for the kind of 'anti-language' typical of subordinate groups (Halliday 1978), as a more recent researcher into children's oral culture suggests. Grugeon combines both perspectives in her commentary on the singing games of primary age girls:

> I want to argue that the games are far more than interesting historical phenomena, relics of a past when there was less TV, traffic and other diversions, but are powerful agents for socialisation, enculturation and resistance. The games both transmit the social order and cultural information – particularly about gender – and provide a means to challenge it.

(Grugeon 1988: 167)

Van Peer (1988) makes similar observations about the nature of social power in relation to 'counting out' rhymes (see also Boyes 1995). Some recent research, then, seeks to redress the implications of a passive role for children, and in the next section I consider some of the evidence from accounts of children's peer culture that they are themselves active both in socialization processes and in creative interpretations of the world they inhabit.

## 4.4.3 Children as social actors

If, until recently, it was research in developmental psychology that had 'firmly colonized childhood in a pact with medicine, education and government agencies' (James et al. 1998: 17), sociological perspectives are rapidly redressing the balance. Both traditions make contributions to our understanding of connections between children and language, and both address ideas about the role of language in the socialization of children. The more psycholinguistic aspects were discussed in Section 4.4.1, whereas sociological approaches tend to stress that '[c]hildren are active agents who construct their own cultures and contribute to the production of the adult world' (Corsaro 1997: 5). The model of the predictable, unfolding path through language socialization is criticized for tending to take 'Society's' needs for granted, and for implying that children must adapt towards these, locating them within the '... broadly conceived sense of order and universality that comprises adult society' (Jenks 1982: 10). Or, as James (1993: 76) describes it, '. . . social processes creep up secretly upon a passive and unwary child'. By contrast, more sociological models highlight children's own interpretations – of their own needs and their own interactions in dialogue. Children's lives are undoubtedly '. . . constrained by the existing social structure and by societal reproduction' writes Corsaro (1997: 18), but children can nevertheless 'create and participate in their own unique peer cultures by creatively taking or appropriating information from the adult world to address their own peer concerns'. (Similarly, see James 1993; Speier 1982 [1970]; Sutton-Smith, 1982; Thorne, 1993; Waksler, 1991.)

Some of these writers have explicitly drawn attention to the discourse traditions in research about children. Sutton-Smith (1982: 75), for example, rejects the idea that children's 'peer groups' are any more 'instructive' than adults' 'clubs': 'Adults do not in general go to their clubs to be made more moral, sophisticated or angelic. Nor, therefore, do children.' Similarly, Thorne (1993: 9) wonders why, since '[a]s adults, we claim "friends" and "colleagues" . . . we so often compress kids' social relations into the flattening notion of "peers"?' She also identifies the difficulty in finding an acceptable referring expression for her subjects: '. . . children use the same practices as adults. They refer to one another by using given names . . . They rarely have occasion to use age-generic terms' (ibid.: 8), and she was influenced by their own practice to write in her book about 'kids' rather than 'children'.

Despite the fact that the 'peer culture' which is the focus of this section is predominantly associated with middle childhood, research perspectives which afford children an active and agential role in their own lives have implications even for the very young child's role in linguistic exchanges. If the social and cultural dimensions of language in use are as fundamental as I would want to claim that they are, then no linguistic interaction between a child and an interlocutor is completely reducible to either participant as an individual, or to the components of the linguistic system. Relationships are, at least in part, emergent from the utterances which constitute conversations; the texts which comprise age-old childhood games and rhymes are 'read' differently by new generations and individuals, and adaptations modify their significance (Boyes 1995). Kress (1997: 60–1) draws attention to this in relation to young children's early interactions with literacy:

> . . . the already shaped cultural world shapes the interested engagement of children with their world. . . . The culture shapes interest, and it provides already shaped objects for that interest to work with. In working with these already shaped objects, children, like all makers of signs, are constantly innovative, creative, transformative.

Similarly, in his analysis of a dialogue between a pre-schooler and her mother, Butt (1989: 82) observes the emergent qualities of the talk, of which neither participant is exclusively in control:

> The exchanges develop . . . according to the principle invoked in the mother's demands and the subject matter tendered by the child. In this way, both interactants are determining the syntagmatic axis of their conversation – what counts as going forward.

Given the traditions in research perspectives on children and language which I have discussed in this chapter, it is not surprising that there are relatively few studies of language in middle childhood which view children as social actors outside school settings.[2] Some exceptions which focus on children in play contexts are Evaldsson (1993), Goodwin (1990), and some of the studies reported in Cook-Gumperz et al. (1986) and Hoyle and Adger (1998). Since this is the context for my own research into children's informal talk, which is reported in Chapters 6 and 8, further reference will be made to these and other relevant studies there.

## 4.5   Summary and conclusions

In this chapter, rather than attempting to provide a comprehensive account of research into children and language – which would occupy at least one volume in itself – I have tried instead to point to some of the main perspectives on children and language from which their connections have been investigated. I have drawn attention in selected instances to the ways in which different emphases and 'angles of telling' are realized in some of the texts which report the findings and theories.

I suggested that one of the dominant perspectives towards 'child language research' is a mainly psycholinguistic approach to initial acquisition, which tells us a great deal about language as a system, commonalities and differences in how it is acquired, and aspects of the interface between the human organism and the human capacity for language. Researchers with more interest in language as a social phenomenon have also contributed to our knowledge about the development of speakers' language and 'communicative competence' in contrast to the characteristics of language as a system.

Children's language is critical to their educational performance and achievements, and different researchers have understood the significance of variations between home language and the language of school in different ways, from deficit theories to greater recognition that school language has its own characteristics which all children need to understand to some extent for educational success, although some are better placed to do this than others. School-based research, particularly that associated with the National Oracy Project in the UK, tells us a lot about language as a tool for learning, while anxieties about 'standards' of oral language and its assessment continue to influence education policy. Very brief attention was given to the dimension of language and literacy, which, while it is a considerable priority in children's initial education, is not a central concern of this particular volume.

Turning away from the school context, the third perspective of research on children's language to be reviewed was its place in children's culture. Studies which locate children in their families and communities illuminate the role of language in socialization, and draw attention to this as a common phenomenon realized in different ways among different groups of people, thus demonstrating links with the home/school language issues considered earlier. Childhood as a discrete culture with its own language and lore was considered next, in research which emphasizes children's separateness from the rest of their communities, and the traditional perspective which portrays children as conservative and relatively powerless was contrasted with later studies which envisage children actively engaging with and seeking to modify the culture they inherit. Finally, some sociological perspectives on childhood were reviewed for the insights they provide on the language of middle childhood. The limitations of a passive process of adult-to-child socialization were reiterated, setting the scene for more detailed consideration in later chapters of children's deployment of their linguistic resources.

In this brief review of some of the relevant research, I have metaphorically held up for consideration three components of the social world, rotating them and their connections, as it were, to see them in different configurations. First there is language: a resource available to human beings, pre-existing them but constantly deployed by them in all their interactions. Secondly, there are children: apprentice speakers of language and members of the social world, from one point of view, active agents and communicators in the social world from the second they arrive in it, from another; rapidly changing, physically, mentally and emotionally, as individuals, but an ever-present segment of the population as a collectivity. Thirdly, there is the social world itself: from one angle this comprises the individuals with whom each child interacts; from another angle it comprises the institutions – family, community, school, communications media, nation state – which constitute the contexts for those interactions. How are we to understand the relationships between these different components of 'society'? What is the significance for understanding children, language and the social world of the representations of children and childhood in public discourse discussed in previous chapters, or the conversations, to be analysed in later chapters, among children themselves and between children, parents and other adults? These are the questions that will be addressed in Chapter 5.

## Notes

1. As recently as 1998, Hoyle and Adger claimed of their edited collection that it '... fills a vacuum that has long been noted ... [and that] [t]his collection is the first to draw together scholarship on language behaviour in the years between early childhood and adulthood' (pp. viii–ix).
2. According to Thorne (1993), as much as 90 per cent of research into children's peer groups is undertaken in schools.

# 5

## Perspectives on Language, Identity and the Social World

*Children's problems are bigger than the ones psychologists assign to their different stages of development. Theirs are the problems inherent in being human.*

(BOSTON 1977: 221)

## 5.1  Introduction

Previous chapters have illustrated some characteristics of language which may have a bearing on how we conceptualize children, and subsequent chapters will consider how children and adults use language in interactions. This chapter sets out to explore some more generic questions about the relationships between individuals, language and society, with specific reference to children. In addressing these, I shall broaden the discussion out from the traditional concerns of child language research, and (within the limits of my own knowledge and expertise) draw on a number of ideas from various disciplines in the social sciences.

The chapter will elaborate on the relevance of the 'domain theory' developed by Derek Layder (1997) to questions of language, identity and the social. This theory provides a framework for conceptualizing the distinct but interrelated influences on people's lives of their own wants, needs and intentions, and of the social structures which are not reducible to individuals. Although I also draw, as does Layder himself, on a range of other theoretical traditions and insights, Layder's approach seems to me to have the distinct advantage over many others of striking a balance between the respective capacities of agency and structure. This version of sociological realism aims to allow not only for people's abilities but also for the constraints on what they can do, both of which are features of our social experience.

## 5.2  The abilities of social actors

### 5.2.1  Individuals, linguistic freedom and the psychobiographical domain

Goffman (1971: 61) claims that '. . . felt self-determination is crucial to one's sense of what it means to be a full-fledged person,' while Archer (1995: 1) suggests that '[a]n inalienable part of our human condition is the feeling of freedom'. We have at our disposal a range of linguistic resources which provides us with the capacity to articulate almost any idea or desire which occurs to us. Thanks to language we can express our feelings, hopes, wishes and needs. We can use our rhetorical powers to persuade others of the correctness of our point of view. We can wheedle, cajole, bully and coerce. Or we can flatter, implore or bargain. We can appeal to the laws of the country, send threatening letters. Or we can appeal to natural justice and individual conscience. Whatever linguistic strategy we turn to in attempts to pursue our own interests, we often experience such decision making as a choice from a range of options, a choice that we are at liberty to make, even as we know that some strategies stand a better chance of success than others, and that nothing in the world is exactly as we might will it to be.

Many of the words I have used in the previous paragraph are from a semantic field associated with the emotions. Even at those times when we are temporarily separate from anyone else in the world, we continue to experience internal states of feeling. And however disrupted our lives might be by changing family circumstances, migration, new spheres of work, bereavement, we experience a kind of continuity, a sense that all the events of our lives, however we may have grown, matured or changed, have happened to the 'same' person. This domain, of 'psychobiography', then:

> focuses on the personal feelings, attitudes and predispositions of individuals. In this respect we can grasp a person's unique individuality only by understanding their identity and behaviour as it has unfolded over the course of their lives, and is currently embedded in their daily routines and experiences.
>
> (Layder 1997: 2–3)

While Layder acknowledges the formative influences of early childhood, as identified by psychologists from Freud onwards, he is not sympathetic to any overemphasis on this period of people's lives as explanatory of their selfhood. Like others who are critical of an equation between 'development' and the early years of one's biography (e.g. Burman 1994; Craib 1998), Layder sees it as important to stress '. . . the equally formative influences of later years and the continuing importance of current bonds and relationships

as inputs into our emotional experiences' (ibid.: 25). Children, then, can be said to occupy the psychobiographical domain, as we all do. Their personal histories are shorter than those of the elderly, to be sure, but the notion of a continuous thread already in existence is important in analyzing children's representations of who they are through the language they use.

Another crucial insight from this social theoretical perspective is that none of the 'domains' is completely separable from the others. Individual existence, although private in some senses, is also social. As Taylor (1985: 8) puts it, writing from a somewhat different tradition,

> a human being alone is an impossibility . . . As organisms we are separable from society – although it may be hard in fact to survive as a lone being; but as humans this separation is unthinkable. On our own, as Aristotle says, we would be either beasts or Gods.

This theme, of a tension between 'separateness' and 'connectedness' is important in this approach to the analysis of the social world. The very fact that we need to negotiate with others, that we are social beings whose wants and needs include social and material goods only obtainable through networks of communications and interactions with other people, means, of course, that we need to pay attention to *inter*actions as well as to individuals. However, as we shall see, these two domains alone (psychobiography and situated activity) cannot account fully for the social world.

What of the part played in our psychobiographies by language? Developmental psycholinguists have taken considerable interest in children's development towards the use of differentiating pronouns, including the demonstration, through language, of an awareness of the 'I', and the ability to distinguish the unique self from everything and everyone else in the world (see, for example, Garvey 1984: 73ff). This 'I', for each one of us, continues to refer to the same person throughout life. It also continues to have a relational status: I am I by virtue of being not you, not them – the pronoun denotes my individuality, true, but that individuality is meaningful only because of the fact of all the others from whom it distinguishes me.

We can make some personal choices too about which varieties of the language resources around us we will use, conveying thereby certain messages about how we wish to be perceived by others. This is particularly noticeable in multilingual communities, where a choice to switch into, say, stylized Indian English, or Caribbean-originated Creole (Rampton 1995), to use African American Vernacular English (Zentella 1998), or to approximate more closely to the 'standard' language, can be viewed as an 'act of identity' (Le Page and Tabouret-Keller 1985). This idea is formulated by these authors thus: '"the individual creates for himself the patterns of his linguistic behaviour so as to resemble those of the group or groups with which from time to time he wishes to be identified, or so as to be unlike those from whom he wishes to be distinguished"' (p. 181). Once again, then, even the most apparently individual, affective decisions about our personal selves cannot be divorced from domains beyond the psychobiographical, since the identification is a relational one: I adopt the pronunciation of particular phonemes (for example) which is *like* that of this group and *unlike* that of other groups (cf. Hogg and Abrams 1988). If this phonological distinction does not serve any function of group identification within a given linguistic community, it may go unnoticed.

To take a slightly different linguistic perspective now: because we are linguistic beings, we can use our linguistic capacities to address our separate selves – we can talk to ourselves even when no one else is present. Thanks to language, we can, quietly or aloud, speak judgementally to ourselves, offering ourselves words of encouragement or blame in an 'editorial voice' (Goffman 1981). Young children, of course, are particularly associated with 'egocentric speech', but Goffman speculates that '[i]t is probably the case that there is a whole array of different forms of talk that are not fully other-involving, that some of these decrease with age, some increase to a point, and still others are not especially age-related' (ibid.: 95n.).

Language also – as the means of expressing one's own emotional states, needs or wishes, or of narrating passages from one's own biography – has an existence external to one's inner self. Our freedom to use language to bargain, negotiate and so on, is a freedom to do that *with other people*. Language is my resource for claiming my rights and stating my desires, but it is also your resource for responding to my claims and for articulating needs, wants and rights of your own. In this sense, language has to serve as a common currency available to both of us.

The metaphorical comparison of language with money is not original. Searle (1995), for example, uses the system of money as an illustration of 'social' and 'institutional facts', which he contrasts with 'brute facts'. It is a central tenet of sociological realism that the world exists independently of our perceptions of it, and independently of our descriptions of it. The social world is not brought into being by talk, as some extreme versions of social constructionism suggest (more of this debate below). However, much of the activity in which human beings in the social world engage involves social and institutional facts, all of which are mediated by the symbolic system of language.

> Symbols do not create cats and dogs and evening stars; they create only the possibility of referring to cats, dogs and evening stars in a publicly accessible way. But symbolization creates the very ontological categories of money, property, points scored in games and political offices, as well as the categories of words, and speech acts.

> (Searle 1995: 75)

Social facts, like the recognition that a piece of paper or metal configured in a particular way is 'money', can only be negotiated because language is available as the symbolic means of communicating them. An individual can undertake a specific action involving money, such as using it to buy material goods, but money in general, as this kind of institutional fact, will 'persist through time independent of the duration of the urges and inclinations of the participants in the institution' (ibid.: 78). Likewise, language itself has a partial autonomy from the individuals who use it to communicate their own individual thoughts and feelings. The deployment of language for some personally motivated end may be an act of choice by an individual, but the nature of the linguistic resources available for such deployment is not. Furthermore, the individual in any interaction is, by definition, only one component of that interaction. Therefore, from this consideration of the psychobiographical domain, we turn now to the domain of situated activity.

## 5.2.2   Intersubjectivity, and the domain of situated activity

As was made clear in the discussion of the psychobiographical domain, individuals experience emotional (as well as cognitive) motivations, so any interaction is imbued with the internal thoughts and feelings of the participants – many of which may not be made explicit – as well as involving the negotiations which comprise the visible and audible dimensions of the interaction.

Another important concept in the theory presented here is the idea of 'emergence'. 'Emergence' refers to the generation of features which are not reducible to their constituent elements and must therefore be regarded as distinct from them. In relation to these two domains, we can recognize that an interaction between two or more participants, each with personal histories and priorities, and linguistic repertoires, becomes in itself something other than the sum of its parts. 'Collective agreements and shared understandings are created during the encounter that influence the subsequent proceedings' (Layder 1997: 85). This echoes the idea of the 'long conversations', presented by Mercer (1995) in the context of pedagogic discourse, but applicable in all those contexts where any specific interaction represents one in a series which can thus be perceived as having its own history, a history which is not reducible to the biographies of each individual participant.

Interactions in the domain of situated activity have long been of interest to linguists. Researchers in the traditions of ethnomethodology and conversation analysis, pragmatics, symbolic interactionism, social constructionism and some versions of discourse analysis have contributed to our knowledge of this domain. Language is the principal available resource on which we draw for communication, and to convey a sense of ourselves to others as well as to position others in relation to that self. 'Situations' are those contexts where face-to-face interaction generates 'definitions' of reality, and where,

correspondingly, actors have varying degrees of influence over these definitions. This perspective emphasizes the dialogic qualities of language, the
ways in which utterances refer back to previous utterances and subtly alter
the existing context within which subsequent utterances will be produced.
The meanings developed by co-participants are intersubjective (even if they
are antagonistic).

Some ethnomethodologists place great importance on paying scrupulous
attention to the interaction itself as the unit of analysis, deliberately exclud-
ing from their accounts anything which is not a visible element in the interaction. For such theorists, the less observable 'domains' identified by Layder
have no place in the analysis of conversation. As I hope to illustrate in the
chapters which follow, it seems to me impossible to make sense of the
moment-to-moment specifics of the children's talk with a range of others,
with which I am concerned there, without reference to those factors beyond
the encounters themselves which nevertheless have a bearing on them. This
point will be developed further below.

Another tradition which gives prime importance to 'the human conversation' as constitutive of the social world is social constructionism, in at least
some of its manifestations. Thus, for Harré (1992: 157) '[t]he intransigent
background to all human action is the human conversation, the elements
of which are the acts produced by the joint actions of speakers'. Various
analysts have detailed how versions of social reality emerge 'on the spot' as
participants interact with each other. Thus Potter (1996: 98), for example,
makes the following claim:

> The strongest version of the metaphor would have the world literally
> springing into existence as it is talked or written about. Ridiculous, surely!
> Perhaps, but I want to opt for something nearly as strong. Reality enters
> into human practices by way of the categories and descriptions that are
> part of those practices. The world is not ready categorized by God or
> nature in ways that we are all forced to accept. It is *constituted* in one way
> or another as people talk it, write it and argue it.
>
> (Original emphasis)

A similar claim is put more succinctly by Shotter (1993b), who says:
'. . . we constitute both ourselves and our worlds in our conversational activity' (preface). As Craib (1998: 141) concedes, '. . . human beings do endow
both the physical and social world with meaning,' but, he continues, 'to
endow something with meaning is not to create it or to rob it of its independent existence'. Constructionist accounts which appear to give almost
unlimited power to social actors are incompatible with realism, which insists
on the existence of less immediate and less perceptible domains than situated
activity. However, there are some social constructionist insights which are
not completely at odds with the version of realism I am presenting here.

The concept of emergence, for example, which allows for conversation being something other than the sum of its parts, and not reducible to them, is not wholly dissimilar from the idea that something is 'constructed' when people interact through language. Furthermore, it is possible for realism to share with social constructionism a recognition that 'meaning' is not given in an object, a word or a text, that it is not given, as Potter says, by God or by nature. Many aspects of meaning are emergent from language in use, and it is only by carefully attending to the details of participants' dialogue that we can understand certain aspects of this process in action. Illustrative of such analyses are several studies by feminist scholars of women's interaction with each other. Coates (1996), for example, argues in a number of ways for talk as a form of social action, having particular meanings for women, who she claims achieve different things from men in friendly interaction: 'Talking with friends is constitutive of friendship; through talking, we do "being friends"' (p. 263). And, again, this kind of research acknowledges the distinctiveness of the group itself from the individuals who meet to talk: 'In a collaborative floor, the group voice takes precedence' (p. 171); '. . . the group takes priority over the individual and the women's voices combine (or meld) to construct a shared text' (p. 117).

In the presence of others, we become co-participants as well as individuals, and here Goffman's notion of an 'interaction order' is important. Language is deployed in the negotiation of appropriate involvement with other people, knowing 'how to go on' socially so as not to intrude or cause offence in some contexts, and so as to demonstrate acceptable levels of intimacy and solidarity in others. Interlocutors carry out rapid monitoring and repair work, as a number of studies in the tradition of Hymes's 'ethnographies of speaking' demonstrate.

The social skills of conveying aspects of the relations between participants, such as relative status, levels of intimacy and so on, for which language is a primary conduit, have been investigated by students of pragmatics. Children may be seen as a special case in this regard, being excused their relatively partial grasp of the interaction order if, for example, they fail to carry out the 'face-work' which conveys a concern with politeness (Brown and Levinson 1978). Patterns of development of pragmatic awareness have been investigated by child language researchers (e.g. Andersen 1990; Garvey 1984; Ochs and Schieffelin 1979), and, again, the focus is typically on very young children, as children of about 6 or 7 years old have already learned a great deal about the pragmatic norms prevalent in their culture.

Children in middle childhood, then, are in many ways successfully involved in utilizing practical knowledge of how to behave in social situations. Ethnographic studies such as that of Goodwin (1990) demonstrate how for the children she observed 'talk [functioned] as social organization'. Similarly, Evaldsson's (1993) study of children's experiences in after-school centres draws heavily on Goffman's work to explore their play as situated activity, with a primary focus on neither the individual, nor the group, but on the dynamics of the interaction. (I shall discuss the definition of children's talk and interactions as 'play' in Chapter 6.)

With such rich sources of data as have been used to such illuminating effect by analysts of co-present interactants, and an acknowledgement of the psychobiographical dimensions of situated activity, have we not, as some social constructionists would claim, now accounted for the domains which comprise the social world? What else needs to be included? At one level, it seems as though the 'conversational realities' (Shotter 1993b) people bring into being may be very largely within the control of co-present participants. Situated activity is the area of social life which most people know most about, since it is the domain most accessible to direct perception. However, even if as social actors we cannot directly perceive them, there are other influences beyond those discussed so far. If we really could talk the world into existence through negotiation with our fellow conversationalists, that world would surely look very different from the way it is.

To understand why this is, we need to account for the existence of all those rules, conventions and expectations which are operationalized in each interaction. Where do these come from? How can we relate specific in-stances of negotiated politeness, or signals of intimacy, or contraventions which cause offence, to the general patterns of which they constitute a part? When children push against the boundaries which govern what is acceptable for them to say to an adult, where are these boundaries located? And what are the patterns of language in use which constitute the discourses available to be deployed in situated activity?

The entities we are dealing with at this level are much less visible to us as social actors. Nevertheless, we do often have a strong sense that there are constraints on what we can say and do even as we seem to be free to make independent choices. The next sections will aim to shed light on the con-straints and enablements of the social world by exploring the domains of social settings and contextual resources.

## 5.3    Structure, and the limits on actors' freedom

Thus we turn now to what Archer (1995: 1) terms 'the vexatious fact of society':

> An inescapable part of our inescapably social condition is to be aware of its constraints, sanctions and restrictions on our ambitions – be they for good or evil. Equally, we acknowledge certain social blessings such as medica-tion, transportation and education: without their enablements our lives and hopes would both be vastly more circumscribed.

Archer goes on to distinguish *social* science from a quest for the 'laws' of natural science, which operate with no reference to (or awareness of!) human wishes, but she does make it clear that society exists irrespective of how we feel about it:

> ... we delude one another by the pretence that society is simply what we choose to make it and make of it, now or in any generation, for generically 'society' is that which nobody wants in exactly the form they find it and yet it resists both individual and collective efforts at transformation – not necessarily by remaining unchanged but altering to become something else which still conforms to no one's ideal.
>
> (Ibid.: 2)

An important insight from this realist approach to understanding the social world is that human societies have a history which is something other than the sum of the histories of individuals. As was discussed in Part I, my childhood or your childhood are not quite the same kind of thing as the phenomenon of 'childhood' for those who occupy it at a specific point in history. The timescale applying to individuals, with their own (linguistic) psychobiographies over their lifespan, is not isomorphic with the timescale needed to identify changes in the language, or in the perceptions and cultural experience of generic stages in the human lifespan, such as childhood, across the centuries. As both Layder and Archer stress, however, we need to be mindful of *both* structure *and* agency, and ultimately it is human beings who cause things to happen in the social world, not some reified, immutable power called 'Society'. Layder explains, for example, how various kinds of interactions between people are differentially coloured by the wider influences of 'social settings', the third of the social domains to be considered.

## 5.3.1   The domain of social settings

The interactions we have with others are of various kinds, some having more predictable patterns than others. Some of the things we need to achieve, for which institutional arrangements are in place, are associated with conventional ways of achieving them, in identifiable social settings. Such experiences as service encounters in shops, for example, or lessons in school classrooms, or consultations in doctors' surgeries, are likely to proceed along predictable lines, which include the patterns of language likely to be deployed. Individuals gain experience of these kinds of interactions (sometimes vicariously through representations in literature or on television), and can then have recourse to a general, stereotypical version of what to expect each time they find themselves involved in such situations. From the individual, psychological point of view, people can make use of, as it were, their personal store of these 'schemas' or 'frames' to negotiate interactions appropriately, drawing inferences as to how the contributions of others are to be interpreted. Thus Gumperz (1982: 209) refers to 'the knowledge of linguistic and related communicative conventions that speakers must have to create and sustain conversational cooperation'. However, 'interactions impose their own rules of involvement, [and] we must see those inferences that are based on involvement as also governed by broader rules of social engagement' (Schiffrin 1994: 103). For Goffman, likewise:

> . . . the organization of framing activity is itself socially situated. Thus . . . we can see Goffman's work as providing an elaboration of the contextual presuppositions that people both use and construct during the inferencing process, and as offering a view of the means by which those presuppositions *are externally constructed and impose external constraints* on the ways in which we understand messages.
>
> (Schiffrin 1994: 103–4; emphasis added)

What Layder's more subtly stratified focus enables us to recognize is that there are different degrees to which participants are free to make their own decisions about the frames, schemas or scripts they will use – or modify – in different social settings. Some interactions are relatively informal and open-ended, while others are relatively formal; some social settings are characterized by quite explicit and significant differentials in power or status (such as that available to pupils and teachers respectively in the classroom), while in others (such as a chance meeting of close friends) any such differentials may be given little salience. Layder's account of this once again alludes to the histories which may not be those of individual actors participating in social practices:

> Pivotal here is the extent to which social relations are already sedimented in time and space and thus become inscribed and enshrined in routinized practices, thus defining the contours of social settings and the macro-patterning of contextual resources. The more sedimented and established they are in certain settings and fields, the reproduced aspects of social relations and practices are more pronounced and 'demanding'.
>
> (Layder 1997: 111)

These claims about features external to interactions which nevertheless have a bearing on them begin to make apparent the weight of social structures and thus the limits on actors' choices. While the 'scripts' we operationalize in many social settings are not handed to us to deliver unmodified – people are not automata – there are costs attached to deviating from certain expected norms. This clearly applies to certain ways of using language. Sanctions are likely to follow instances where, for example, pupils disrupt the (tacitly) prescribed sequences of moves typical of much classroom interaction. Recent classroom-based research (e.g. Edwards and Mercer 1987; Mercer 1995; Norman 1992) presents a more varied set of possibilities than the canonical three-part moves of teacher's 'initiation' followed by the nominated pupil's 'response' and the concluding 'evaluation' or 'feedback' (Sinclair and Coulthard 1975). Nevertheless, there are traditions and expectations underlying the institutional nature of classrooms, and pupils are not well placed to overturn these by individual actions. (Cf. the news story about the 'disruptive' schoolboy analysed in Chapters 1 and 2.) In Layder's analysis, while no social setting is 'entirely free-form' (Layder 1997: 110), there are some settings which are particularly defined by institutional objectives:

> The bureaucratic rules and regulations that inform and shape the working practices in many employing organizations . . . are good examples of the demanding or mandatory character of reproduced relations and practices. Workers *must* take account of established practices or risk censure (a reprimand), some kind of deprivation such as the withholding of certain rewards (such as promotion, a pay increase or better working conditions) or even a more serious penalty (such as being fired). In more positive terms anyone who flouts the established practices and social relations – and therefore challenges the discourses and powers that underpin them – has to be willing to forgo the inclusive benefits that accrue from general (though not necessarily unquestioning) conformity.
>
> (Layder 1997: 111–12)

For children, for whom paid employment is largely a proscribed activity (in the West, that is), the equivalent social setting is obviously the school, and we can easily imagine the passage above rewritten with 'pupils' substituted for 'workers', 'excluded' or 'expelled' for 'fired' and so on. Children can bring creative and imaginative uses of language to the classroom, some of which will be explicitly encouraged, but the contexts in which these are permitted are tightly circumscribed. (For some specific examples of teachers' proscription of dispreferred discourse moves by inexperienced or non-compliant pupils, see Merritt 1998; Thorne 1993; Willes 1983.)

The mention of 'discourse' in the previous extract highlights a particular kind of connection between language and social relations which is of central concern to (critical) discourse analysts (e.g. Fairclough 1993, 1996; Fowler et al. 1979; Sarangi and Slembrouck 1996). Extensive debate about the nature and influence of 'discourses' has led to the term being used in a range of ways, not all of which are mutually compatible. For example, analysts working within a linguistic tradition may interpret 'discourse' as the kind of move analysis pioneered by Sinclair and Coulthard (1975), while social and cultural theorists may be more familiar with contemporary work, influenced by Foucault, which portrays 'discourse' as almost comprehensively constitutive of social relations.[1] 'Discourse' in this latter sense incorporates extra-linguistic phenomena, but it is helpful in the present context to restrict the term to refer to the manifestations through language of the relationships of people to each other and to social structures. Stubbs (1996: 158) provides a helpful definition of discourse:

> . . . recurrent phrases and conventional ways of talking, which circulate in the social world, and which form a constellation of repeated meanings. . . . Vocabulary and grammar provide us with the potential and resources to say different things. But often this potential is used in regular ways, in large numbers of texts, whose patterns therefore embody particular social values and views of the world. Such discourse patterns tell us which meanings are repeatedly expressed in a discourse community. . . . Such recurrent ways of talking do not determine thought, but they provide familiar and conventional representations of people and events, by filtering and crystallizing ideas, and by providing pre-fabricated means by which ideas can be easily conveyed and grasped.

This formulation recalls the 'established', 'sedimented' routines and practices which characterize the more institutionalized of Layder's social settings, and a realist account acknowledges the existence of orders of discourse as influential in situated activity and social settings. However, it also insists that people are not entirely at the mercy of discourses, and retain the option of modifying or even rejecting the discursive resources available:

> Discourses . . . are elements of a more general cultural context of resources that both enable and constrain the behaviours of those within their sphere of influence. At the same time within situated encounters people transmute, transform and refashion these resources by the very act of utilizing them and making them work in real-life contexts.
>
> (Layder 1997: 85)

Both Stubbs and Layder suggest here the idea that linguistic practices have cumulative effects which are observable beyond the fleeting passage in time of specific interactions. Indeed Stubbs's observations are made in the context of reviewing the contribution to discourse and text analysis of linguistic corpora, which can be seen as physical manifestations of patterns and conventions in language use of which individual speakers and writers may be only dimly – if at all – aware. The notion of 'contextual resources', including these linguistic resources, brings me to the last of Layder's four domains.

## 5.3.2  The domain of contextual resources

This is the domain which is furthest from our immediate perceptions of the world as individual social actors within it. It is concerned with people as collectivities, and with the recognition that, from this macro perspective, people are – involuntaristically – located as 'social agents' in distinctive ways. For Archer (1995: 257) agents are '. . . defined as *collectivities* sharing the same *life chances*' (original emphasis).[2] In addition to our individual psychobiographies, and the many personal relationships in which we participate, we are all 'agents of the socio-cultural system into which [we] are born' (ibid.). 'Life chances' are related to prior distributions of resources, including both the material resources associated with money and goods, and the cultural resources associated, for instance, with texts and discourses in various media. Thus '. . . we are dealing primarily with a group or collective level of analysis in terms of the possession, distribution or ownership of cultural, material and authoritative resources throughout the whole social system' (Layder 1997: 4). Agents clearly do not all have equal access to these kinds of resources, and there is a relational connection between the collectivities concerned. In other words, being working class of necessity only makes sense in the context of the relationship between the working class and the class(es) that define it as such in terms of the distribution of resources. Thus:

> . . . the major distributions of resources upon which 'life chances' pivot are themselves dependent upon relations between the propertied and the propertyless, the powerful and the powerless, the discriminators and the subjects of discrimination: and these, of course, are relationships between collectivities.

> (Archer 1995: 257)

Archer goes on to point out, echoing some of the observations made by Bell (1991) and discussed in relation to the analysis of news text in Chapters 1 and 2, that agents are not equally empowered to 'have their collective say'. Collectivities that have not chosen to identify themselves as such, nor to organize around their collective vested interests, are likely to be less influential than those that have. And the interests and concerns of some collectivities are simply kept 'off the agenda' of those with decision-making powers: many people would agree that children, who cannot vote and whose property is rarely unambiguously their own, are a relatively powerless group on both these criteria. Differential degrees of access to decision-making and political power are thus not simply a matter of numbers, which is why the distinction between structure and agency is not simply a distinction between the macro and the micro dimensions of social life: a single, dyadic interaction between two individuals who are structurally located as the presidents of nation states may have much more far-reaching social consequences than another inter-action participated in by large numbers of, for example, children.

Children, as was argued above (Chapter 2), constitute a collectivity in the sense of being collectively defined in relation to adults (or parents). They also occupy the collective position of pupils in relation to teachers when participating in the enterprise of schooling. They may simultaneously be-long to other collectivities which are contrastively defined. By virtue of the family into which they are born, they will belong to one among the social classes identified by the differential distribution of wealth, for example. By virtue of whatever differences are counted as significant in the 'racializing' practices of the society in which they live, they may be classified in the school's records as belonging to a specific 'ethnic group'.

In terms of language as a cultural resource, some children have access to the more prestigious varieties, while others are excluded from the benefits these bring unless they make conscious efforts to incorporate them into their repertoire. This observation links with the idea of language as 'cultural capital', as expounded by Bourdieu. In addition to knowledge of the grammar and vocabulary of the standard language, there is also the consideration of discourses as contextual cultural resources. Some commentators (as was dis-cussed in Chapter 4) believe that children from particular social backgrounds are systematically excluded from social and educational opportunity by not being helped to master the discourses and genres needed for certain kinds of economic success. This is expressed provocatively by Martin (1989: 60):

> In capitalist countries the major function of education is not to train chil-dren for jobs, but to control a large sector of the community for which cap-italism cannot provide work. . . . Education is concerned with controlling children and withholding powerful writing until the last possible moment in order to do so. But as well, education ignores almost completely the kinds of writing that would enable children to enter the workforce.

Identification of the genres of 'powerful writing' – principally 'factual' writing – has been the concern of various educationalists seeking to counter-act the inequalities in access to this kind of cultural resource. To my mind, Martin's claims take too little account of the powers and potentials of agents and actors, who are rarely, even as children, 'passive receptors of the status quo' (ibid.).

A similar (over) emphasis on structures is familiar from the work of some of the discourse analysts who, from a macro perspective, seek to identify how the news media, for example, influence readers' and viewers' percep-tions of politics, economics, and their own location in the social world. Motivated, like Martin, to 'unmask' manipulative discursive practices, they sometimes over-stress the hidden power of ideology, characterizing speakers' and readers' responses to and uses of linguistic configurations which 'code a world-view' as 'largely automatic' or even 'totally determined' (Fowler and Kress 1979: 185, 186, 194).

Thus the linguistic and discursive configurations which are a component of people's contextual resources are of considerable significance. The analyses in Part I of patterns in the representation of children through the language of many texts are evidence of my own commitment to discourse analysis as one worthwhile way of investigating the links between language and social relations. But the exploration of Layder's domain theory should also serve to demonstrate the importance of actors' ability to 'make a difference', and to deploy language for their own ends and in their own interests, which is why I include in subsequent chapters some more 'micro' level analyses of relatively powerless individuals in spontaneous conversation.

## 5.4   The relations between domains

I want to conclude these sections, where I have attempted to set out the relevance of domain theory for a consideration of children, language and the social world, by reiterating that the domains should not be thought of as separate spheres of social life. Somewhat as water refracts the colours of the spectrum so that they can be seen as a rainbow, analysis can theoretically separate structure and agency, as Archer does, and can further separate for consideration and reflection the four domains identified by Layder; however, lived experience is not separated out in this way, just as light is usually perceived as the full visible spectrum.

It should be acknowledged that some writers have sought to abolish the dualism between agency and structure by regarding them as mutually con- stitutive. Put simply, in relation to language, we could consider each instance of the production of a particular way of saying things as the 'micro' level, produced by individuals. The repetition of these forms over many micro instances would then generate the 'macro' level of system, or structure. For example, Halliday (1991) considers the relationship between the system and the instance to be one of observer viewpoint, the same phenomenon looked at from different perspectives: in his own analogy, a climate is simply many instances of the weather.

Stubbs (1996: 58) writes approvingly of this formulation, and explicitly identifies it with the work of Giddens and his notion of structuration:

> Human agency constitutes social structure. Social structure is the medium for human agency. . . . A key concept is the recursive nature of social life: drawing on convention reconstitutes it. When I produce a grammatical sentence, I intend to communicate something to someone. I do not intend to reproduce the English language: but this is the unintended outcome of

all those people out there producing grammatical sentences. . . . This is what Giddens calls duality of structure: social structure is both the medium and the outcome of the behaviour it organizes.

The main claim with which I would wish to take issue here is that agency and structure are mutually constitutive. Archer and Layder have both drawn attention to the fact that if agency and structure are seen as 'two sides of the same coin', it becomes impossible to examine the interplay between them. Indeed, Stubbs himself writes of the 'changing *relations between* occurrences in a text and the underlying language system' (1996: 92, my emphasis), which strongly implies that there are two distinct strata involved, and that the issue is therefore not merely one of different perspectives on the same thing.

I noted earlier the realist claim that social structures have distinctive properties which are not reducible to the actions of individuals. This insight is lost when structure is regarded as no more than the repeated, cumulative actions of individuals, and makes problematic Stubbs's contention that 'It is the continuous reinforcement, through massive repetition and consistency in discourse, which is required to construct and maintain social reality' (ibid.: 92). Properties of language as structure include those patterns which are to be found only in corpora comprising many instances. Likewise, only at the level of system can language have a history (as Halliday notes (1991: 34)). Again, the different temporalities implied by analytical dualism, to which I referred above, make it possible to see that the anteriority of language to any individual speaker, and the maintenance and change of language across long periods of time, are systemic properties not reducible to specific individuals or specific individual instances of language in use.

The theoretical claims underpinning the discussion, then, are as follows. The social world is stratified, each domain within it has distinct properties, and the different domains are not reducible to each other, although they are mutually interpenetrating. People act within this stratified social world, and it is ultimately human beings who take actions, not discourses, nor ideologies, nor any other reified entity. But the complex mediation by the social world of what people do results in social action having all kinds of unintended consequences – and generating further emergent features – which in turn help to shape the social environment for subsequent actors. Language is indispensable to social life, and plays a crucial role in each of the domains.

## 5.5  Identity: language, structure and agency

Language is an essential element in the social world, which is inconceivable without it. Even those 'brute facts' of the natural world, such as 'cats and dogs and evening stars' (Searle 1995: 75), are represented differently in different language systems or discourses. Our perceptions and experiences of inanimate things can be given various shades of meaning, angles of telling, as they are negotiated and mediated through language. This is even more the case for all the *social* experience which is, necessarily, conducted primarily through the medium of language. Thus for many writers on social identity, language is fundamental to the very concept. Shotter (1993a: 17), for example, claims that '. . . one's social identity is structured like a language, to parody Lacan'. Also, Gumperz (1982: 7) states: 'The key point of our argument . . . is that social identity and ethnicity are in large part established and maintained through language'.

There are two, related, conceptual problems to which those concerned with language and social identity have drawn attention, and which I shall address briefly here. The first is the nature of the social categories within which 'identities' are be classified (are identity categories to be regarded as given, or are they context-dependent, malleable?), and the second is the nature of the relationship between the self and the social world (is 'identity' a property of the individual or an intersubjective construction?). Although, once again, these are large issues, worthy of extensive discussion in their own right, my limited aim is to demonstrate how the realist theory I am putting forward can be helpful in conceptualizing the relationship between language and identity.

## 5.5.1   Varieties of language and identity

Traditional variationist studies in sociolinguistics have identified correlations between speakers' membership of specific social categories and patterns in their use of specific linguistic variables. Prototypical categories include social class, sex, 'ethnicity' and age; prototypical linguistic correlates include phonemic, lexical and syntactic variables. However, some recent debate has focused on whether the *a priori* identification of the social categories is justified. For one thing, sociolinguists have to confront the methodological complexities of assigning speakers to a social class category, for example, which, as sociologists know only too well, is a persistent challenge (Chambers 1995; Hasan 1992; Le Page and Tabouret-Keller 1985). Some researchers have refined discussion of the nature of correlations so as to distinguish social *class* categories and social *network* affiliations in explaining speakers' adoption of linguistic variants (Milroy 1992; Milroy and Milroy 1992). This distinction may be read as a recognition of the 'macro' and 'micro' dimensions of the influences involved: 'Whereas the guardians of social class norms are more or less ineffable, the guardians of network norms might very well buy you a pint' (Chambers 1995: 68). In whatever way class and network are identified, however, the causal mechanisms linking membership of such categories to phonological variation in the speech of individuals remains problematic (Lass 1980): *how* does social class membership lead to the use of particular language variants? and *why* are such correlations always probabilistic and not categorical?

Similar questions have been raised in relation to gender and linguistic variation (Bergvall et al. 1996), with analysts exploring afresh whether membership of the category 'male' or 'female' should automatically be assumed to lead to differentiated linguistic behaviours. James (1996: 119), for example, lists a number of factors which 'are important in accounting for the choices that women and men make in the speech forms that they use', including 'local economic conditions, employment and educational opportunities that are open to each sex, social conditions giving rise to differences in social network strength, the amount of status and respect accorded to women in particular communities and the extent to which they can participate in public and economic life'. Or again, as Freed (1996: 56) suggests, rather than assuming gender as a given variable, research should attend to 'economic privilege, subcultural phenomena, setting, activity, audience, personality, or . . . the context-specific communicative goals of the particular speakers who are being studied'. Belonging to a broad category such as 'women' cannot determine one's linguistic behaviour. Similarly, recent research among boys and girls has, by not assuming difference from the outset, identified similarities in their styles of interaction (Goodwin and Goodwin 1987; Thorne 1993).

The unproblematic classification of speakers by 'ethnicity' has also been called into question, in ways which lead to a rethinking of the classification of language varieties themselves. Le Page and Tabouret-Keller (1985) point out that the creoles they studied pointedly disrupt commonsense assumptions about boundaries between languages. Moreover, their method of grouping speakers on the basis of their linguistic behaviour *before* determining 'what non-linguistic attributes membership of the same linguistic group implied' (p. 152) helps to weaken further any absolute notions of ethnic identity.

All of these examples contribute to a growing recognition that the canonical categories of sociolinguistic studies may be difficult to sustain. Gumperz (1982: 1), for example, has questioned the way '[w]e customarily take gender, ethnicity, and class as given parameters and boundaries within which we create our own social identities'. While my own argument does not support his claim that these parameters and boundaries are entirely 'communicatively produced', it does recognize that the language forms a speaker uses are not the manifestation of some *essential* attribute, such as being female (Cameron 1996), or middle class. Also, as will be suggested in Chapter 7, it seems likely that similar considerations apply to age gradations as social categories. The recognition of a range of linguistic options, interrelated with a range of factors influencing speakers' choices, leads to a consideration of 'identity' as itself many faceted.

### 5.5.2   Multiple identities?

Some relevant research explores speakers' active part, through the language they use, in presenting – or indeed 'constructing' – particular social identities. For example, in the context of considering 'discourse and lifespan identity', Coupland and Nussbaum (1993: xix) conceptualize the self as a narrative project, reflecting on '. . . the discursive *means* by which identity formations are achieved across the lifespan'. In the same volume, Shotter (1993a: 6), also stressing the relational nature of identity, claims that '. . . we . . . craft our unique selves. In other words, we become and are ourselves only in relation to others.' He goes on to acknowledge the contextual limitations on these acts of creation, including differential access to opportunities, so that 'we cannot just position ourselves as we please' (ibid.).

Other writers too highlight the significance of the contexts of the interactions in which speakers participate for their 'identities'. This perspective may elide 'identity' and 'role', particularly in contexts where the relatively predictable discourse of institutions requires speakers to occupy the respective roles of, for example, 'bureaucrat' and 'client'. Sarangi and Slembrouck (1996: 79) provide an illustration of this perspective on the issue: 'We take the view that language use is instrumental in inscribing social identity, including the construction of role relationships. . . . identities are often imposed one-sidedly and clients' attempts to resist a role or, in their turn, define the institutions' role, rebound.' Implicit in this formulation is the notion that one individual can possess several identities. Used in this way, the term 'identity' would feature to name participation in the relational categories considered above: one could have the identity of mother, employee, sister, doctor and so on. In a critique of gender as a unitary category, Meyerhoff (1996) proposes just such a conception, that people have many identities which become salient at different times in different contexts: 'Individuals may have a number of identities, some of which are characterized as social (i.e. identities linking an individual to social groups and providing a group basis for interaction with others), some of which are characterized as personal (i.e. identities based on more one-to-one relationships)' (p. 204). (Cf. Hogg and Abrams 1988; Zentella 1998.)

The perspectives reviewed here are useful in drawing attention to the limitations of essentialist notions of identity, and to the relational nature of the social categories to which people belong. Hasan (1992) summarizes these two aspects well, emphasizing in addition the importance of structures such as social class which are outside the control of the individual, given observable differences in life chances as indicated by, for example, reports on effects of poverty, which show:

> . . . the essential interdependencies of human destiny, the extent to which
> an individual's position in the social universe is defined not by what is 'in'

that person, but by that person's relation to others in the community, and by the possibilities of his/her action, non-action and exploitation.

(p. 86)

For the purposes of my own analysis, while drawing on much of the work discussed here, I would nevertheless want to maintain a distinction between 'role' and 'identity', and to retain a recognition of the tension between structure and agency, as social identities are mediated through language.

## 5.6   Summary and conclusions

The picture of the social and linguistic world which I have sought to sketch in this chapter includes analytically separable elements, which are irreducible, mutually influential, and productive of emergent features. The social world is both reproduced and changed over time, and children are participants in both these processes.

People have an embodied existence in a physical world, where the law of gravity, for example, exerts its effects whether we choose to recognize it or not, and whatever we choose to call it. People are biological organisms, with the innate capacity for language, and there are physical constraints on what they can do. Thus young children whose brains and vocal apparatus have not yet matured sufficiently for them to deploy the linguistic resources of their community are not social actors in the same way that adults can be said to be. Even at this stage of life, however, a human being's existence is fundamentally social.

Each human being has a unique psychobiography. To my mind, this is the sense in which it is meaningful to speak of people's 'identities'. 'Social identities can come and go,' writes Craib (1998: 4), 'but my identity goes on as something which unites all the social identities I ever had, have, or will have.' Our psychobiographies are formed in relation to others, and are not separate from the other domains: '. . . the influences of language, discourse and power are centrally important in the construction of personal identity . . .' (Layder 1997: 43). *But* '[j]ust as social processes cannot be reduced to the effects of individuals operating as if they were separate psychological atoms, so individuals must not be dissolved into social processes or reduced to their effects' (ibid.: 44). The children whose informal talk I analyze in Chapters 6 and 8 have distinct personalities, and, of course, each of them, in conversation with other people, has generated linguistic data that is not identical to the talk produced by any other person.

Informal, spontaneous talk with others is the kind of language that is most within the control of speakers, but the very interaction of the participants generates a conversation that is not the exclusive responsibility of any of them. In the context of situated activity, speakers may seek to project aspects of their 'identities', aligning themselves with some of the participants present and distancing themselves from others, or demonstrating familiarity with items in the wider cultural system, thus claiming affiliations with collectivities beyond the participants in the interaction. The children occupy various relational roles, which are both reflected in talk with others, and also constituted through that talk: it is partly through the way in which one addresses one's younger brother that one 'does', being an older sister. The linguistic resources for constructing the relationship through the interaction are 'always already there', as one half of Bakhtin's formulation has it (Clark and Holquist 1984: 217). Or, as Taylor (1985: 232) says, any

> . . . new coinages are never quite autonomous, quite uncontrolled by the rest of language. They can only be introduced and make sense because they already have a place within the web [of language], which must at any moment be taken as given over by far the greater part of its extent.

However, because of the creativity of human agency, the utterances any speaker produces are, simultaneously, 'never ever before' (Clark and Holquist 1984: 217). As Taylor observes: '. . . if the language capacity comes to be in speech, then it is open to being continuously recreated in speech, continually extended, altered, reshaped. And this is what is constantly happening' (Taylor 1985: 232). These immediate, situated interactions are continually negotiated, generating their own emergent histories over time. These, though, are the most malleable kinds of relationships with the social world in which most children are involved, while the more opaque domains of social settings and contextual resources exert different kinds of conditioning effects, which are less amenable to actors' interventions.

Children find themselves participants in various of the social settings in which routines are repeated and into which linguistic formulae are often tightly woven, and they gradually learn the schemas and frames associated with them. As apprentices in these enterprises of the wider social world, they are excused a certain degree of ineptitude, but are gradually made aware of the costs of asserting their personal interests in contexts where their social location and membership of a collectivity – as 'pupil', 'minor' or 'juvenile', for example – is more salient. These relational roles too may be *aspects of* specific children's identities, but I find this formulation more convincing than the fragmented conception of 'multiple identities'.

Finally, there are the contextual resources, including the resources of language, which pre-exist individuals and are distributed unequally, exerting a conditioning, but not determining, influence on all social actors. Despite offering a less finely stratified model, Taylor's (1985: 232) description of language allows for a balance between agency and structure:

What then does language come to be on this view? A pattern of activity, by which we express/realize a certain way of being in the world, that of reflective awareness, but a pattern which can only be deployed against a background which we can never fully dominate; and yet a background that we are never fully dominated by, because we are constantly reshaping it. Reshaping it without dominating it, or being able to oversee it, means that we never fully know what we are doing to it; we develop language without knowing fully what we are making it into.

Considered on this larger, composite scale, language may be thought of as existing in Popper's 'World 3' of objective public knowledge (as distinct from the 'World 1' of physical bodies and 'World 2' of 'subjective know-ledge'); thus language 'as a product, . . . is a World 3 artefact, self-existent in that world, but manifested by an infinitely complex and delicate World 1– World 2 interaction' (Lass 1980: 129). (See also (Stubbs 1996: 243).) In this sense, language may be thought of as partially autonomous. Taylor's descrip-tion continues:

> From another angle: the background web is only there in that we speak. But because we cannot oversee it, let alone shape it all, our activity in speaking is never entirely under our conscious control. Conscious speech is like the tip of an iceberg. Much of what is going on in shaping our activity is not in our purview. Our deployment of language reposes on much that is preconscious and unconscious.

The development of corpus linguistics is beginning to allow us to witness linguistic phenomena beyond 'the tip of the iceberg', including some of the properties of language of which individual users are unaware. Such proper-ties (patterns of collocations, for instance, and connotations attaching to lexical items) which native-speaker introspection does not fully reveal, can be classified as 'relations between relations' (Archer 1995), where a system is more than the sum of its parts, and macro is more than micro writ large.

All of this may seem a long way from research into children's acquisition of modal verbs, or a headline about fashion-conscious pre-teens, or a dispute between sisters about whether being allowed to watch a video on the last day of term is 'fair' or not. However, I think that in order to understand the complex relations between children, language and the social world we do need an analytical framework which helps us to situate both the individual utterance and the predictable patterns of children's language development, to recognize both the power of media discourse and the potential of each child's human agency. In my view, this version of realist social theory offers such a framework, and I shall draw on it further in the analyses presented in the chapters that follow.

## Notes

1. James et al. (1998) identify 'the socially constructed child' as one product of recent theory, which addresses itself to the '. . . analysis of modes of discourse whereby children are brought into being' (p. 27). Two authors who have applied such a perspective, for example, to 'agendas of child concern' are Stainton Rogers and Stainton Rogers (1992). They describe their analysis of 'shifting agendas of child concern' as 'a stylistically hetero-geneous collection of stories' (p. 132), and claim that the socio-economic system which is the context of contemporary childhood '. . . is no more – and no less – than a human product. It has neither reality nor force nor momentum of its own, outside of our discursive engagement in it. We have made and make it; only we can unmake and change it' (p. 197). By contrast, however, James et al. point out that social constructionism '. . . does run the risk of abandoning the embodied material child' (James et al. 1998: 28). Furthermore, I think it is important to understand who is meant by 'we', and to know whether, for Stainton Rogers and Stainton Rogers, all society's members are implicated equally in 'making' and 'unmaking' social systems.
2. Archer in fact refines further the distinctions between 'actors' and 'agents', who for her are always collectivities; and between 'corporate' and 'primary' agents. I hope it does not do violence to her theory to omit these distinc-tions from the present discussion, where I do not believe they are crucial to the points I want to make.

# Children's Talk

# Introduction to **Part III**

*Compared with adults, children enjoy less extensive rights not only in respect to space, but also in respect to information and conversation. Almost any adult can ask a child 'What's your name?' 'How old are you?'*

(GARVEY 1984: 105)

Previous chapters have discussed how the English language *represents* children as a distinctive social group. This third part of the book is concerned with what 'being a child' might mean in relation to childly ways of *using* the English language. Age-grading is an area of sociolinguistics which is receiving increasing attention, as one of the social categories by which we intuitively classify speakers, given the expectations we have of 'characteristic linguistic behaviours which are appropriate to and typical of the different stages in the speaker's lifespan' (Romaine 1984: 104). One of the considerations for research in this field identified by Coupland et al. (1993) is 'age-appropriate behaviour', including linguistic behaviour, and the authors raise the questions 'how (when and why) is age-appropriateness implied or inculcated prescriptively ("act your age"), such as in relation to moral responsibility, health, sexuality, appearance, social control, maturation, achievement?' (p. 289). Although these authors identify such considerations particularly in respect of older people, they reflect similar social preoccupations to those illustrated in Part I, about what children should do and should refrain from doing.

How do we make judgements about speakers' age categories? As an experienced speaker of English, you will probably have little trouble in determining – even with no discourse context – which of the following was said by (a) a very young child, (b) a speaker in middle childhood, (c) a mature speaker and (d) an elderly person.

(1) everything was done for me I was well looked after (.) you can't expect much at eighty eight can you? (chuckles at length) still I see some of them are flying across the world at ninety (.) true (laughs)

(2) I'm not——(pretend cry). Mummy——off. I'll tell my Daddy come back home.

(3)   she said well we'd wanted to move in she said within six weeks /
      she says could you do that? so Mandy said well if you really
      wanted to so she said yes / it was obviously a confirmed sale and
      everything went through all right

(4)   well erm we were allowed to bring a game in and we played them
      all afternoon and we watched the jungle book / the jungle book
      the video

In their discussion of the end of the lifespan furthest from the theme of this book, Coupland et al. (1991: 5ff) have identified several ways in which 'elderly' attributes of speakers may be interpreted, and their insights are relevant to children's self-representation through talk too. They discuss 'inherent causes' of identification of a speaker as elderly, such as changes to the body, brain or voice, and we may note that children's voices can be similarly distinguished from those of adults. In addition to their higher pitch, young speakers may continue to have difficulty articulating the full range of speech sounds in a language until their vocal apparatus is fully mature, despite an ability to hear salient sound distinctions in the speech of others.

Another of Coupland et al.'s categories is the 'historical causes' of 'elderly' speech attributes, such as the use of vocabulary or pronunciation styles learned in earlier times which when used in later life mark the speaker as elderly. Young children enter the ever-changing language when particular influences are operative on pronunciation, particular words or phrases fashionable or current. In infancy, young speakers' own invented vocabulary or approximations to standard names for people or objects may become generally used, at least for a while, within the family. By middle childhood, children may develop a quite conscious awareness of the implications of talking in particular ways. Some 10- and 11-year-olds with whom I worked (Sealey 1992) – Martin (M) and Wendy (W), for example – were very articulate about the need to keep up with 'fashionable' slang, explaining in discussion:

M:   people / like / some people / who aren't like / who don't get in
     with the gang and all the fashionable words / they just say normal
     words but um the other people that are with it all they say all
     fashionable words so it's like a fashion show
W:   it's like a fashionable gang and a gang what's left out

Thus particular vocabulary can be a marker of age-category for both older and younger speakers.

Coupland et al.'s third category is 'environmental causes', such as being cut off from the domains of talk – work, for example – that were important to elderly people at earlier stages in their lives. Children too talk *about* those things that are important and meaningful to them in their day-to-day experience at that stage in their lifespan.

In the absence of detailed phonological information, we are not in a position to respond to the voice quality of the utterances quoted above. And perhaps the topics which, as propositional content, are arguably not purely linguistic clues are the easiest markers to use, but we can also respond to vocabulary and syntactical peculiarities in determining which speaker is the infant, which the child, which the adult and which the elderly person. In case there is any doubt, the 'answers' are: 1 = d (Coupland 1997: 37); 2 = a (Dunn 1988: 37); 3 = c (author's data); 4 = b (author's data).

So age and language use are clearly related, and the preceding discussion also illustrates again the different timescales relevant for a consideration of these issues: from an individual perspective, one speaks as a child at one period in one's life and then 'puts away' childish talk; from the perspective of society as a whole, there are always children there, and their use of language *as children* may be different from that of previous generations and thus a source of adult anxiety ('I would never have spoken to my parents like that!' – unattested).

In terms of the domain theory outlined in Chapter 5, age-grading can be viewed as partly related to psychobiography. As was noted in Chapter 4, children's language is exclusively linked in much research literature to *development*, as though each member of this human category follows a predetermined blueprint, so that 'comparison between child, prehistoric man (*sic*) and "savage" presupposes a conception of development, of individual and of evolutionary progress, as unilinear, as directed steps up an ordered hierarchy' (Burman 1994: 11). However, one problem with many psycholinguistic accounts of children's language influenced by these presuppositions is that they fail to take account of the other domains.

With reference to the domain of contextual resources, access to the language itself is different for people who belong to the social categories of children and adults respectively, but these resources are not stored under lock and key. Some aspects of syntax and vocabulary, it is true, are so unfamiliar to most child speakers that we would be surprised to hear a child utter them. At the level of lexis and syntax, there is evidence that linguistic features associated with the written mode are the most salient distinctions between the language of middle childhood and that of adults; the use by a child of linguistic forms found more frequently in writing can make an utterance sound uncharacteristically mature. Perera (1984: 157), for example, mentions 'structures such as complex grammatical subjects, non-finite and verbless clauses and certain types of ellipsis – all of which occur much more frequently in writing and formal, planned speech than they do in spontaneous speech'. (See also Adger 1998.) It is likely, for example, that the phrase 'a confirmed sale' in (3) above, provides as much of a clue to the speaker's age category as the topic it refers to. We *can* use such a phrase in informal speech (as this speaker did) but it is more typical of the less transient mode of writing (Halliday 1989). (Contrast this construction with the less nominalized alternative 'they were definitely going to buy it'.) There are various features, particularly at the level of syntax, then, which adults use and children in middle childhood rarely do. Thus it is perhaps these omissions, rather than any errant 'commissions', which we can surmise will help to distinguish adult and middle-childhood talk.

Both the topic of an interaction and the relationships between the participants may also be related to age-grading. In (4) above the reference to 'a game' and 'the jungle book video' both suggest childly interests, while reporting what one is 'allowed' to do implies a subordinate relationship to someone in authority. This will turn out to be a recurring theme in my analyses of children's informal talk in the chapters that follow.

However, all these are probabilistic tendencies, not categorical certainties, so that membership of the social category 'child' cannot be definitive of a speaker's behaviour. The dialogic, organic, social nature of language means that child speakers will draw on its resources as any other group of speakers does, and different children will do this in different ways, influenced both by individual psychobiography and by unevenly distributed contextual resources.

At the level of 'social settings', there is some pressure on children to conform to expectations about the childly use of language. It was clear that the child involved in the school closure news story in Part I did not have the power to affect events through any speech acts of his own in the way that the adult news actors could. And children's access to social and political institutions (even to a range of public spaces, as discussed in Part I) is severely limited. Within the institutions where children do spend their time, of which the main one is of course the school, children's roles are prescribed and deviations from adult-sanctioned linguistic behaviour are censured. All these circumstances mean that children do not have much opportunity to practise certain kinds of discourse, but such inexperience is not the same as an individual, developmental explanation for children's use of language differing from that of adults.[1] Thus, as Hoyle and Adger (1998: 4) observe:

> the difference between younger and older children is largely attributable to developing communicative competence . . . Moreover, the competences displayed by eight-, twelve-, or sixteen-year-olds are not merely immature reflections of those of adults; rather, the nature of those nonadult but well-formed competences is the issue.

Finally, the respective generic status of children and adults is locally marked in the domain of situated activity. In sociolinguistic accounts of interactions, children are almost prototypical of low status participants, as can be seen from explanations of the distinction between formal and intimate 'you' in many languages, for example. Learners may be warned to avoid being disrespectful by choosing, if in doubt, the more formal variant – except, 'of course', to animals or children. In relation to address forms in general,

Holmes (1995: 146) explains that many endearments are potentially express-ive of intimacy between equals, but that 'used non-reciprocally they suggest one is talking to an inferior or subordinate. . . . Parents, older relatives, neigh-bours and even shopkeepers address children with terms such as *sweetie, darling, lovie, sugar plum* and so on. But they would be shocked if the child were to reply in kind.' The limitations on children's rights to expect equal status in interactions with adults are also exemplified in Holmes's discussion of the range of ways apologies may be expressed. The seriousness of an offence, she explains, may be calculated relative to the status of the offendee, so that '. . . bumping into a child may not warrant an apology at all' (ibid.: 173). Similarly, Garvey (1984: 50) observes that '[a]dults interrupt children with relative impunity'.

Hymes claims that this kind of differentiation is universal, with optimum status associated with the stage in the lifespan which comes after childhood but before old-age:

> . . . In all societies there are age-graded terms for persons. If unmarked usage is to refer to a person by the term for the category in which, by age, he or she belongs, then derogation can be expressed by referring to a person by a term for the category below that to which, by age, he or she belongs (calling a man 'boy', a boy 'big baby'). Praise can be expressed by referring to a person by a term for the category above that to which, by age, he or she belongs (short of decrepitude[2]) (calling a boy 'young man', an infant 'little man').

> (Hymes 1974: 157)

Both Thorne (1993) and James (1993) provide recent empirical evidence for this kind of derogation and praise from schools in the USA and the UK respectively, while the latter highlights the strong cultural connection between size and age.

In the next chapter, I shall use transcripts of recordings of children talk-ing to consider what might mark certain kinds of interaction as childly. Interactions among children are often deemed to be 'play', yet sociologists of childhood have criticized the automatic assumption that play is what children do, in contrast to work, the occupation of adults. This assumption, say James et al. (1998: 93) 'underscores the suggestion that integral to the identity status of "child" in Western cultures is the devaluation and disempowerment of children as competent social actors'. Some of the re-cordings discussed in Chapter 6 shed light on children as people who play, but others reveal a wider range of capacities and interests. The recordings were made by equipping the children with compact portable tape-recorders for short periods, during which they recorded themselves in conversation with different interlocutors, predominantly friends and family members. They were simply asked to make recordings when it was convenient and accept-able to all participants, as they engaged in their usual activities, with no *a priori* classification of these interactions as play, nor prompting to record jokes, games or 'verbal lore', those rituals identified in the literature on children's peergroups which James et al. describe as 'material argots of a youthful subculture which children swap with one another' (James et al. 1998: 82).

In Chapter 6, after considering how ideas of children as 'play-ers' are illuminated by the recordings, I explore a type of interactive exchange in which social status is fairly clearly marked – the request, or directive – to illustrate how belonging to the category of 'children' corresponds in patterned and predictable ways with how requests are formulated. However, my data also suggests that these patterns are interwoven with other dynamics in the social world, so that 'being a child' conditions, but does not determine, how this kind of linguistic interaction will unfold in the context of situated activity.

To extend the exploration of how age-grading might, like many of the other 'fuzzy categories' found in linguistics, have its own rather blurred boundaries, I consider in Chapter 7 whether, how and why speakers deploy the linguistic resources usually associated with people occupying another stage in the lifespan. This chapter will present some examples of adults using childly language, of older children using baby talk, and of adults being addressed as children often are, and it will analyse what the rhetorical func-tions of such 'code-switching', or 'crossing' (Rampton 1995), might be.

Chapter 8 returns to data from the informal conversations among chil-dren and various adult interlocutors discussed in Chapter 6, to investigate further the idea of children's identity in the social world, and how an appre-ciation of the different domains of social life as introduced above can help in understanding the language used in children's interactions with others.

## Notes

1. Ochs and Schieffelin (1995) discuss a wide range of grammatical forms in different languages of which children have passive knowledge but which they do not use themselves because it would be inappropriate for their status as children, as well as other forms used *only* by children, for similar reasons. Or, as Burman (1994: 141) puts it, '. . . an understanding of chil-dren's status and speaking rights . . . enters into the form and structure of what they say'.
2. Hudson (pers. comm.) points out that this quotation may suggest as univer-sal an attitude to old age which is perhaps less respectful in the West than in some other societies.

# 6

## The Social Status of 'Child' in Informal Talk

*It should be noted that children at play are not playing about; their games should be seen as their most serious-minded activity.*

(MONTAIGNE)

## 6.1 Introduction

This chapter will be concerned with two themes which are closely associated with being a child: playing, and being subject to adult authority. Some of the (adult) speakers in Chapter 3 suggested that 'play' was a defining characteristic of childhood, and that the loss of opportunities for children to play portends the potential disappearance of childhood itself. However, one commentator who strongly rejects the idea that childhood is disappearing from contemporary society highlights a different core characteristic of this age-phase, in view of children's economic dependence. 'To be a child', writes Hood-Williams (1990: 163), 'seems commonly to be an "immediate" relationship of command and obedience; notwithstanding the variety in the exercise of command and the forms of compliance.'

The first section of this chapter, then, will explore different kinds of 'play', using transcripts of some children's informal talk. The second section of the chapter will consider how the various participants in the conversations negotiate what Ervin-Tripp et al. (1990) term 'control acts'. Adults typically tell children what to do; children typically have to ask for what they want. In this chapter I explore how these patterns are realized – but also modified – in some of the family conversations recorded.

There were three boys and three girls in the study which provides the data for this chapter and for Chapter 8. Through initial contacts with schools I recruited families who would be willing to make recordings, and the children who eventually participated were from three areas within the west midlands of England. All the children lived with both of their parents and their sibling(s), and all were either 8 or 9 years old at the beginning of the six-month period during which recordings were made. Their parents worked in a wide range of occupations: although such a small number of children could not provide representation of different social classes (or any other variable), my interest in what might be distinctive about children as language users meant that I was keen for there to be some heterogeneity in their social experience (rather than confining my investigations to the talk generated by the children of academics, for example). This book is about children and the English language, and apart from the practical difficulties of processing data in languages other than English, the different kinds of question raised by bilingualism led me to select children who were monolingual in English, although more than one variety of English is represented in their talk.

Each child made a number of recordings at different times during the period of the research, keeping a written note of the time, location, participants and context. The corpus consists of 36 such recordings, ranging in length from two or three minutes (telephone calls) to extended interactions lasting up to an hour. Contexts included telephone calls to friends and relatives to make social arrangements, family meal times, informal talk after a church service, car journeys on the way to swimming practice, interactions with friends and siblings in the house and garden and, less frequently, at school.

It was not possible to video the interactions recorded, so little paralinguistic information is available, but after each recording was made I visited the children so that they could review it with me, and they provided supplementary, contextual information. I used this very open-ended method because I was interested in how the children actually used spoken language to negotiate their relationships, talking, usually in my absence, to the people they encountered in their normal routines. Thus there was no attempt to prestructure the kinds of interaction recorded so as to elicit 'play routines' or 'control acts'.

While the children always knew they were being recorded, and therefore may have censored themselves in various ways – or 'performed' in others – the talk recorded was *ipso facto* talk which they knew how to produce and use. In addition, the talk of the children's interlocutors is – within the same constraints – equally authentic.

## 6.2  Children's interactions and the idea of 'play'

The following extract of dialogue was recorded by 8-year-old Nadine, who took a tape-recorder to school to record herself with her friends in the playground. In this extract, the recorder itself becomes incorporated into an episode of role-play, in which Nadine pretends to be a television presenter and interviewer, although she told me that this was a popular game even before she began making recordings. As Nadine instigates this role-play, she mimics the intonation and discursive style of an adult in charge of a television show: 'right right right / let's go // we're going up now the TV crew's coming up right right Sarah / how many friends have you got in your class?' It has been noted that '. . . older children generate fictional reality by jumping to the fictional level immediately, without any preparing steps. They do not define or explicate the parameters but they simply presuppose them' (Auwärter 1986: 226). Nadine's minimal scene-setting achieves this here, and she proceeds to interview a series of children about how many people in their class they number among their friends:

(6.1) Nadine (N) and Julia (J)[1,2]

> N:  hello this is Nadine Jenkins at Hightree School / we're inter-
>      viewing Julia / <u>just</u>
> J:  <u>no you're not</u>
> N:  <u>a few ques</u>tions / okay no comment from Julia / moving onto
>      the next one // no comment from Ceri // moving onto the
>      next one Leon [*adopts a Caribbean accent*] don't try to be bad
>      like you're fresh you know 'cos you'll not come fresh with me
>      [*resumes more standard accent*] right / have you got any friends
>      in your class?

## 6.2.1   Role-play, imagination and fantasy

One way of describing this extract is to say that Nadine is 'playing' at being a television interviewer, in the sense that she is enacting a fantasy scene. Her choice of topic is childly: while involvement in friendships is by no means peculiar to children, it is for young children that 'simply "having friends" to enumerate is important' (James et al. 1998: 95; James 1993), and this is not a topic likely to form the basis of any genuine television interview. Nadine explicitly retains her own name: 'this is Nadine Jenkins', and the actual location of the school, rather than imagining herself in a studio or on the street stopping members of the public.

Within its own terms, however, Nadine's manipulation of her fantasy is perhaps not so childly, since it is within the play frame that '. . . children can control the adult world they represent to themselves' (Steedman 1982: 122). As Romaine (1984: 143) notes in respect of children observed playing house:

> . . . the new context was marked paralinguistically, prosodically and lin-
> guistically; or, in Goffman's terms, it was bracketed as a new frame. The
> play itself was clearly childish, but the management of it was adultlike in
> competence, since adults too use similar devices to negotiate identities and
> manage interactions.

The roles which Nadine attempts to allocate to other children present rely on her own persona as an adult interviewer. When she meets with resistance, although she has no real power to compel her peers to co-operate, she responds to one refusal in terms consistent with the scene, by representing it in a news media formula as 'no comment'. Children role-playing interviewers have been observed to achieve 'an adult-style flavour' to their talk through the use of discourse markers and forms 'that they use sparingly, if at all, in other talk' (Hoyle 1998: 52–3). When Nadine is met with a refusal from another 'interviewee', she temporarily relinquishes the interviewer role but not the adult component of it, in the utterance beginning 'don't try to be bad . . .'. She has access to both standard English and the regional variants used in the area of the inner-city school she attends. Her father has links with the Caribbean, and at the start of the study she alerted me to the fact that she might use 'patois' in some of the recordings. In the event she did not do this very often, and when she did use non-standard English it was actually as little different from standard English as this extract exemplifies. Her very explicit direction of Leon using these particular linguistic resources suggests that Nadine is drawing on a speech style she has heard adults use to put misbehaving children back into line.

Somewhat paradoxically, then, linguistic 'play' may involve temporarily moving outside one's designated role as a child (one who plays), and experimenting with how it feels to be someone with more status in the social world, someone who directs others as to what they should do, someone with more contextual resources at one's disposal than are routinely available to children.

It is noticeable that most of the roles adopted by the six children in these recordings move them 'up' the status hierarchy, so that they choose to be adults rather than younger children or babies. (Other studies have noted children's reluctance, in directed role-play, to be 'the baby' – see Andersen 1990; Ervin-Tripp 1986; Garvey 1977.)

Nadine's 'interview' scenario is obviously influenced by television, as are many of the characters adopted by these children in their role-play: sports competitors, sports commentators, television and radio entertainers and personalities (including Mr Blobby, Hulk Hogan) and action figures (where the role-play consists in moving the toys and providing their dialogue). These cultural influences have been identified as a source of anxiety to parents and educators, but analysts have also pointed out the creativity in children's use of media material (e.g. Kline 1993; Meek 1985). This kind of 'play' involves deployment of the available cultural resources to experiment with alternative possibilities, including alternative relations of power. According to Whitehead (1995: 48), it is children's routine vulnerability which partially accounts for their abiding interest in 'power and its misuse', expressed in a tendency to exaggerate the speech styles of 'authoritarian figures' in role-play. Further, a fascination with fiction and fantasy is not exclusively childly, but among adults it is more institutionalized, as 'art' and 'literature'. For both groups, make-believe makes possible an engagement with 'powerful, formless, un-named sensations' (Meek 1985: 49).

This is one way, then, in which the boundaries between children's and adults' use of talk may be less clear cut than some kinds of research would suggest. If researchers, assuming that particular topics and experiences are familiar and relevant to children, choose a 'playroom' as a setting for the research, and toys (often dolls and puppets) as content for the talk which is to be studied, there is a danger that the research design may make an *a priori* distinction between children's talk and that of adults. A focus on children's 'culture', as was demonstrated in Chapter 4, often highlights those aspects of children's uses of language which are most distinctively childly, while their negotiations over toys and playthings, which similarly foreground childliness, are another common focus for research into children's language (see, for example, Allen 1995; Garvey 1977; Goodwin 1990; McTear 1985).

Several sociologists of childhood are critical of accounts of children's play which associate it with 'ossified cultural forms (jokes, games and childhood lore)' (James et al. 1998: 89), while from historical accounts of children's culture it emerges that childhood as necessarily a time for play is a relatively recent idea (Kline 1993). It has also been noted that this linkage is not universal across cultures (Archard 1993). James et al. (1998: 90) maintain that 'children's culture', if there is such a thing, is 'a form of social action, a way of being a child among other children, a particular cultural style, resonant with particular times and places'. This model allows for diversity in children's management of interactions with others, which, in terms of domain theory, will emerge from variety in different children's social and temporal locations as well as their unique personal histories.

## 6.2.2   Playing games with rules

All of these observations make the simple classification of children's freely chosen activities as 'play' problematic. The children in my study did refer to many of their interactions as 'play', as did the adults around them, but the word was used to denote more than one activity.[3] Apart from 'playing' music (or the radio, or a record), there is the sense of the word which denotes unambiguously the 'playing' of childly games. These include games with rules, often involving linguistic formulae. Some are the age-old games prob-ably taught to the children by their parents, some are more specific to these children. There are a number of examples from the transcripts in which this kind of 'play' is enacted; just two are presented here:

(6.2) Simon (S), 8, in the car with his family, including Theresa (T), 12.

S:   shall we play I spy then?
T:   yeah

> S:   erm erm i+ [laughs] I'll start / I spy with my little eye
>       something beginning with T
> T:   Tesco's
> S:   no // we just passed one
> T:   telephone box
> S:   yes / your turn

Some accounts of 'children's culture' (particularly their activities away from adults) stress the similarity of formulae like these in children's games over centuries, highlighting continuity and the fact that children claim as inventions games which in fact have a long history (see Opie 1993; Opie and Opie 1959; Thomas 1989). However, there has been a reaction against the 'conception of play as just imitative rather than creative social action' (James et al. 1998: 93). The 'rules' of the game proposed in the next extract are rather obscure to non-participants, but this is clearly not simply a rehearsal of a sterile formula:

(6.3) Emma (E), 9, is playing with her friend and next-door neighbour, Gemma (G), 10, at home. Emma's sister Jenny (J), 7, is with them. They have been playing a game involving the listing of animals – hence Jenny's first contribution in this extract (l. 2)

> G:   hang on I've got an id<u>ea</u>
> J:   <u>bat</u>
> G:   what we can play I've got an idea what we can play
> E:   what?
> G:   what we do / you have+ you're going to go in a            5
>       wardrobe and you can take / two / two+ (<u>***</u>)
> J:   <u>two (ants)</u>
> G:   you've gotta say if you can take them or not / all right?
> E:   take them where?
> G:   now I'll take // a canary / and //                         10
> J:   take
> E:   take where?
> G:   into the cupboard
> J:   I know
> E:   I'd take+ //                                               15
> J:   why would you take a canary and a fox?
> G:   you can take anything at all

Unlike 'I spy', the conventions of this game have to be made explicit, as indeed is the fact that it is a game (1.3). The game is some kind of fantasy, perhaps drawing on children's adventures in magical worlds found in cupboards, or more cerebral 'games' such as debates in which participants identify what is most vital for survival. Gemma, as originator of the idea, has the right to sketch out the scenario (ll. 5–6), specify what players 'can' do (l. 6, l. 8), and take questions of clarification. Some other features of this kind of co-construction of activities will be discussed in Chapter 8.

### 6.2.3   Play as sport

'Play' also has connotations of imitative action as a preparation for adult life, which once more implies adulthood as authentic and normal, and childhood as a period in waiting. Functionalist explanations of children's play suggest an analogy between human children and other species whose young play-fight their siblings as practice for later hunting and self-defence. A version of 'play' as socialization is represented in my data in the context of discussions about particular activities (which are not confined to children, and are clas-sifiable as 'play' because of the need for rules and equipment), of which the most frequently mentioned was football.

> (6.4) Chris (C), 8, at the dinner table with his mother (CM), father
>       (CF) and sister
>
> CM:   well Thomas's quite good at football isn't he
> C:    yeah / so is Tom now
>       ...(***)...
> C:    what d'you say dad?
> CF:   (***)
> C:    he plays in hi+ er with his dad in the back garden about
>       twice a day // he plays after school every night or until the
>       every evening
> CM:   does he?
> C:    and at the weekend he plays about six times / and he goes
>       to football training about two or three times a week

Exchanges like this exemplify children's involvement as apprentices in cul-tural practices validated by the wider community, particularly in the mention of 'training', an overt form of socialization. However, in some episodes in my data, this more mainstream meaning of 'play' as sport overlaps with fantasy or role-play. The children may be 'playing' with a ball in the garden, but simultaneously pretending to be adult sportspeople. Chris manages such a game, in one recording, using talk in this interaction to:

– instruct his younger friends on their roles:
  'Thomas / you're Liverpool / Tom you're Man United'

– negotiate the rules:
'it's not a kick-off / it's a free kick in isn't it Thomas'
– comment supportively on his friends' performance:
'cor good goal Tom'
– and, in role as (part of?) a spectating crowd, chant the score:
'two-one' [*pronounced wu-un, with falling intonation*]

In another example rather like this, Emma moves through a comparable range of 'play' contexts. She uses talk to negotiate with her younger sister Jenny and, in role as a commentator on her own actions, she makes explicit the imaginary elements of the game.

(6.5) Emma (E) and Jenny (J)

E:   okay / let's do some more football // with **my** ball
J:   don't like that one
E:   well you threw yours next door / I want to do it with my new ball that Grandma bought me [bounces ball] [*as commentator*] and Emma has the ball / oh and it's hand ball // the game's changed / and the game's changed to basketball
J:   Mum
E:   Emma gets the ball she's bouncing it and [*shouting exultantly*] she hits the barbecue

The 'commentary' is rapidly established, partly through the simple present action verbs (cf. Hoyle 1998) but despite its authentic generic features, any notion of the social function of play as preparation for sport in later life appears quite irrelevant. Clearly children have little power to influence which of their activities are to be defined as important, a point made by Thomas (1989: 58) as relevant in earlier periods of history too:

Of course, when we say that children preferred play to work we mean only that they liked to spend their time doing serious things which adults regarded as trivial and frivolous. . . . since in early modern England, as today, it was the Grown-ups who decided what was or wasn't frivolous, 'play' was officially what children did, not adults.

The automatic designation of children's activities as 'play' also troubles Thorne (1993: 5–6): 'Observing on school *play* grounds, I saw not only play but also serious and fateful encounters; I witnessed anger, sorrow, and boredom, as well as sport and jest' (original emphasis). If everything which children do when unsupervised is 'play', there is no room to make distinctions between different activities from the children's own point of view.

## 6.2.4   Play as socializing

Looked at from another perspective, 'play' as inconsequential relaxation may be something adults do too. Coates (1996: 1), for example, asserts that for many groups of women friends 'talk is our chief form of recreation: we meet our friends to talk, and our talk is a kind of play'. Coates's point is made in relation to gender-related differences in uses for talk, and some researchers into children's 'play' have noted a marked contrast between girls demonstrating their friendships through talking together and boys demonstrating theirs by acting together (Davies 1989; James 1993; Opie 1993, although cf. Goodwin and Goodwin 1987; Thorne 1993, who note similarities as well). Although gender differences between the children were not the focus of my study, I did indeed find that two of the girls, in particular, spent time on several of the recordings engaged in interactions with others which might easily be designated 'socializing' if the participants were adults rather than children. Their talk recalls the 'women talk' which Coates (1996: 151) describes, when friendship is accomplished through 'talk-as-play', and women 'improvise on each other's themes, share painful and funny experiences, laugh at ourselves and with each other'.

For example, in one recording, Emma was visited by her friend Louise (9), and the latter's twin sisters Helena and Abigail (7). At the beginning of the period recorded, when the girls go up to Emma's room together, the question 'what are we going to play?' is uttered four times. Several activities are suggested and rejected before Emma produces the *Guinness Book of Records*, as a contribution to the debate about what they should 'play'. Although two of the girls are initially unenthusiastic, Emma's suggestion is taken up, and subsequent conversation over a prolonged period constitutes a joint reading and discussion of this book.

> (6.6) Emma (E), 9, with her friend Louise and Louise's sisters. Apart from Emma's, the girls' voices in this recording are not clearly distinguishable, and their utterances are therefore attributed to unidentifiable female speakers (F??). As with Coates's recordings, there is a large number of overlaps in this extract
>
> E:     have you seen this? the Guinness Book of Records?
> F??:   <u>what can we do?</u>
> E:     <u>it's really</u> good / it's got erm
> F??:   it won't be interesting
> E:     <u>it **is**</u>
> F??:   <u>it's just a lot</u> of boring+
> E:     the+ the shortest woman erm
> F??:   <u>in the world?</u>
> E:     <u>she's only</u> thirty-two at the moment and she's only about that high

F??:    oh my god
F??:    is she higher than me?
F??:    (***) I'm taller than her
E:      I know / she's she's only erm sixty-five centimetres
F??:    oh my goodness
F??:    that's smaller
E:      she's+
F??:    than me
E:      yeah
F??:    hold on a minute (***) smaller than me
F??:    it's about she's about that big isn't she
E:      she's not that big actually
F??:    she's just a bit bigger than a ruler
E:      no she's not seventy-two / she's thirty+
F??:    she's five more centimetres than a ruler
E:      mm
F??:    you know what? she's only that big
F??:    (***) she's seventy-two (***)
E:      she's not seventy-two
F??:    (***)
E:      she's thirty-two / she's middle aged

The transcript of the conversation on this topic lasts for another seven pages, with discussion about the heights and weights of people featured in the book eventually leading to the topic of the girls' respective positions in their families, and the pros and cons of cast-off clothes. Thus collaborative, and occasionally competitive, reflections on shared experiences and exchanges of personal accounts may be the main activity when these girls gather, away from the adults, to 'play' in Emma's room. While there are certain distinctive qualities of the talk they use which mark it as childly, in other respects it is hard to see a clear boundary between this kind of talk and that presented by Coates, for example, as informal conversations among friends. As Garvey (1984: 161) maintains:

> Just conversing . . . is one social activity that increases in frequency and in diversity of topic over the preschool years to become an important type of sharing among children and a major constituent of the interactions of most close friends, both displaying and reinforcing solidarity and intimacy.

## 6.3   Requests, directives and being a child

The previous section aimed to explore whether the talk of the children in my study could be seen as distinctively childly by considering various meanings of 'play', and it considered general characteristics of the exchanges rather than their detailed linguistic features. This section will focus at a more specific level on exchanges in which individuals ask – or tell – each other to bring about some change in the state of affairs. Children's relational status is prototypically that of novice or apprentice, so:

> ... there appears to be no analytic basis on which to exclude *any* sphere of children's conduct as being potentially rule governed. There can be a right and wrong way of requesting, interrupting, eating, sitting, standing and playing. The list is *essentially* undefinite.
>
> (Wootton 1986: 149)

So childliness is apparently closely related to being told what to do and how to do it. However, children too have to find ways of negotiating their own needs and interests, which often involves seeking to influence others to act. What does it mean to have the status of 'child' in these interactions?

## 6.3.1   Variations in requests and directives

According to politeness theory, requests carry a potential threat to the face of both speaker and addressee (Brown and Levinson 1978: 81), and, while 'there is nothing intrinsically polite about any linguistic form' (Holmes 1995: 10), variation is found in the forms used to realize requests (imperatives, imbedded imperatives, hints, offers and so on; see Ervin-Tripp 1977; Schiffrin 1994). Something requiring greater inconvenience to the addressee may be requested in a form which demonstrates recognition of the imposition: the degree of aggravation or mitigation in the way the directive or request is framed is thus related partly to the degree of 'expectancy on the part of the speaker of compliance by the addressee' (Ervin-Tripp 1977: 194). The relationship existing between speakers is also a factor in this, so that the degree of formality in putting a request may be linked to the continuum of distance-intimacy, and the degree of deference linked to differential power or status. The influence of such variables is a conditioning, rather than a determining one, and perceptions of how they are to be read, as well as the details of their realization in speech, may vary among individuals and groups, and even during the course of an interaction (Erickson 1981).

Nevertheless, the principles of patterned variations of this kind are found across cultures (Blum-Kulka and Olshtain 1984; Brown and Levinson 1978; Holmes 1995). Furthermore, each instance of a request sequence may be seen both as an indication of the nature of the relationship, and as (partly) constitutive of it. Thus Goodwin (1990: 70) claims that sequences of requests and directives constitute '. . . a research site where one can investigate in an especially clear way ties between the details of linguistic structure and an encompassing cultural world of social action'. Although Goodwin's own research (1990) identifies contrasts between boys' and girls' use of directives in the context of peer interaction, it is a concern with communicative development which has largely driven research into children's use of requests and directives (for example, Cook-Gumperz 1977; Ervin-Tripp 1977; Ervin-Tripp et al. 1990; Gordon and Ervin-Tripp 1984; Levin and Rubin 1983; McTear 1985; Mitchell-Kernan and Kernan 1977). Thanks to such studies we know that, with increasing age, children extend their repertoire of requests and their tendency to differentiate the form of a request according to the kinds of social factors outlined above – and that young children find the use of 'tactful deviousness' (indirect hints) least accessible (Ervin-Tripp 1977).

However, as my interest is in children as a social category, the discussion of my own data will be concerned not with the children's developmental stages, but with how adults explicitly directed their behaviour, and how the children sought to influence the actions of adults and attempted to position themselves 'above' various interlocutors. Finally, I shall discuss some examples where the hierarchy is less clearly determined.[4]

## 6.3.2   Directives 'down': adult to child

In these recordings, the children are often the recipients of directives from parents and other adult relatives. One area in which it is culturally legitimate for parents to address unmitigated directives to their children is to prohibit undesirable behaviour, such utterances being in themselves markers of the role-relationship.[5] The following directives, for example, are among those addressed by Ian's father to his two sons during a car journey from home to swimming practice. About the tape-recorder: 'don't start messing with it please Ian'; 'just forget it's there'. About some behaviour unidentified in the recording: 'don't be silly'. Indeed, 'don't be silly' occurs several times in the data, and is a directive which assumes that the addressee is aware, in context, of what constitutes unacceptable behaviour without the need for explicit specification (cf. Wootton 1986: 153).

Researchers have documented ways in which parents in different cultures instruct their children about how to speak (Ely and Gleason 1995; Ochs 1983; Schieffelin 1983; Schieffelin and Ochs 1986), and in my study too linguistic behaviour can itself attract censure. For example, when Ian's father asks him about his day at school, and Ian, apparently deliberately, chooses a pragmatic misinterpretation of the question, his father disallows it.

> (6.7) Ian (I), 9, and his father (IF)
>
>     IF:   what did you have for dinner?
>     I:    food
>     IF:   don't be cheeky

Like 'silly', 'cheeky' implies 'tacit cultural knowledge' (Hymes 1972: 279) shared between parent and child. Other syntactic forms of directive can convey the parent-speaker's assumption of authority in behaviour regulation, such as Chris's mother's reprimand to his sister Vicky, who is copying every gesture her father makes during a family meal: 'I really do think you'll have to leave the table in a minute.' This formulation makes Vicky the subject of an abstract obligation, while her mother's 'I really do think' establishes the link between her perception of how things are and the obligation placed on Vicky.

Parents also have the right – and the duty – to regulate the children's behaviour in less censorious ways, informing or reminding them of matters of hygiene, safety, cultural norms and so on, and one would expect greater mitigation to be employed in these more positive directives. One Sunday morning, Gemma accepts an invitation from Emma to go round to her house. As Gemma's brother is ill with a cold, her mother checks that Gemma won't be risking catching cold. While the exchange leads up to a parental directive, this is embedded in reasoning which implies (a) the adult's responsibility to protect her daughter from the cold; (b) the transmission of knowledge about matching clothing to weather conditions; and (c) the child's own responsibility to act on this awareness.

> (6.8) Gemma (G), 10; her mother (GM) and Emma (E), 9, as the girls leave Gemma's house to go next door to Emma's
>
> GM: do you need your coat?
> G: er
> GM: you going in the garden?
> G: no
> E: no
> GM: well if you go in the garden come and get your coat ok<u>ay</u>
> G: <u>ok</u>ay
> GM: 'cos I don't want you ill as well

Ian's parents also address directives to their sons about their swimming. Again, the stance taken is consistent with a parental role, but, unlike the behaviour-prohibiting examples cited above, these directives are embedded in reasons, including giving information about the conventions of the swimming trials, and also advice in the more abstract domain of emotions, about how to cope with failure:

> (6.9) Ian (I), 9, his father (IF), mother (IM) and brother Jason (J), 7, on their way to swimming practice in the car
>
> IF: you need to erm // swim as fast as you can tonight because your / swimming times are going to count for the team on Saturday
> I: mm

> J:     I might even get my silver on my front crawl
> IM:    bronze
> IF:    you've got to get your bronze first
> IM:    I don't want you to be disappointed if you don't get it /
>        right?

In both (6.8) and (6.9), the parents state what is good for the child in terms of their own wishes: 'I don't want *you* to [have a negative experience which I could help to prevent].' This could be interpreted as simply a formulaic softening of a directive, but it could also invite a shared response to potential occurrences.

Occasionally, an adult has reason to express a need or desire on his or her own individual account, and in such cases the lesser salience of childly status is indicated in the interaction. For example, Leanne and her cousin Angela ask if they can leave their grandmother's house to go to Angela's, but their grandmother is also looking after their sleeping baby cousin Cherelle. She says: 'Well could you just wait while I go to the toilet so's there's someone here with Cherelle please.' Firstly, this formulation provides a reason for asking the girls to delay; secondly, it emphasizes Cherelle's dependence while positioning the older girls as equivalent, for these purposes, to herself: even if she goes, so long as they stay there will be '*someone* here with Cherelle'. Finally, the conditional modal 'could you' and the inclusion of 'please' acknowledge a potential threat to the face of the children, which is not necessary in those exchanges which emphasize their childly status as people whose behaviour is legitimately subject to adult regulation.

### 6.3.3   Requests 'up': child to adult

If the topics of adults' directives to children are frequently children's behaviour, those of children's requests to adults are, like many requests, their own local needs and wishes. The dependence associated with child status is evident in children's need to ask more powerful others to do or provide things for them (Ervin-Tripp 1977: 165). The most typical formulation of such requests in my data is 'can I . . . ?'. This construction involves the modal auxiliary *can* and implies that the addressee has the power to grant or withhold permission. Thus Chris demonstrates in the following exchange a recognition that it is in his parents' power to decide what kind of a party he will have.

> (6.10a) Chris (C), 8, and his mother (CM), talking during a family
>         meal. (The instances of *can I* have been capitalized)
>
>         C:     Mum when it's my birthday
>         CM:    mmmm?

> C:    what thing CAN I have for a party? CAN I have erm
>       quite a big party with all / all of my cousins and about
>       five friends or CAN I just have like // go to a football
>       match with about three friends or stuff like that?

In addition to the parental power, however, the exchange also implies an expectation that the child's wishes are likely to be acted upon. The question, 'what thing can I have for a party?' suggests that for Chris, as a child with a birthday, some kind of party is almost a right. His list of alternatives, which invites his parents to make a choice, does not include the option of denying him any party at all (although his words cannot in themselves rule this option out). He continues with a more indirect request form: 'I would like to have a really big party with all my cousins and about five friends now', and the reformulation suggests that he has chosen his preferred option from those available, almost as though it is offered to help with the joint decision. This sense of a negotiation among the participants, related tightly to the childly topic, continues later in the conversation, with each participant providing justifications for their preferences:

(6.10b) Chris (C), 8, with his father (CF) and mother (CM)

> C:    can I have another treasure hunt?
> CF:   it took a lot of organizing
> CM:   be nice to do something (different)
> C:    yeah but it was good

The potential refusal to provide 'another treasure hunt' is hedged by both parents with 'face-supportive' reasons (Holmes 1995: 155), which help to endorse the interpretation already suggested that all participants accept Chris's expressed wishes as legitimate. Whether children's requests will be recognized and/or granted obviously depends on a number of factors: what the requests are and how the parents view them; whether it lies within the parents' power to fulfil them; the immediate context and the broader relationship between parent and child. Where there is ambiguity about such factors in relation to the children's requests, further negotiations are necessary.

For example, in one recording, Nadine tells her mother that she may decide to go outside and play. Although she is not explicitly challenged by her mother, merely asked to repeat her utterance (her mother uses a hearing aid to compensate for hearing loss), it changes in the repetition from an independent statement of intention, through a form which may have begun as a modified version of the original statement, to an explicit permission request.

(6.11) Nadine (N), 9, and her mother (NM), in the house on a hot summer afternoon

N:      I hope it stays nice // I might go outside the front later
NM:   eh?
N:      if that's okay with you
NM:   you what?
N:      if it's okay with you erm / later on can I go outside the front and play with Dionne?

A renegotiation also occurs when Chris expresses very indirectly a wish for some mint sauce to accompany his dinner.

(6.12) Chris (C), 8, and his mother (CM), talking during a family meal

C:      is there any mint sauce?
CM:   don't have mint sauce with beef
C:      can I have it to / try it out?
CM:   it's really hot (this meat)
C:      Mum can I have some to try it out?
CM:   no

His formulation 'is there any mint sauce?' could be interpreted as a proto-typical hint, at the extreme of polite indirectness and, if taken as an isolated utterance, not typical of the childly speaker. He is repositioned in the exchange as a supplicant child when his mother tells him that mint sauce is inappropriate for this dish, and this cultural information is implicitly linked with a direct refusal to his request. Here, Chris's formulation becomes 'can I have . . . ?', and includes an allusion to his inexperience – 'to try it out' – which could be seen as a bid to justify the request in a manner which capitalizes on his childly status.

These examples illustrate the fact that the 'childliness' of these children has various dimensions and is open to some negotiation. Children's power is limited partly by the fact that they have relatively few material resources of their own to bring to their relationships with adults. A (limited) exception is their labour, and, as we have seen, Leanne's grandmother solicited a brief period of child-minding from the older children with a face-supportive request. At a different point during this recording session, the girls help with the domestic chore of preparing a meal. Their grandmother asks them to fetch things necessary for the task, again using 'please', and Leanne offers to peel the potatoes, formulating the offer as a request:

(6.13) Leanne (L), 9, her grandmother (LGM) and her cousin Angela (A), 12

LGM:   get me the big saucepan please Leanne / you get me the bag of potatoes

L:       Nan can **I** peel them / please?
LGM:     Eh?
L:       can **I** peel them?

Again, the situation itself allows for the child to have a role in general domestic labour, which makes Leanne's childliness less salient. On the other hand, the fact that the utterance is framed as a permission request marks the speaker as childly, making the utterance perhaps an obverse of parents' and teachers' formulation of requests as offers, as in 'who would like to help me carry these books / make some pastry?' (unattested). Being 'allowed' to contribute to necessary tasks can thus imply entry to the more statusful world of adult activity (recall the variety in attitudes towards 'child labour' and 'children's work' discussed in previous chapters), but the fact that permission is needed identifies the participant as a child. As these examples show, the children have some room for manoeuvre in formulating their requests to adults, and can clearly make use of different strategies, but this flexibility is not limitless, since the interaction must be negotiated collaboratively.

## 6.3.4   Directives 'down': child to toys and pets

It would seem that there are relatively few opportunities for children to occupy unequivocally high status positions in many of their interactions, but, as already noted, there is evidence from the recordings that fantasy play can provide at least a simulation of more powerful roles. The children in the study had toys of various kinds, including figures representing characters (dolls, cuddly toys, action figures) and some of them had pets. Addressing these various characters, playing fantasy games in role as adults, and talking to pets all gave the children opportunities to use directive forms that would not be appropriate to use towards adults. In several recordings, Ian tells his budgie what to do, and Emma her rabbit likewise, using even more aggravated directives than those from adult to child discussed above. In addition, the exaggerated intonation, voice pitch and vocabulary used in this context are reminiscent of the 'baby-talk' or child-directed speech (CDS) identified by researchers (e.g. Snow 1976), positioning the character addressed noticeably lower in age hierarchy than the children themselves.[6]

(6.14) Ian (I), 9

I:    talk you little budgie // [ . . . ] come on / mind the wire you
      little rascal / come on talk // Alison's+ Alison's checking your
      language as well you know

The descriptive address term 'you little rascal' implies Ian's right to evaluate his 'addressee', and is interpretable as both critical and affectionate, like address terms used towards young children by adults (Holmes 1995). Ian's choice of 'checking' probably also indicates why he thinks adults would be interested in recordings of children's talk (it was not a formulation I had used!). Emma addresses her rabbit with a possessive which indicates her power/ownership of the pet and a diminutive endearment 'how are you my Cloveykins?'. This is dropped when she directs the rabbit to leave its hutch: 'Clover get out.' At one point when showing Clover the rabbit to her friends, Emma makes explicit the way she is adopting (or perhaps parodying?) an adult approach towards the animal.

> (6.15a) Emma (E), 9, tries to persuade the rabbit to come out of its cage and into the garden shed
>
>> E:    [tuts] this calls for mummy (stuff) // this is how the mummies get her out [*in role as a mummy:*] get 'ere or I'll pull your ears off / come 'ere / ugh
>
> (6.15b) Later in the same episode
>
>> E:    I'll get her / I'll get her / [*in a sing-song tone:*] now Clover you're being impolite to our guests / [*in a mock-threatening tone:*] get out / now come on / out you come

Here, Emma signals her adoption of a role explicitly: 'this is how the mummies get her out,' but, as I have noted, the children sometimes move into role simply by imitating the voice and behaviour of the persona concerned. In the recording made by Nadine during a school lunch break, from which Example (6.1) was one extract, she tests the boundaries of the rights afforded by adopting such a role and evokes comment from her school-friends when she addresses an adult in similar terms to those she has used with friends. She is using the tape-recorder in role as an interviewer, asking each of her friends in turn whether they would like to form a singing group ('choir') to perform with her on television. One friend 'dares' her to put the same questions to a dinner supervisor (Lorraine), and the children express shock when she does.

> (6.16) Nadine (N), 9; several pupils (P1, P2); dinner supervisor, Lorraine (DSL)
>
>> P1:    ask [*pronounced 'aks'*] Lorraine ask Lorraine Lorraine Lorraine Lorraine
>> P2:    oh no she's done it
>> P:      oh look
>>          [ ... ]
>> N:      would you ever join a choir to go on T V?

DSL:   hang on / repeat the question?
N:   would you / ever go+ / join a choir to go on T V?
DSL:   no 'cos I can't sing
N:   you could learn / would you like to <u>learn</u>?
DSL:   <u>I</u> could scream at the kids if you want me to [laughs]
N:   right

In this interaction, Nadine uses two resources to mitigate her childly status. She is able to use the tape-recorder as if to legitimize the things she is saying in this context. She also uses her assumed role as an interviewer to ask questions about other people's ambitions as entertainers, thus side-stepping some of the conventions applying to childly status. Her role places her in a position to make a potential offer – 'you could learn / would you like to learn?' – in an unchildly modality.

Thus the children found opportunities to place themselves on a different level in the social hierarchy from that typically associated with their status as children when engaged in fantasy and role-play. They know how to use directives such as those typically addressed by adults to children, but are more likely to deploy this resource in the context of the childly activities of playing out fantasy roles.

### 6.3.5   Directives and requests between children

Among the children, the power relations were less clearly defined than in the contexts discussed so far. Some researchers (Ervin-Tripp 1977; Goodwin and Goodwin 1987; Mitchell-Kernan and Kernan 1977) suggest that 'children use imperatives less to get something done than to test and make assertions about relative positions among participants' (Goodwin 1990: 68). In my data there are certainly several examples of sequences in which, despite the fact that compliance with a speaker's directive is not assured, he or she does not mitigate the directive/request, which could thus be interpreted as a face-threat. Thus Emma's (apparently playful) directive to her friend receives an equally assertive response.

(6.17) Emma (E), 9, and Gemma (G), 10, walking to school together

E:   oh shut it
G:   why don't you shut it

At other times, particularly in those recordings involving schoolfriends, the children tell each other to 'get lost', 'shut up', and occasionally 'piss off'. In my data, these directives do not usually lead to prolonged arguments, although, as in the exchange above, the addressee may make a short response which marks their right to reply. By chance, five of the children in the study were older siblings, so that, in talk between them and their brothers and sisters, they could adopt a higher status role. Immediately after Nadine's statement-request that she wants to go and play outside (Example (6.11)), her younger brother, Adam, objects.

(6.18) Nadine (N) and her brother Adam (A), 4, indoors with their mother

> A:  she's not / she's not / she's not playing nobody / you c+ you stay in this house
> N:  oh so you're my **moth**er now
> A:  no I'm just a boy

Nadine's response to Adam refers implicitly to the different status of mothers and younger brothers, while Adam's 'I'm *just* a boy' is even more explicit. This exchange echoes an example quoted in Mitchell-Kernan and Kernan (1977: 204), where a younger child told an older child to 'Bring your li'l self here'. This elicited the challenge 'Who do you think you are?', and the reply, 'I think I'm somebody big', prompted general laughter. The subtle distinction between different stages of childhood is exploited by Chris when he directs his younger friend Thomas, on one recording, and his sister Vicky, on another, to say childly things as though on his behalf, including rude words and nonsense which his parents find irritating (see Example (8.15) below). In a different way, Emma often demonstrates her seniority in dialogues with her 7-year-old sister Jenny by commenting negatively on her behaviour, as though she is more aware of how children ought to conduct themselves.[7] Sometimes this is by means of directives reminiscent of those used by adults to naughty children, although, as in this example, there is movement between an adult stance and occasional childly lexis and syntax.

(6.19) Emma (E), 9, trying to handle the rabbit running round the shed

> E:  and this calls for+ no don't do that Jenny that's the most stupidest thing you **could** do // I might have known **you**'d do it though // don't squish her
> . . .
> E:  no // we need+ / Jenny stop stomping your feet / you're scaring her

The children sometimes tell their friends and siblings what to do and what not to do in ways that draw on adult-like justifications – safety, the preservation of objects, appropriate dress and other norms of behaviour. For example, Emma and her friend warn a fellow schoolfriend about stamping on a frozen puddle.

(6.20) Emma (E), 9, talking to her friend Mark, with another female
      pupil (FP) in the school playground

    E:    don't
    FP:   Mark / you're breaking the ice
    E:    and you're going to fall in
    FP:   you'll get wet

In some of the interactions where children are directed by other children,
however, even in these adult-like terms, the addressee may question the
directive, and either child may then invoke an adult-like voice of authority.

(6.21) Emma (E), 9 and her sister Jenny (J), 7, playing outside and
      arguing about retrieving a ball from a neighbour's garden

    E:   [sighs] oh gosh // Jenny // <u>stop it</u>
    J:   <u>uh oh</u> / I forgot I'd got my slippers on
    E:   oh go and put your shoes on
    J:   (I don't want + ) I don't have to do I Grandma?

Sometimes, then, a child will attempt to establish or to capitalize on a
more senior position in more or less distinctly childly ways. The addressees
in such exchanges may accept this definition of hierarchy, but may challenge
it, sometimes referring to an adult (or an adult's perspective) as a means of
arbitration. The converse of this occurs when one child positions another as
capable of providing something the speaker wants or needs. Younger siblings
and friends sometimes directed requests to the children in the study, with
this implication. A refusal may be absolute and unmitigated or softened with
a justification, as when Nadine tells her brother Adam why she won't get
him the hot drink he asks for: 'I can't make a drinking chocolate I'm not old
enough / you shouldn't play with matches so I can't make you one.' In this
example, it is the older child who makes explicit and quotes the norms of
childly behaviour (which include the implication that any contact a child has
with matches is dangerous 'play'), but applies them to herself in order to
refuse a request. Whether she actually concurs with the idea that in lighting
the stove she would be 'playing' with matches, quotes the phrase wholesale
without questioning it, or finds it a convenient if inaccurate formulation
cannot be determined.

    I suggested earlier that children, subject as they are to both material and
cultural dependence, rarely find themselves in a position to make offers to
adults, and that requests and offers can perform similar pragmatic functions
(Schiffrin 1994) (see Example (6.13)). In my data, it is in the child–child
interactions that these categories become most blurred. In the following
exchange between Leanne and her brother Richard, for example, where they
negotiate over how to use stones for chalking on paving in the garden, the

ambiguity of the prevailing power relationships is apparent in the forms which the utterances take. Leanne has the clear status advantage of her greater age, but Richard has the power to grant or withhold co-operation in the game.

(6.22) Leanne (L), 9, and her brother Richard (R), 4

L:  do you want to play hopscotch Richard? // Richard
R:  (play) hopscotch? // (no 'cos) you don't let it be **my** turn
L:  it **is** your turn look / you can+ it will be your turn I promise you // give me it here / so I can draw it I need to draw it first / you don't do it like that
R:  look all the numbers / then
L:  no you don't do it like that
R:  (I I want to play the the with them) numbers
L:  don't you want to do this? please [*drawn out pleadingly to 2 syllables*] / please play with me
R:  (just) pictures Le<u>anne</u>
L:  <u>please</u> play hopscotch with me
R:  these are for pictures
L:  get me a stone then so we can draw pictures

Leanne's opening question could be interpreted as either a request or an offer. Richard's reluctance and Leanne's subsequent persuasions indicate that the speakers interpret it as the former, positioning Leanne as supplicant. Simultaneously, the remarks about turn-taking suggest that she is the more powerful one, with the gift of allocating turns ('it will be your turn I promise you'). Leanne uses the directive forms often associated with superordinates: bald imperatives, a need statement and an unchildly 'corrective' ('you don't do it like that'), but she moves back to 'please' imperatives before conceding that Richard's choice – to draw pictures – will prevail. Her final directive once more suggests an assumption that her brother will do as she asks – within the negotiated choice of activity.

Finally there are a number of exchanges between the children where power differentials seem relatively insignificant, and negotiations seem co-operative rather than competitive. Among friends, where the children have the opportunity to negotiate what they will do as peers, directives and re-quests may have the properties associated with adult intimates in informal contexts, where 'we do not bother to use a great deal of explicit politeness' and can use linguistic strategies which '[emphasise] what people share, thus minimising the [social] distance between them' (Holmes 1995: 13–14).

(6.23) In the school playground, Helen (H) and Emma (E) show each other the hats they have made for an Easter hat parade

H:  oh look that's coming undone (***)
E:  quickly put it back

(6.24) Leanne (L) and Angela (A) discuss the research Leanne is
       contributing to and whether I might be asked to include Angela
       as well. (I suspect the topic was introduced partly so that I would
       hear it)

L:  Angela you're really keen in taping conversations ain't you?
A:  I know I do like it you see I wanted to do <u>one</u>
L:  <u>you</u> should ask her when+ next time she comes

(6.25) On their walk to school, Gemma (G) and Emma (E) bemoan the
       difficulties of crossing the road

G:  the cars told you to walk slow / [*loud traffic noise*] eeow //
    they never let you cross / shall we cross? cross
E:  let's go on the / safe side and cross

(6.26) During a phone conversation, Chris (C) and Ryan (R), who live
       at some distance, plan for Ryan to come and visit during the
       holidays

C:  do you know them little sucker guns we got?
R:  yeah
C:  why don't you buy some more of them? // you can even
    bring your money over
R:  I've still got three missiles I can't find any more yet

Directives here are formulated as suggestions and offers, and position speaker
and hearer as sharing needs and interests: 'you should', 'you can', 'shall we,'
'let's', 'why don't you'.

## 6.4    Summary and conclusions

The first part of this chapter problematized the idea that children interact-
ing with each other are invariably engaged in 'play', as well as challenging
the notion that 'play' is necessarily frivolous. If the idea of 'child labour' is
disturbing (see Part I), the idea that children's unsupervised activities are
'play' is perhaps comforting to adults. However, the data presented has
suggested both that play may be one of the most common ways in which
children seek at least a simulated entry into the activities associated with
adults, and that it may be used for immediate purposes devised and directed
by the children themselves as much as for any rehearsal of priorities identified by adults.

In the second part of the chapter, the small corpus of informal conversation was used to illustrate how both adults and children use directives and requests in pursuit of personal and shared goals. The interactions recorded illustrate the existence, maintenance and negotiation of differential status and relationships through choices from the linguistic resources available, although these are not usually made at an explicit and conscious level. Even without recourse to quantitative evidence, it is possible to observe in the extracts of transcribed talk presented here the realization of probabilistic patterns in the children's use of language which confirm other studies of how differential status and degrees of intimacy are indicated in situated activity. In addition, there are glimpses of unchildly language, and of the children's testing of the limits of available roles and 'subject positions'. The porous nature of the boundaries of childly language will be explored further in the next chapter.

## Notes

1. All examples of the transcribed talk which are set apart from the main body of the text in this chapter and Chapter 8 are numbered sequentially. Line numbers are included, where applicable, to assist in the location of items discussed in the commentary.
2. The transcription conventions I have used are intended to make the examples accessible while indicating the basic features of the dialogues which are relevant to the analysis. There is always a balance to be struck between accuracy and readability. I hope that, given the emphasis in my analysis on the semantic and syntactic features of the talk, I have not erred too far towards the latter. The conventions I have used are as follows:

   ?      marks all utterances I have interpreted as questions
   /      short pause or silent beat in the rhythm, which marks speaker parcellings of talk and makes long utterances readable
   //      longer pause
   +      an incomplete word or utterance
   **text**      emphatic stress is marked by bold print
   <u>text</u>      overlapping parts of utterances are underlined
   [*text*]      additional information
   [text]      non-verbal contribution
   (text)      indicates some doubt about the accuracy of the transcription (i.e. where the recording is indistinct)
   (***)      inaudible / unclear section
   . . .      indicates that material has been omitted

3. According to Thorne (1993: 191), it is impossible to define play satisfactorily: 'for every list of characteristics (such as spontaneous, voluntary, unproductive),

counter-examples can be found, perhaps in part ... because the line between "play" and "real" is inherently problematic'.

4.  In the analysis of these exchanges, in which speakers seek to influence
    addressees to bring about a change in the state of affairs, I refer to either
    'requests' or 'directives', according to which term seems best to fit each
    example.

5.  The micro-political aspects of parent–child interactions have been con-
    sidered by Ochs and Taylor (1992) in the context of family narratives. They
    found that children in their study were often the protagonists in anecdotes
    recounted by one parent to the other, and were thus represented as poten-
    tial 'objects of scrutiny' (p. 301).

6.  CDS is one kind of 'speech to incompetents', according to Garvey (1984,
    following Ferguson). It seems to me that, regardless of whatever function
    it has in enabling conversation, this register has an important role in
    designating the addressee *as* a member of an 'incompetent' or 'not fully
    accredited' group, defined by Garvey as 'babies and young children', 'the
    senile and the infirm', 'the very ill', 'pets', 'prisoners', and 'foreigners who
    have not acquired the language or cultural conventions of the members'
    group' (pp. 102–3). She documents children of 3 using 'motherese' to babies,
    yet in other contexts adults and older children address 3-year-olds in the
    same register. These issues are explored further in Chapter 7.

7.  Although models of 'language socialization' often assume that the 'trans-
    mission' is from parent to child, older siblings are also involved in any such
    process (Burman 1994; Dunn 1988).

# 7

## Blurred Boundaries: Speaking to Children, Speaking as a Child

*When I was a child, I spake as a child, understood as a child, I*
*thought as a child: but when I became a man, I put away childish*
*things.*

(I Corinthians, 13: 11)

## 7.1 Introduction

The topic of this chapter is the use of language features that are closely
associated with one phase of the lifespan by speakers who belong, object-
ively, to a different one. In the previous chapter, I illustrated how 8- and 9-
year-olds draw on the ways adults often speak to children, and reported that
they did this both when adopting adult roles in play and when talking 'down'
to pets and younger children. I also noted that there is rarely a status advantage to be gained by playing 'the baby' in fantasy games, but the use of baby
talk occasionally has its place. For example, 9-year-old Emma adopted the
intonation of a much younger child in one interaction in the school playground, as she admired her friend's 'easter bonnet' with its decoration of
daffodils. She also phrased her remark with an object pronoun in subject
position, as beginning speakers sometimes do: 'oh it's pretty . . . me want it.'
Maybin (1996: 45) discusses how one of the 10-year-old girls she studied
'announced "Me got this little dog to swap"', and Maybin links this baby
talk, in context, with 'the cuteness and vulnerability of the dog'. The same
girl uses 'a high pitched baby's voice' when reporting to a friend her younger
sister's request to 'bowwow' [i.e. 'borrow'] a rubber. Maybin reviews some
potential evaluations of the younger sister's behaviour 'as stupid, annoying,
or cute and naive'; in fact the friend responds, 'Ah, isn't that sweet!' This
example is quite clearly located in the reported speech of a specific other
speaker (Julie's younger sister), but the two previous examples are more in
the category of quoting from the language resources at large, where drawing
on the way a younger child might have made the utterance seems somehow

appropriate. In the sections which follow, I shall consider the contexts within which adults, as well as older children, may use various childly language resources, and those within which adults may find themselves addressed in ways usually associated with child addressees, drawing on data from literature written for adults and an elicitation survey I carried out among 40 adult speakers of English.

## 7.2   Adult speakers using childly language

One example of an adult speaker using 'baby talk' is given by Dunn (1988). In her study of children in their third year of life, she was interested, among other things, in children's developing ability to empathize with others, and illustrates one 2-year-old's (C) response to his mother's (M) involvement in building with his bricks. My concern here, though, is with the mother's contributions.

M:   No? Can't I build a little building? Here, look. A little station.
C:   No. No.
M:   Oh all right then (pretends to cry). I want to play! At building!
C:   No you can't . . . (Looks concerned at M) You can!

(Dunn 1988: 97)

We have no phonological information to indicate *how* the mother uttered the turns quoted here, although intonation and prosody are likely to have been significant. However, there are other features which mark her utterances as childly. At the level of the interaction itself, the mother reverses the conventional relationship between the participants by asking permission of the child (see Chapter 6 above). What most children may own is limited (toy bricks but not mortgaged houses), but the permission request here confers the power associated with ownership of desired goods on to the child.[1] The mother's response to the child's refusal could have been to draw on parental authority, but within this game she opts instead to maintain the reversed roles and imitates the childly response of forcefully stating one's own wants, showing the kind of distress which, as children know, sometimes leads the interlocutor to relent – as indeed the child does in this case. We cannot know the mother's motives for playing this role, but can speculate that there might be mutual pleasure in occasional role-reversal, and that she might see episodes like this as opportunities to develop the child's ability to empathize with others, giving him a brief period of power in contrast to his customary dependence on others. (Such motives could well be intuitive, not necessarily entailing conscious reflection in the terms stated here.)

Given that, as far as I am aware, the linguistic research that has been conducted in this area has focused on speech patterns associated with babies and infants rather than children (Ferguson 1996 [1964], 1996 [1971]; Haynes and Cooper 1986; Menn and Berko Gleason 1986), I have again turned to narrative fiction as a source of data. From various novels I have noted instances when an adult character is described as speaking like a child. While this can only provide us with snapshots, it is one indication of the cultural norms available to the novelist for conveying particular aspects of an interaction. If the author writes that someone spoke 'like a child', there is a presupposition that the reader will know what this means. Sometimes the childliness is made explicit. Here are three examples.

1.  In the novel *Alias Grace*, a doctor interviews the convicted murderess, Grace, trying to probe the hidden motives for what she has done. In her first-person account of one interview Grace describes how she explained embroidery designs to the doctor, telling him that the Tree of Paradise design, even with four trees, is still known as 'the tree'.

    Why is that, do you suppose, Grace? he says. Sometimes he is like a child, he is always asking why.

    (Attwood 1997: 113)

    (There is a layer of irony here: the doctor presumes that he has greater insight than his patient into her hidden motivation, which simple questions may uncover; addressing the reader, Grace claims to interpret this style as genuine naivety; aware of Grace's perspicacity, the reader may draw yet further inferences about which of the characters is really naive.)

2.  In another novel, *Yesterday in the back lane*, a character comes to view the body of her recently deceased sister which is laid out at the home of the dead woman's adult daughter.

    'I can't eat until I've seen her,' Auntie Annie said suddenly. 'Will you come with me, girl?' she asked. She sounded like a child who was afraid of the dark.

    (Rubens 1995: 221)

3.  Another scene from fiction involves an argument between a married couple. The wife has had a breakdown, on account of which the husband has left his job.

    'You blame me for it, don't you? It's not *fair*.' It was the anguished wail of a child.

    (Bawden 1989 [1963]: 71)

In these examples, three different speakers are described as using childly ways of talking, glossed as repeatedly asking why, seeking moral support to face a frightening experience, and expressing distress over a perceived un-fairness. We might link these qualities to some associations with childhood noted before: relative ignorance and powerlessness, and also the child's sense of 'positive justice' which is very evident in studies such as Dunn (1988). She found from her observations of 3-year-olds that:

> [w]hen it is in their interest to do so, they point out that a rule applied to them also applies to others. And these rules used as sources of humour, attack, and self-justification are, it must be emphasized, principles of the wider culture in which children are growing up.
>
> (pp. 70–1)

Complaints about unfairness were cited extensively in another source of data I have used for this chapter, an elicitation procedure by means of which adult respondents were asked to reflect on the circumstances in which an adult speaker might comment on another adult's use of language as being childish or childlike. I give more detail below on the method used, but will first present some examples of the responses to the following vignette, which was one of the stimuli given. For future reference, this vignette will be labelled 'Argument'.

> Ashley and Jo are having a heated argument, which gets increasingly angry and frustrated. Ashley responds to something Jo says with 'That is such a childish thing to say.' What might Jo have said to warrant this?

Among the suggestions given were:

> It's not fair
> It's not fair – you always . . .
> It's not fair. I don't care what you think. It was your fault.
> That's not fair!
> You always do that and it's not fair

The 'not fair' accusation was indeed made in several contexts by the children in my study, and the fact that it is supplied intuitively by a number of the respondents in this research adds weight to its association with childliness.[2] As Dunn points out, the principle of fairness is a general cultural one, not confined to childhood, but there are several reasons why we may recognize the link between this particular expression and childliness. Perhaps the con-cept of 'justice', which is more complex and nuanced than 'fairness', is more applicable to adult perceptions of morality[3]? Perhaps only those who are relatively powerless appeal to a general principle rather than to the other resources at their disposal for justifying why things should be otherwise than they are? Perhaps with social and emotional maturity is supposed to come (at least in this society) greater suppression of self-interest, a code of co-operation (Grice 1975) and politeness which preserves the face of all parties (Brown and Levinson 1978)? If this last suggestion is valid, it would also help to account for some of the other suggestions made by respondents to this stimulus vignette, many of which make explicit the separateness and different interests of speaker and addressee.

Before presenting these results, I shall explain the method used. A single two-sided sheet was distributed to adults known to me and in some cases to contacts of these individuals. The study was on a small scale, and could be no more than indicative of 'the things which [these particular] native speakers of [British] English immediately recognize as drawing on the ways children speak and are spoken to', as it was expressed on the sheet. The introduction further explained:

> I am investigating how adult people sometimes speak to each other in ways similar to those in which children speak and are spoken to. It would be very helpful for this research if you would be willing to take just a few minutes to consider the following examples of some situations where particular kinds of language might be used, and suggest, drawing on your own experience, what exactly the people in each case might have said. There are no right answers and there is no need to think about this for long.

The method has some similarities with that used in the much larger cross-cultural study of speech act realization (CCSARP) (Blum-Kulka and Olshtain 1984), a controlled elicitation procedure specifying a setting, inter-locutors and an incomplete dialogue. This method can be criticized on the same grounds as any collection of reported speech behaviour rather than actual utterances – that speakers do not necessarily speak as they believe and claim they do. However, in this study the method allowed for a compromise between recording long hours of spontaneous interaction in the rather unrealistic hope that the situations in which I was interested just might arise, or else relying entirely on my own intuitions. It was interesting that several respondents recognized the gap between receptive awareness of a speech phenomenon and the ability to reproduce it, with some people reporting that they found the completion task harder than they anticipated. Some who did not return the sheet stated this as a reason, and among those who did respond one added the following footnote: 'I must say I found it extremely difficult to think of actual bits of dialogue. If I could do this easily I might consider a career as a scriptwriter. Sorry I couldn't be more productive.'

Despite the challenges of the study, however, 40 completed elicitation sheets were returned, 24 by women and 16 by men. Most respondents supplied details about their age-group and occupation. Of those who did 4 were (adults) aged under 25; 6 were between 26 and 40 years old; 23 were aged 41 to 60; and 6 were over 60 years old. Respondents' occupations were predominantly within education, mainly as lecturers or teachers – including those who had retired from such jobs – (21), and students (5). Others were or had been in clerical or secretarial jobs (4), and the remainder of those who supplied the information were in other jobs, retired or unemployed (6). Obviously with such a small and arbitrarily selected group of respondents no claims can be made about the population in general, but certain patterns do emerge from the data which provide an indication of what these 40 speakers of English intuitively feel is distinctively childly language.

Two of the vignettes were of situations where one speaker explicitly commented on the 'childish' speech of another. One was the argument between Ashley and Jo presented above. The other, labelled 'Meeting', was as follows:

> After a meeting at work, two colleagues discuss a third member of staff, Chris. Of Chris's intervention in the meeting one of them says, 'It's the way Chris always puts things like this across. It sounds so childish.' Can you suggest what Chris might have said?

In both cases, a speaker draws attention to the 'childish' nature of the remark, implying that this quality marks it as inappropriate for the context. Respondents were also given opportunities to consider less negative connotations for childly ways of speaking, as will be explained below.

Responses were coded according to categories derived from the data and entered into a database. Each respondent had the opportunity to make several suggestions for each scenario: some made no suggestions for certain items; some made one per item; some offered up to four or five for one item. This means that the total numbers of suggested utterances for each item were variable. Also, although respondents were asked for suggestions as to the exact words spoken, they sometimes supplied instead descriptions of the utterance. For example, in relation to 'Argument', one respondent wrote: 'It is possible that Jo has allowed the argument to become too personal or have [*sic*] brought another topic into the argument that is really irrelevant but is certain to upset Ashley.' I classified these responses according to the categories used, but could not include them in the collated lists of actual dialogue suggested. However, these more discursive responses are useful in describing the features of talk described as childish, and serve as a reminder that in genuine interactions the discourse *as a whole* is highly relevant in determining what might be seen as childish: an identical utterance might not provoke Ashley's criticism in a different discursive context. As Hymes (1974: 101) expresses it:

Some assertions, requests, commands, threats, and the like are known to be such on the basis of a knowledge, *jointly*, of the message-form and the relationship in which it occurs. For example, the same sentence commonly serves as a serious insult in some relationships and as a badge of intimacy in others.

Nevertheless, respondents were able to suggest a range of specific utterances for one speaker which they felt might well be met with another's accusation of childishness. One large category in relation to 'Argument', exemplified by the suggestions given above involving 'not fair', is of utterances in which Jo draws attention to a perceived disparity in goods, resources, conduct or responsibility between him/herself and Ashley. Out of a total of 60 suggested utterances, 22 were assigned to this category. Some responses consisted simply of 'it's not fair', a claim which implies something along the following lines: S(peaker) deserves more than H(earer), or H has something which S should have, or should have the equivalent of, or H has evaded responsibility, and so on. Note, however, as Dunn has pointed out, that such claims appeal to a general cultural norm about equity. Other examples from this category include:

*Category 1 (fairness)*

It was your turn anyway

That was supposed to be for me

You always get more than me

Well it's my ball anyway

A very similar group of suggestions includes those in which Jo's utterance *presupposes* a disparity between the two protagonists and is used to threaten actions that will redress it. Thirteen suggestions were assigned to this category, including:

*Category 2 (redress)*

Well if you're going to . . . then I'm going to . . .

That's the last time I do anything for you.

And I'll have my jumper back, please, that you borrowed.

The third category I identified was used for those utterances involving criticisms of the addressee's actions, or other insults. Indeed, the suggestion from this group 'All you ever want is your own way' could arguably have been classified in Category 1. However, since it focuses exclusively on how Jo perceives Ashley, rather than explicitly identifying contrasts between them, I assigned it to a separate group, of 22 suggestions in total, which include:

*Category 3 (criticism/rejection)*

Don't be so stupid

To top it all you finished off the last piece of bread and left the lid off the Clover

Yeh, well you're ugly

You have no dress sense

Just because you have a chip on your shoulder

Shut up you. You make me sick you do.

In relation to the content of the suggested utterances, then, the character-istics which respondents identified as childish seem broadly to be: state-ments of a disparity between protagonists which flouts an unsophisticated, simplistic notion of fairness or equity; threats to withdraw goods or services in response to such a perceived disparity or state of unfairness; insults based on personal qualities such as appearance, or even on nothing other than simply-stated dislike. These hypothetical utterances which are classified as 'childish' fail to take account of the complexities of social relationships which recognize that life isn't fair, that conflicting interests usually have to be negotiated with some degree of give-and-take, or that the qualities by which people will be judged are not confined to their appearance. Perceptions of the social world in limited terms like these are associated with immaturity, with speakers at an early stage of social and emotional development – and yet all the remarks were supplied by adult respondents as suggestions of what adult speakers might, in some circumstances, be heard to say.

The social context of 'Meeting' was presented as somewhat more public and inherently more adult: a meeting at work. While 'Argument' was explicitly presented as a conflict, respondents had more scope in 'Meeting' to interpret the kind of 'intervention' that Chris might have made. Also, in this scenario, the criticism of being 'childish' is levelled at a third party in his/her absence. In the light of these differences, it is striking that (although there were only 33 suggestions in total) the categories which emerged from the data have much in common with those devised for 'Argument'. Again, seven sugges-tions were classified as having a concern with 'fairness' and equity. Examples include:

*Category 1 (fairness)*

It's not fair

I don't think it's fair – you're always picking on me

If they're doing that, why can't we?

It's nice that some of us have the time for all this; I know I certainly don't

In the second category I included the closely related stance which polarizes the speaker in relation to others, often suggesting that the speaker is being afforded a lower status than others. Eleven responses were of this kind, including:

*Category 2 (polarization of the self and others)*

I think my way's best, but if you don't want to listen

No one ever listens to me!

I know you all think my ideas are stupid, but I can't help the way I feel about these suggestions

I don't think it will work but then nobody listens to me

Reinforcing this stance of separateness from colleagues, Chris was sometimes portrayed, like Jo, as threatening to withdraw goods, services or co-operation. The four responses in this category are:

*Category 3 (threatening to withdraw goods/services/own company)*

Well of course, if my suggestions are so stupid, I'll shut up

If you're not going to look after it properly then I shan't bring it in again

I'm not prepared to share my wordprocessor with anyone from the typing pool, I've worked hard to establish my position, and anyway I would probably have to train them. After all, they're still using Tippex – no idea of the delete key

If Dorothy insists on smoking, I shan't come in here again. I'll take my lunch and have it in Pete's room.

In addition to the four further responses that I was unable to classify, I identified one other category as being childish because of vocabulary or phrasing, drawing on expressions conventionally used in talk with children. I classified seven suggestions in this group, including (emphasis added to childish features):

*Category 4 (childish in vocabulary/phrasing)*

Can't we talk about this like friends instead of <u>squabbling</u>?

I don't want to do that – <u>so there</u>!

We can do this if we <u>really really</u> try

This final group of examples highlights the limitations of considering only content in identifying what makes an utterance seem childish. As with 'Argument', some respondents offered descriptions of what Chris might have done and said, rather than supplying dialogue, and several of these suggestions point to style rather than content. For example:

> He probably spoke petulantly or without due reflection or in an attention-seeking way

> He may have spoken anecdotally, referring only to his own personal experience, when the focus was more general. He may have taken criticism personally, or demonstrated emotion openly

These are familiar themes, linking childishness to egocentricity, a well-established notion in developmental psychology. Other suggestions draw on similar perceptions, but in relation to cognitive or linguistic development rather than social and emotional maturity. These include:

> Using things out of context or using the wrong meaning for words is one way adult language can sound childlike. Also using simple childlike metaphors/explanations can affect the sophistication of speech

> Putting things in the form of a story with voices in role

> Basic vocabulary

> Chris spoke of marking children's work 'very carefully' and that comments should be 'polite' (rather than 'thoroughly' and 'constructive')

This final point reinforces the claim made above that children's speech may be distinguished from that of adults in being less influenced by the written mode. However, the boundaries between speech and writing are themselves somewhat porous (e.g. Graddol et al. 1994) – communication via electronic mail is one celebrated example. As suggested above, speakers can draw on their experience of written texts, and literate adults are likely to have more of this experience than children. This distinction is only a probability, however, with many exceptions.

Another approach to identifying what makes the style of the suggested utterances childly is to explore patterns in the lexis. The total number of words included in the database for both 'Argument' and 'Meeting' is itself very small at 919, so any statistical findings are of very limited significance. However, it is still interesting to note that of the words used in suggested utterances which speakers feel would be criticized as childish, there is a ratio of 33.51 per cent tokens : types. In other words, only 308 different words were cited, many of which were used a large number of times. Among these, the first person singular and second person pronouns figure prominently: *you, you're, I, I'll, I'm, me, my,* and *your* account for a total of 17.64 per cent of all tokens in the 'corpus', while *you* and *me* are found in close proximity to each other, all of which is consistent with a linguistic realization of the pattern already identified in the content of the utterances, that one protagonist contrasts himself or herself with the other, emphasizing the speaker's separateness from others. The collective pronoun *we*, however, features only nine times, and *us* only three. *Fair* is the most frequent content word in these suggested utterances. *Always* occurs 15 times, in the context of claims such as 'You always get more than me' ('Argument') and 'I always have the late lectures on Fridays and I'm fed up with it' ('Meeting'). The association with childishness here would seem to be the exaggerations and black-and-white representations of an egocentric world-view, in contrast to the more measured, 'shades of grey' outlook expected of a mature speaker. Speakers are depicted as emphasizing 'separateness', shoring up the boundaries and barriers which are relinquished in the 'connectedness' of social relationships (Goffman 1971).

Finally, before leaving this collection of intuitively generated utterances suggested by adults as typical of inappropriately childish speech, let us consider some actual children's utterances. Selected from much larger studies of children's talk, these examples illustrate children's use of 'always', 'fair', first and second person pronouns, and repetition of 'really' as an intensifier, as were identified by my adult respondents.

One child criticizing another for putting the hood of her jacket down on a cool day (black American community):

> Kerry:   ***You*** always showin' off. You always actin' smart. I'm a spank you. Always gotta show off . . .

> (Goodwin 1990: 155)

Children's grandmother (EG) asks them about their last day at school before the holidays. The younger sister Jenny (J) had to work, but her older sister Emma (E) was allowed to watch a video:

> J:   oh / you're being horrible
> E:   I'm not
> J:   **we** didn't+ we didn't do any of that stuff / we had to work
> (Later)
> J:   it's not fair 'cos . . .
>      (Author's data – note that 'we' here is used in an exclusive, contrastive sense)

Children arguing about seating space in their after-school centre (translated from Swedish):

> Tim:   Tony you're always sitting there you are
> Fia:   You're not allowed to sit there any more

> (Evaldsson 1993: 160)

Emma explains a reward she had for good work at school:

> at school we have these things called smiley faces . . . and you get and you only get them / when / when you've done a really really really good piece of work.

(Author's data)

Leaving aside their phonology, these children's utterances do not contrast with the adult language system in lexis or syntax in the way that younger children's language does. There is no developmental reason why an adult should not produce any of these utterances. In some contexts, though, to do so would be to make oneself vulnerable to a charge of being childish.

## 7.3   Adult speakers addressed as children

This section will consider another 'blurred boundary' – the phenomenon of adults being addressed in ways usually considered appropriate for talking to children. Let us briefly consider first what marks features that are conventionally associated with speech addressed to children.

### 7.3.1   Child-directed speech

While 'baby talk' refers to older speakers approximating to the talk of infants, the phenomenon of 'child-directed speech' (CDS) has been noted and discussed extensively within language acquisition research. Described also as 'care-giver speech' or 'motherese', it refers to all those features of simplified speech which seem likely to make the 'input' more accessible to the apprentice language user. These features include 'consonant cluster reduction, reduplication, exaggerated prosodic contours, slowed pace, shorter sentences, syntactically less complex sentences, temporal and spatial orientation to the here-and-now, and repetition and paraphrasing of sentences' (Ochs and Schieffelin 1995: 76). Recent comparative research has demonstrated that some aspects of the CDS style once assumed to be universal are not used by all care-givers everywhere, and that cultural assumptions about infants' communicative competence influence the ages at which children are included in 'conversation' with others (Ochs and Schieffelin 1995; Schieffelin and Ochs 1986). Such research has been almost exclusively associated with language learning, and assumed to be relevant only to infancy, but, as we shall see, the features of CDS identified here are also found in other discursive contexts.

The account given by Hymes (1974) – quoted in the Introduction to Part III – of how status is so profoundly linked with age reminds us even as it makes this explicit that speech acts themselves can be used, at least metaphorically, to shift an addressee's status within the interaction in spite of their objective age category. He draws attention to variation in this potential when he continues: '. . . there are of course also emergent meanings, as when unexpected concurrence of two or more relations, intended or imputed, produces humor, irony and other effects' (p. 158). Respondents in my elicitation study drew on their own experience to provide examples of adults being spoken to as though they were children.

## 7.3.2    Being patronized

Writers of fiction make use of readers' familiarity with the subtle potential of this aspect of language, including adults' experience of being 'talked down' to, or 'positioned' as a subordinate, like a child. Wall (1991) identifies the problem of 'writing down', when adult authors address child readers, as 'the dilemma of children's fiction'. She also provides a definition of 'talking down': 'Speakers *over*-simplify, are condescending, that is, stoop metaphorically, perhaps even literally, towards those they see as lower than themselves, and assume – falsely – that the listeners are ignorant' (pp. 15–16). 'Talking down' is likely to provoke comment if experienced by the addressee as unwarranted or offensive, as this example illustrates. In the novel *What a carve up!*, a character disagrees with his (adult) niece about the high priority she gives in her business career to making a profit.

> She stares at him. Perhaps it is her fury at finding herself addressed in a tone which she remembers from many years ago – the tone which an adult would adopt towards a trusting child – which provokes the insolence of her reply. 'You know, Daddy always said you and Aunt Tabitha were the odd ones of the family.'
>
> (Coe 1994: 19)

Another example comes from a short story by Umberto Verdi, where a woman is invited by the sweep who has cleaned her chimney to go outside and see the brush sticking up out of the chimney. Her reaction prompts him to explain that this invitation is to check he has done the job properly: what she says is 'I'm not a child you know', the implication being, of course, that his invitation is a threat to her 'face', rather than his own.

Similarly, the scenarios in the elicitation sheet in which an addressee feels positioned as a child by another speaker assume that the addressees experience this as inappropriate enough to warrant comment. The two scenarios given were:

*Visit*

Terry shares a flat with Pat. After a weekend's visit home, Terry returns to the flat and Pat asks how it went. 'OK,' says Terry, 'but I do wish Mum/Dad wouldn't talk to me as though I was still eight years old.' Can you suggest one or more of the things Mum/Dad might have said?

and

*School*

Mr and Mrs Taylor attend a parents' evening at their children's primary school. On the way home, they discuss the conversations they have had with the teachers. They agree that one teacher in particular has a way of speaking which 'makes you feel as if you're still at junior school'. Can you suggest some of the things this teacher says to parents?

As before, some caution is needed in drawing conclusions from speakers' intuitions about such dialogues, but on the whole respondents were able to supply more suggestions for these scenarios than for the previous two discussed. Some of the younger adults, in particular, reported examples from their own recent experience with their parents, although of course their memories for the exact words of the utterances they quote are likely to be fallible.

In terms of the content of items suggested for 'Visit', the majority reflect the parental role of being responsible for the child's basic needs. Twenty-five suggestions were classified as relating to Terry's diet and/or health – the most fundamental responsibility for a new human life, assumed by parents from a child's birth onwards. Six respondents suggested 'Are you eating properly?' and another four items were variations on this question, such as 'Are you eating enough/well?' Other suggestions included 'Come on, eat up, it's good for you' and 'What do you usually have for dinner?' Items relevant to other aspects of basic care for the self included clothing and warmth: 'Are you sure you're going to be warm enough, dear?', 'Have you packed enough warm clothes?'; sleep: 'Are you getting enough sleep?', 'You look very tired'; and safety: 'Be careful with those knives', 'If you're going into town be careful how you cross the road'.

Obviously, the tendency of parents to express a concern for the health, safety and well-being of their offspring has its basis in objective facts about the social world: young children are literally dependents, and parents – or, if they fail, members of adult society at large – have to fulfil this responsibility. Thus, as was the case with linguistic patterns in news reporting about children, there is one sense in which these suggested utterances unproblematically articulate the original basis of parent–child relations. Terry's objection, then, is with what he/she feels is the inappropriate extension of an originally justified responsibility for him/her into a phase in his/her life where it is no longer necessary. Some respondents' descriptive comments about 'Visit' make this explicit, for example: 'assuming child can't cope away from home.' If there is a continuum with dependence + freedom from responsibility at one end, and independence + responsibility at the other, there is a mismatch between Terry's and the parents' perceptions about the point on this continuum where Terry is now, or should be.

The fact that there can be these different perceptions, however, immediately exposes how little reliance can be placed on 'objective' facts to determine what is appropriate in such dialogues. Furthermore, because human beings are not simply biological organisms, but social and linguistic creatures inhabiting a world of cultural norms and potentials, parental care and concern extends to involvement in ways of behaving in that social and cultural world. As we saw from the literature about children's socialization through language (Chapter 4), parents are in a position to convey simultaneously three kinds of thing through interactions with their children: the way language is used interactively, the way things are/should be done in the world, the nature of the parent–child relationship. One respondent suggested the utterance 'you shouldn't do it like that – you should do it like this', which epitomizes the socialization stance of a parent, no matter what action the child is undertaking (cf. Wootton 1986). Similarly, the words 'properly' and 'enough' presuppose a 'right' way of doing things, and each occurs ten times in these suggested utterances ('Are you eating *properly*?', 'Are you getting *enough* sleep?'). Some respondents suggested that Terry's parents would comment on practical matters:

> I like your new shoes, Terry. You must look after them.
>
> Just make sure you have paid the bills.
>
> Make sure you get to work on time.

Other suggestions concerned relationships with others:

> I hope you don't make as much noise as you did at home – how will the people in the other flats cope?
>
> I wish you wouldn't use language like that.
>
> It's about time you got married / started a family.

Of course, Terry's sense of being addressed like an 8-year-old cannot derive from the propositional content of comments about getting married or getting to work on time, since both are proscribed activities for young children. This in itself is an indication that the effect is partly a product of the less tangible, pragmatic dimensions of the interaction. I shall now look briefly at some of the features of the suggested utterances which are distinctive in these terms.

It is noticeable that 53 of the items are interrogatives, many of them including the word 'you', and they raise the possibility of Terry's behaviour being presented as a topic for discussion. The discussion, and perhaps evaluation, of children's behaviour is acceptable as a feature of family conversation in a way that parents' behaviour is not (cf. Ochs and Taylor 1992). Examples include:

Are you wearing a vest?

Have you got your umbrella?

When are you getting married?

The pragmatic function of questions like these – in the context sketched for respondents – is closer to a scrutiny and assessment of the addressee's competence than a request for information.

Many of the other items suggested are imperatives, including seven beginning 'make sure':

Make sure you get to work on time

Make sure you wrap up warm

Make sure you remember your sister's birthday.

Other imperatives suggested include:

Remember to get enough sleep

Terry! Wipe your feet

Put your coat on. You'll catch your death of cold.

Many of the imperatives are proscriptions on behaviour:

Don't slouch on the settee

Terry, blow your nose and don't sniffle

Don't touch it. I'll do it'

and three begin 'Don't forget to . . .' ('send Gran a birthday card', 'switch off the fire').

Other elements of the suggested utterances also position the speaker as superordinate and the addressee's behaviour as subject to the speaker's control. Some of these include deontic modal verbs, indicating what the speaker thinks Terry ought to do. For example (emphasis added to modals):

You *should* be wearing a scarf in this wind

Couldn't you eat your greens? You really *should*, what with all that junk food you get during the week

I like your new shoes, Terry. You *must* look after them.

A similar pragmatic effect is achieved in utterances where the speaker's statement of their perception of the way things are implies how they ought to be (emphasis added to speaker's mental state verbs):

> I *hope* you don't make as much noise as you did at home – how will the people in the other flats cope?
> I *wish* you wouldn't use language like that.
> I really *don't know* what you see in that girl.
> I *hope* you're not squandering your money.
> I *don't think* you should be riding that motorbike.

Several of these features of parent–child interaction, particularly directives, were discussed in Chapter 6, and the reader is referred in particular to Examples (6.8) and (6.9), which illustrate once again that some of the features which emerge from this small-scale elicitation of speakers' intuition are to be found in actual interactions. The suggestions supplied by the respondents were utterances directed to adults occupying the relation which has already been identified as ambiguous, that of the child as offspring who is no longer child as very young member of society.

The final example to be discussed takes us once again out of the home and into an institution, in this case the school. Since the teacher in 'School' was said by respondents to deploy some of the same linguistic behaviour as Terry's parents, I shall discuss this example more briefly. However, it illustrates once again that superordinate–subordinate status relations are relative rather than essential, as is demonstrated in Chapters 6 and 8, with examples of children themselves finding ways to occupy a superordinate role with interlocutors who permit it. Again in this scenario, the speaker finds appropriate some ways of speaking with which the addressee is not comfortable, and again some respondents recalled their own experience, including, from one young adult for whom parents' evenings were a recent memory: 'my parents have found that my teachers treat *them* as the child'.

Some of the suggestions for this scenario included a version of the speaker's right to direct and/or evaluate the addressee's behaviour, indicating the teacher's assumption of higher status in interaction with the parents. This group includes imperatives:

> Sit there for a minute while I do this.
> Use these chairs please.
> Quiet please!
> *Always* remember, Mr and Mrs Taylor, that . . .
> *Never* forget that . . .

and expressions of the speaker's perspective (note the 'I' in the following examples):

I can't have . . . / I will not have . . .

I really don't think that it applies to your son

I haven't got time for that now.

I do wish parents wouldn't use the playground as a turning circle for their cars.

Suggestions also included questions of the kind identified in 'Visit', whose pragmatic function seems to be at least partly monitoring of the addressee's competence:

Do you really think you should dye your hair my dear? (glossed by the respondent as an authentic instance)

You help her with her homework? Oh that does please me

And tell me, how is she at home?

Can you do this for them?

If Terry's parents were imagined as attending to matters of his/her health, safety and social competence, respondents suggested that Mr and Mrs Taylor's competence as adults and as parents was called into question by the teacher's linguistic behaviour:

Have you ever thought about helping them with their homework?

As parents, you really should show enthusiasm and a little more commitment if you want your child to do well. Perhaps I could give you a few suggestions

Such responses also threaten to undermine the addressees' cognitive abilities, an idea expressed by some respondents in the following terms:

being over-explicit, conceptually and empathetically underdeveloped

slowly, clearly, gently, repeating things, checking comprehension

explains things they already understand

over-basic explanations of material listener already knows

and by others in these examples:

I'll show you if you don't know

Do you understand?

However, in addition to the propositional content, the implication of relative status in the use of imperatives and priority given to the speaker's perceptions, and the suggestion that the speaker is entitled to evaluate the addressee's competence and knowledge, many respondents emphasized the significance of another dimension to being positioned as a child in this interaction. One respondent, for example, wrote:

> Perhaps suggests rather the *way* in which she speaks, rather than the language, i.e. . . . repeating things, checking that they've understood her. May also say something about her body language: maintaining direct eye contact throughout, sitting in close proximity to them.

and another:

> . . . on re-reading these examples I have realised how important tone is in childlike language – possibly more so than actual vocab

Two respondents mentioned a 'Joyce Grenfell' style of talking, and another wrote:

> It's *tone* here rather than content . . . the royal 'we', the tag question . . .

These comments reflect an awareness of a 'tone' or 'style' which is effected by a combination of certain prosodic and syntactical features.[4] As one respondent identified these:

> I've noted two characteristics of utterances as if to a child: (a) rhetorical questions delivered in a (b) bated-breath Joyce-Grenfell-like intonation e.g. 'And what do you think we saw?'

Although the inclusive 'we' suggested by these respondents does not, in my view, have precisely the same function as 'the royal "we"', it is noticeable that this pronoun occurs more frequently in suggested responses to this scenario than in any of the others, as do tag questions. Some examples include:

> Now, what do we want to talk about?
>
> We don't do that do we?
>
> Of course, we know that . . . don't we?

If adults sometimes use such speech strategies to 'talk down' to other adults, and many of my respondents recognized this phenomenon, why might they do it? Two respondents suggest that teachers need to adapt their talk for children, and continue to do so with other interlocutors:

I believe this is more to do with tone of voice, the teacher may have been used to addressing children, thus does not adapt to 'adult-talk' so readily. A patronising way of speaking . . . involves repetition – clarifying what's been said as one might have to with a child.

It doesn't have to be *what* was said. Teachers through their daily exposure to children of a certain age, adopt methods of phrasing and emphasis, together with a deliberately limited vocabulary, thus giving the impression that they are still talking to children. . . .

If this rather stereotypical perception has any validity, it is consistent with empirical findings about 'over-accommodation' to the perceived speech styles of a number of groups of people. Giles and Coupland (1991) report on studies which have found that members of various social categories may be addressed in an 'over-accommodating' register, whose features include: 'grammatical and ideational simplification, overly polite forms of language, and a slowed speech rate' (p. 162). As well as 'institutionalized elderly people', there is some evidence that 'the elderly in general', 'the visually impaired', 'the handicapped' and 'the hospitalized young, too, in some settings' are 'recipients of over-accommodation' (ibid.). This register – 'a form of baby talk' – is used to the elderly, for example:

irrespective of their functional autonomy. In other words, these nurses use a blanket speech register which linguistically depersonalizes those in their care; . . . Ryan et al. (1986) have noted that this might be mediated either by stereotypes of elderly's incompetence or sensory decrements and could also be encoded as a means of establishing social control.

(ibid.)

If what has been discussed in this section has a connection with Giles and Coupland's observations, then, it may be that this version of child-directed speech is available to adults ostensibly to make information more accessible, but also, and crucially, to attempt to assert power and status in certain kinds of interaction. One interesting question is whether children in middle child-hood need or want this degree of linguistic 'accommodation' from teachers and other authority figures, or whether its social controlling function is in fact the more salient. I shall return to this issue in the final two chapters.

## 7.4   Choosing childly language

The scenarios and examples explored in this chapter so far have been concerned with adults assuming a childly way of speaking, or being addressed as a child by others, in ways which other speakers find inappropriate or offensive. Given the observations by sociolinguists cited above, about child-hood as an inherently low-status category, these negative connotations are understandable. However, as has been demonstrated in Part I, there are cultural norms about childhood which can be drawn upon for positive reasons too, and respondents were given the opportunity to reflect on cir-cumstances in which speaking, or being spoken to, as a child can be a positive thing.

Two main kinds of reason were given for consciously choosing to address another speaker as though he or she were a child. The first is for reassurance, especially where the addressee is of lower status. Some examples include:

> When pointing out an error, so as not to undermine confidence/hurt feelings
>
> Direct honesty and openness can reassure, console, gain trust (in counselling)
>
> Giving encouragement and praise
>
> When one is ill or over tired, being told what to do – e.g. to rest – can be comforting and supportive

This accords with findings reported by Giles and Coupland (1991), that although some elderly people experienced the over-accommodating register as distasteful, 'others frame it more positively – as a nurturant' (p. 162).

The second main reason given for addressing someone as a child is for simplicity or clarity, for example:

> In helping someone to understand something . . . in a way that will not offend them or degrade them . . .
>
> Helps with explanation, rather than complicated jargon
>
> Complex instructions expressed very simply as though to a child can often be helpful.
>
> In a naive way e.g. 'I don't understand what you mean by that'

As for choosing to speak as a child oneself, the qualities culturally asso-ciated with some versions of childhood are reflected in responses related to deeply felt and openly expressed emotions, simplicity and sincerity (consist-ent with many of the meanings associated with *childlike*, as discussed in Chapter 3). Some examples from this group include:

> Extreme grief, where speech must be pure and straight from the heart
>
> Occasionally it can mean speaking simply or with naive(?) honesty
>
> Speaking frankly may be seen as childish
>
> If one is poorly or depressed sometimes it may only be the child that responds

Occasionally it is seen as honest and exploratory – 'I don't know' as a response instead of waffle?

When something is deeply and personally felt.

Can mean directly, honestly, openly, without guile

A second group of responses identified the link between childly speech and solidarity or intimacy. This idea is the obverse of the use of a patronizing register to raise one's own status, either deliberately or unintentionally. (Indeed, some respondents admitted to choosing to speak to another adult as though to a child 'to "put people down"', and 'If I want to patronise someone'.) Choosing childly language, with its connotations of low status, makes the speaker vulnerable, and several respondents identified it with the context of sexual intimacy:

When speaking to husband or lover using pet names

affectionately, 'lovey-dovey': 'Oh – are you okay, baby'

in courtship, where people's sexual desires are aroused

Sexual negotiations often involve talk as between children

The association between diminutive terms and affection is borne out by some actual Valentine's messages which have appeared in newspapers. Senders and addressees are 'down-sized': 'little minx', 'little devil', 'me [sic] little flower', 'babe', 'little smoothie', 'baby'; they use 'baby-talk', with rhymes and repetitions, declaring quantities of love as 'millions and billions', 'lots and lots', 'to bits'; and they use 'pet' names: 'honey-bunny', 'squiggy', 'pookie bear'.

Respondents in my survey identified the potential inappropriateness and fragility of this context, however:

Appropriate signal of intimacy, provided participants agree to 'play' at being dependent

Affection often expressed in terms more commonly used to a child can help to break down barriers. If used inappropriately, it can create barriers

Less specifically, some responses suggest other kinds of relationship where the positive connotations of childliness can be deployed, including simply having fun:

being caring/looking after someone

informality/comradeliness is advisable

Mother [to adult daughter] 'Come on [diminutive name], have a cuggle'

It can sometimes be used humorously, as a way of breaking ice or helping
someone to relax

A little fun or silliness helps to bind individuals together through humour

To make people realize you are joking

## 7.5   Summary and conclusions

This chapter has suggested that by middle childhood categorical distinctions
between 'child language' and 'the adult language system' begin to break
down, and boundaries become more blurred. Not only are children potentially able to deploy linguistic resources from a much wider range than is
possible for pre-linguistic infants, but adults too may have reasons for adopting the speech styles more centrally associated with childhood. This was
illustrated by some examples from fiction, and the idea was extended by an
analysis of suggestions made by 40 adult speakers of English of utterances
whose use by adults might attract comment because of their association with
the way children speak.

Exploration of the range of responses revealed some tendencies which
are posited as possibly identifying features of childly language, and some
authentic data produced by children was set alongside the elicited suggestions. One characteristic was identification of the speaker as separate from,
and in comparison or contrast with, the addressee, or the salient community
(family, peer group) in general. Linked with this was an explicit concern with
fairness, a desire to evaluate the distribution of goods, services and responsibilities, and to ensure that the speaker had a fair share. A lack of concern for
the 'face' of addressees (Brown and Levinson 1978; Holmes 1995), shown by
unrestrained expressions of dislike, jealousy or hostility also emerged as
characteristic of speaking childishly. In addition to such propositional content, the features of this register, it was suggested, included a high incidence
of all of the first and second person pronouns *except* the collective *we* and *us*,
and discourse markers such as *so there*, *well* and *anyway*, used contrastively
between speaker's and hearer's points of view. Although the data was generated intuitively, respondents' suggestions for 'childish' utterances are
consistent with talk recorded in some studies of children's arguments which
identify conflict and opposition as highly salient in their negotiations of
relationships (Brenneis and Lein 1977; Goodwin and Goodwin 1987; Maynard
1985).

The child-directed speech (CDS), which is usually referred to in the
context of carers addressing children at the earliest stages of language acquisition, was found from the elicitation study to be a resource capable
of deployment with any speaker whom one wishes to patronize, and some
illustrative examples from narrative fiction were cited. The canonical charac-

teristics of CDS (explicitness, oversimplification, repetition and exaggerated intonation contours) were identified by respondents as features of speech addressed inappropriately to adults-treated-as-children. While the empirical advantages are recognized of simplifying material for addressees – of whatever age – who might find it inaccessible, this process is easily elided with an assumption by the speaker of social power, status and control, and the question was raised as to whether teachers in particular might have an interest in continuing to deploy a version of CDS with addressees in middle childhood for micro-political reasons as much as pedagogical ones.

Finally, the more positive characteristics of childhood and the way children talk were identified and discussed, and some familiar themes were evident from the elicitation study, including the association of children with naivety, simplicity and innocence. The voluntary relinquishing of the status accruing to adulthood makes a speaker particularly vulnerable, and respondents identified social goals such as indicating solidarity, support and good humour, as well as the intimacy of close family and sexual interactions as the contexts where speakers may willingly adopt childly language for positive reasons.

The 'blurred' nature of the 'boundaries' discussed in this chapter is important as a context for Chapter 8, which returns to the study of children's informal talk to explore how, and within what limits, they negotiate identities and relationships – as children and as participants in the wider social world.

## Notes

1. As was illustrated in Chapter 6, children find that even small-scale involvement in the economy and the associated world of work can confer status. Various writers have exemplified this in descriptions of swapping and trading small objects, including toys and foodstuffs which, though they may be financed by parents, become children's own property, to be used in the negotiation of friendships on the children's terms. See, for example, Katriel (1987), Seiter (1993) and Thorne (1993).

2. Maynard (1985: 219) has noted that, in relation to the negotiation of conflict, 'the traditional development question might . . . be usefully reversed. That is, the regular approach to socialization asks how children are becoming like adults. With respect to conflict, the problem might also be to see how adults are like children.'

3. Developmental psychology provides a model for the development of children's moral understanding, but linear, individualistic accounts are criticized for underestimating the significance of research contexts (Siegert 1986), cultural contexts (Burman 1994) and situated relationships (Dunn 1988).

4. In the context of analysing 'voices' in children's literature, Wall (1991: 83) defines 'the all-controlling, all-knowing voice of the person in the nursery – kind, comforting, reassuring, wise, firm and safe'.

# 8

## Children's Negotiations of the Social World

*... even among children we need to understand the importance of politics, power, and social control in the constitution of social organization.*

(Maynard 1985: 210)

## 8.1  Introduction

In this chapter, my aim is to explore further the concept of social domains, as outlined in Chapter 5, in analysing extracts from children's conversations. I want to suggest, following on from the ideas presented in Chapter 6, that the children's negotiations of their experiences and relationships through language have features which in some ways distinguish them from adults, as inhabitants of the social world, while in other ways these negotiations and the language resources used in them are not distinctive to children. In other words, the 'blurred boundaries' identified in Chapter 7 are porous in both directions. A crucial difference, I shall suggest, between what adults and children can do with language in interactions is their respective locations in the domains of the social world.

This is one way in which the patterned differences between children's and adults' formulation of requests and directives, as discussed in Chapter 6, can be accounted for. These patterns both reflect and realize actual social relations which obtain between children and adults. Thus, if there is an established expectation that parents are entitled – sometimes indeed obliged – to direct children's behaviour with unmitigated imperatives, for example, while children are expected to demonstrate their subordinate position in relation to their parents, then many of the dialogues presented in Chapter 6 represent a realization of these existing interactive patterns. It is partly the nature of this relationship between instance and pattern which highlights the relevance of domain theory.

To understand what an 'identity' is, or a 'self' or 'person', involves seeing the individual in the context not just of the surrounding 'significant others' at different times of his or her life, but also in terms of position in the wider social structure and of the wider historical processes which provide us with the stage on which we act out our lives. We are each of us given a starting point and we do something with it.

(Craib 1998: 28)

The conversations which the children in my small study recorded, as I have explained, were not structured in any predetermined way, and may or may not be representative of their conversations in general at this time. In any case, they are all examples of the social domain of situated activity, where participants co-construct representations of experience, as well as negotiating their respective needs and interests. In addition, each participant is an individual with his or her unique psychobiographical experience of the social world, and at the same time all the interactions are encased in social settings of one kind or another. In these particular dialogues, the social settings are relatively informal, although in some cases institutions beyond the family impact explicitly on the immediate interaction, while in others their influence is less visible. The analyses which follow will also seek to demonstrate the differential access of participants to contextual resources, and how the children draw as best they can – as all social actors do – on those which are available to them. In the following section, I shall discuss one extract of conversation which exemplifies a number of these themes, which will then be explored further in the remainder of the chapter.

## 8.2  Emma's win on the lottery

The following extract of dialogue involves Emma, aged 9, at home on a Sunday morning with Jenny, her sister. Emma has called next door and invited her friend Gemma to come round to play at her house. The three girls have gone upstairs so that Emma can show Gemma her 'display' of cuddly toys, and they have been chatting about the toys laid out on Emma's bed. Emma remembers a new toy Jenny has bought, and this apparently supplies an introduction to the topic of some money won in the national lottery.

(8.1) Emma (E), 9, her sister Jenny (J), 7, and her friend
     Gemma (G), 10

    E:   Jenny bought / oh we won+ we won the lottery yesterday
    G:   did you?

E:   a tenner
G:   oh
E:   [laughs]                                                          5
J:   and we got five <u>pounds</u>
E:   <u>we get</u> five pounds each
G:   [laughs]
J:   we've <u>got five pounds</u> [*in a sing-song voice, crowing,
     but quietly*]                                                     10
E:   <u>because Jenny chose</u> the numbers / a+ / and so she
     gets five / and it wouldn't be fair if I didn't get five so
     we got five each
G:   oh [*drops something*] oop sorry
J:   five for me and Dad cos I got five cos Dad's spending            15
     the money on getting the lottery numbers
E:   oh if only you had told me **I**'d spend the money if I
     knew it was going to win
J:   yeah but erm we're not allowed to (purchase the lottery
     tickets)                                                          20
E:   no but they can still give us the money
J:   who?
G:   mm I suppose so
J:   **you** didn't even do a thing
E:   [laughs]                                                          25
J:   **I** did / **I** chose the numbers
E:   Gemma the lottery started on my birthday
G:   did it?
E:   yep
G:   oh erm                                                            30
E:   look <u>at this</u>
J:   <u>you're a lott</u>ery girl aren't you Emma

An initial level of analysis can demonstrate how the three participants
negotiate this conversation (or 'situated activity'), and how each of them is
positioned in relation to the others. The topic as Emma introduces it represents Gemma as an audience for an account of an experience involving
the two sisters. Gemma's 'did you?' functions as feedback for the story, with
the minimal utterances 'mm', 'oh' and so on also providing back-channel
support for the telling of the anecdote.

Emma's introduction of the account specifies who did what, and her first
use of 'we' could be read as denoting the family as a unified group to which
she and Jenny belong and Gemma does not. The 'tenner' that was won was
the total prize, presented at the beginning of the story as a single sum
acquired by the family. However, Jenny's first contribution (l. 6) uses 'we' in
a new sense: now it means only the two sisters. Jenny's modification to the

story, explaining that they got 'five pounds' is ambiguous, and in clarifying that they 'each' received five pounds, Emma simultaneously distinguishes herself from Jenny. She elaborates on this distinction in ll. 11–13, when 'Jenny' becomes the third party in the account of events addressed to Gemma, repeating the grounds on which she and Jenny, separately, 'each' received half of the total. In Jenny's next contribution (ll. 15–16), she realigns herself in stating her role alongside her father's in the sequence of events. Emma's response (ll. 17–18) sets up a revised contrastive relationship between herself and Jenny. While the import of her claim that she would have spent the money herself is ambiguous (she uses an ironic intonation, suggesting scorn for Jenny's supposed foresight in choosing winning numbers), this statement repositions the girls in respect of their father. Emma echoes Jenny's formulation 'Dad's spending the money', but makes herself the subject in 'I'd spend the money' (ll. 17–18). So now it is Emma who is connected to their father, until Jenny reminds her that she could not have done what he did. The 'we' in ll. 19–20 may mean children in general or it may mean just the two sisters, but its effect is to place Emma back on a par with Jenny, with the status of a child. Within the role of children, collectively, who are involved with the lottery enterprise, Jenny once more contrasts herself with Emma, distinguishing her as the 'you' who made no contribution (l. 24), and emphasising 'I' in l. 26. At this point (l. 27), Emma addresses herself to Gemma to distinguish herself as someone who can claim a birthday on the day the lottery started.

In this dialogue, then, Emma is represented as an individual 'I', with a specific psychobiography: the 'I' who has a particular date of birth, the 'I' who received five pounds, the 'I' who invents a brief fantasy in which she buys her own lottery tickets. Emma is simultaneously a member of more than one collective 'we'. She is part of her family unit and also one of the members of her particular generation within it. In this particular extract, she chooses a designation as the former (ll. 1, 3) and is assigned a designation as the latter by Jenny (ll. 6, 19–20). Emma is also designated as belonging to the collective group of 'children' in general, as well as, indirectly, girls rather than boys, when labelled a 'lottery girl' by Jenny.

Conversations like these are transitory and mundane, relatively inconsequential compared with, say, a press briefing given by a senior politician. Yet over time they constitute part of the fabric of relationships and experience which are significant components of who people are. They are also necessarily intersubjective: the children's understanding of what winning the lottery 'means' may be partial, and uninflected by knowledge of the political controversy surrounding its introduction, or the big business deals transacted among those who organize it, and so on, yet no single individual – adult or child – 'knows' what a win on the lottery 'means' from every angle; discourse about it – like discourse about any topic – utilizes available language resources in ways which must have degrees of shared meaning, in order to communicate at all, as well as areas of subjective meanings, only some of which are made explicit.

Another theme of the book which is illustrated by this brief dialogue, then, is the status of children as both inside and outside the wider social world, which is symbolized here by the lottery: in reporting the win itself, in speculating about buying her own ticket and in making the link with her birthday, Emma is included. The language associated with this social institution becomes part of childhood experience for these people (Emma, Gemma and Jenny) in a way it was not for previous generations: the fact that the children refer to '*the* lottery' signals their shared terms of reference. Certain aspects of the conversation are also consistent with an adult account of an incident shared among peers. On the other hand, direct participation in the lottery can only be a fantasy for Emma, because of legislation, while her freedom to negotiate her own actions is constrained even within the family by parental authority and potential resistance from a younger sister with her own needs and interests.

## 8.3   Children talking about growth and change

The reference to her birthday by Emma was not unique in the recordings made by these children, and it is consistent with the finding in Part I of the book that ages and stages – physical growth and intellectual development – have strong associations with the childhood phase of the lifespan. However, we do in fact continue to change physically throughout life; birthdays in mainstream culture in the UK continue to carry social significance (a quick perusal of age-graded greetings cards in a shop is an indication of the similarities and differences between cultural associations with various ages); and psychobiographical development is also a life-long process. Nevertheless, the rate of change is much faster in childhood, and the social and cultural significance of even a few months can be quite marked in a society characterized by 'the hegemony of developmental stage monitoring' (James et al. 1998: 19; see also Burman 1994). So both spatial and temporal change are important in children's lives, with both physical growth and years clocked up associated with increased status.

Thorne (1993: 136) found that the children she studied were 'keenly aware of physical size', while James (1993) notes that the 3- to 5-year-olds she observed often introduced the body as a topic of conversation, expressing a range of attitudes towards themselves and other children in their comments on the height, shape and appearance (as well as gender and performance) of children's bodies. She also points out that children learn from much adult discourse the implication that bigger is better: 'The received emphasis for children is clear. It stresses the importance of the growth and development of the physical body in the present for future social identities' (p. 111), and notes that '... the term "grown up", while primarily used as a metaphor for adult social status, is also more literally a representation of the corporal changes that accompany the move out of childhood into adulthood' (p. 117). She quotes from an interview with an 8-year-old girl who comments explicitly on her ambition to be seen as an autonomous person:

> What I like [is] to be big and what [why?] I want to be older is because everyone treats me like I'm a little kid, like a baby. They say 'Camilla, will you do that?' Like I'm a little baby. And my [older] sister gave me this little toy to play with and, guess what, my mummy picked me up and put me in the chair and she goes 'I'll feed you in a minute' and I said 'No, I can feed myself'. . . .

> (James 1993: 114)

The vocabulary found in this extract supports James's claim about associations between age, size and status ('big', 'older', 'little kid', 'baby', 'little baby', 'little toy'). Further, most of the transitivity relations represented in the account are consistent with patterns that have been highlighted elsewhere in the book. Thus the agents of the clauses are people other than the child: 'everyone', 'my sister', 'my mummy'; the processes are experienced by 'me', the child, as goal or beneficiary: 'treats', 'gave', 'picked up', 'put', 'feed'; the one exception is the verbal claim: 'No, I can feed myself.'

Example (6.6), in which details about the smallest woman recorded in the *Guinness Book of Records* were discussed, illustrated the interest of these children in disparities between age and size, and particularly the possibility of a 'grown' ('middle-aged'!) woman being smaller than themselves. All of the children in my study refer at some point on the tapes to their ages, often in the context of a comparison with people of other ages, or with themselves at previous or future periods in their lives. The following are some examples.

(8.2) Emma (E), during the walk to school one morning with her friend Gemma (G), discusses the preparations her class have been making for Easter

    E:   and an easter hat parade / we all had to make an easter hat / we made them in reception and we're too old for it

    G:   [laughs]

    E:   [laughs] but she still made us wear+ make one

Note the casual reference to adult compulsion: 'she' is recoverable as Emma's teacher, positioned as having the authority to 'make' children do particular things, the things they 'had' to do. The 'we' which defines Emma in this context is her age-graded class, who were 'all' required to do this task:

perhaps the implication is that there could/should have been differentiation or choice, but there was not. Rather like the adults in the scenarios discussed in Chapter 7, children can feel that they are being treated, inappropriately, as though they still have the characteristics they once did (as Camilla also observed, see above).

Chris, at the dining table with his parents and younger sister, turns the conversation to preparations for his ninth birthday and recalls previous parties. His father reminds him about the time a 'bouncy castle' was arranged for his party as a surprise.

(8.3) Chris (C), 8, his mother (CM), father, and sister Vicky (V), 5:

C:      that's what+ / I think that's what I'd been asking for earlier on / in the+ in the year hadn't I

CM:   it was when you were five wasn't it / I can't remember whether you wanted it but you <u>didn't</u>

V:      <u>I'm five now</u>

CM:   know (***)

C:      I was six

Vicky claims a right to make a contribution by relating Chris's age then to her own now, and it is apparently important to Chris to be accurate about which party was arranged for which birthday. As a corollary to the relation-ship between parents and children which positions the latter as subordinate to the former – illustrated by the patterns of requests and directives dis-cussed in Chapter 6 – this conversation illustrates the potential of parents to be benefactors and children beneficiaries, another theme identified in Part I. Chris, as a child, can/must 'ask for' things he wants, and it is parents who provide. There are various examples in the dialogues of children referring to things adults have given them: Emma's and Jenny's 'five pounds each', various toys bought for them by relatives and so on. Although these are examples so commonplace as to be hardly worth remarking, I think they are likely to be contributions to the patterned ways in which, because of differential social locations, children may deploy the same language resources in slightly different ways from adults, with relatively few opportunities to represent themselves as benefactors. Hence the importance of trading and swapping small goods, identified above and in Katriel (1987), Seiter (1993) and Thorne (1993).

In another conversation recorded by one of the children, 8-year-old Simon engages a member of his church congregation, 17-year-old Luke, in con-versation after the service, and tells him an anecdote about when he used to attend a mothers and toddlers group (in which, incidentally, he itemizes the designated spaces for children of different ages: 'and there's a room for / the+ the mums and younger babies and there was a room for erm toddlers').

(8.4) Simon (S), 8, and Luke (L), 17

S: I don't think many people remember that far [laughs]
L: no it takes a good bit of memory to do that / mind you you haven't got to think as far back as many people have you
S: pardon?
L: you haven't got to think as far back as m+ some people have you
S: [laughs] yeah
L: only six years [laughs]
S: s+ it seems longer but erm mm the time seems to go really fast
L: sure does / I remember when you were down there not down there [laughs]
S: [laughs]
L: you weren't that far down but
S: mm / I remember when I was about down to my waist
L: someone could have given you a fishing rod and a little hat and they could have put you in the garden by the er
S: [laughs]
L: pond you know just like a gnome [laughs]
S: [laughs] just give me some quick freeze or perhaps a coat of cement [laughs]
L: yeah that's it
S: and a fishing rod like that

Some of the references to the children's former selves, in extracts like these, are very like the observations one would make about a third party. Emma's 'we made them in Reception and we're too old for it' contains a suggestion that the referents for each of the two 'we's are not identical. Chris's seeking of confirmation about what he had asked for and when would not be out of place in a question about what his younger sister, or some other third person, had said and done. This phenomenon is perhaps most noticeable in Simon's good-humoured fantasy about how, when he was younger and smaller, he could have been used as a garden gnome.

The way in which Example (8.4) is constructed collaboratively again illustrates the intersubjective relationships between child, (young) adult and the resources of language. In Simon's first assertion he identifies himself as one among a particular group of 'people' – those who can remember their own toddlerhood. Opie (1993: 3) finds the self-description as 'people' by the children she observed worth commenting on: 'Children call themselves "people" rather than "children". They say, "You need six people for this game," or "There's some people playing marbles over there,"' and this is perhaps a claim by these speakers to be regarded as 'person' rather than 'child'. (See also Thorne's discussion of children's self-naming choices, p. 100 above.) Luke's reply distinguishes Simon within his self-identified group, however, as younger than most people who might try to remember early childhood. In accepting Luke's account of this earlier phase in his life, Simon implicitly aligns himself with the perspective of those who can look 'down' on his younger self. Note particularly the construction 'I remember when I was about down to my waist': if each 'I' and 'my' have the same referent, the utterance cannot make literal sense. This does not cause problems for the audience (i.e. Luke, and the readers of the transcript), though, in a context where physical growth and significant distinctions based on age are an accepted feature of being, and talking about being, a child. They could also be interpreted as a device to distance the child as current speaker from the child who once was a baby, toddler, Reception-year-pupil or 6-year-old.

In addition to these most obvious and explicit references to the self as classified by age, the children sometimes comment, in various kinds of conversation, on other aspects of their personalities, skills and abilities. Chris, for example, in a telephone conversation with his friend Ryan, remarks on his ability with hand-held computer games.

(8.5) Chris (C), 8, in a phone conversation with Ryan (R), 10

> C: erm [sighs] // when I went to my friend's house / erm Dylan / he gave me this little game / you know that dinosaur game I had?
> R: yeah
> C: erm well he gave me one of them except it's smaller and it's a different game
> R: oh
> C: mm / and erm / it's good I'm good at it now / gave it me last Monday

This example also includes an implication of change: one learns to be good at a practical skill and expects to improve over time, and reporting these achievements to peers can perhaps signify something slightly different from telling adults about them, since the contextual frame in which they 'count' is shared among the interlocutors. Ryan does not follow up Chris's claims in this extract, which digresses into a clarification of when Chris got the game, but other researchers have noted how skill with play objects is a regular topic of children's conversation, and, among boys particularly, a site of competitive demonstration of skill (see, for example, Evaldsson 1993; Goodwin 1990). When Emma reports an academic achievement to her grandmother, she has to explicate the school context in some detail before receiving an approving comment.

(8.6) Emma (E) and her grandmother (EG) in the garden

E:      Grandma

EG:     yeah

E:      at school on Friday we erm had a congratulations assembly /
        and erm // we ha+ at school we have these things called
        smiley faces

EG:     oh yes / oh right

E:      and you get and you only get them+ when when you've
        done a really really **really** good piece of work

EG:     and had you done a good piece of work?

E:      yeah and I got and erm / you get a prize if you get a certain
        amount of these smiley faces / and erm / if you get ten you
        get a / handwriting pen and if you get twenty you get a
        certificate

EG:     and did you get any?

E:      I got ten

EG:     oh so you had a

E:      <u>yeah</u>

EG:     <u>what</u> did you have?

E:      a pen and erm

EG:     ink pen or was it a biro <u>pen</u>?

E:      <u>ink</u>

EG:     oh that's nice . . .

Emma's 'we' here is the whole school community, and the pupils are designated by the generic 'you'. The subsequent discussion of Emma's performance individuates her as 'I' and 'you', but Grandma is clearly external to the social setting to which these matters are integral. In children's day-to-day experience, a degree of power and significance is possible within the informal social setting of the peer group at 'play'. Seiter (1993: 8) suggests that part of the attraction for children of the toys and games associated with children's television is that they can '. . . feel their knowledge and mastery of consumer culture to be a kind of power: something they know, but of which adults are ridiculously ignorant'. In the more formal setting of school, one can demonstrate achievement, as Emma has done, but the rules and conventions for doing so are much further from children's control.

The changes in age, size and status referred to in the children's talk are both predictable and consistent patterns of growth, common to most children, and also specific and personal – events, experiences and relationships which are unique to them and constitutive of their individual psychobiographies. Woven into their talk about what these events mean to them, however, are references to other domains – social settings like age-graded institutions (schools, playgroups), and the cultural significance attached to 'growing up'.

By way of contrast with these examples, Leanne sometimes represents herself in dialogue as though she has a sense of herself as a more stable member of the social world. In the following group of extracts, Leanne is at her grandmother's house. She has negotiated with her 'Nan' that she will stay there for her tea, as will her cousin Angela (aged 12), and they begin to help to prepare some potatoes. Her grandmother is working out how many are needed.

(8.7) Leanne (L), 9, and her grandmother (LGM)

> LGM:    How many do you want Leanne?
> L:       I'll er I'll eat as much+ as as much / as you give me Nan
>          / I don't really care / I just eat / what / what's put in front
>          of me / I'm not fussy

Leanne's style in this contribution suggests a continuing state of being, an ability to describe what one is like with some certainty. This effect is created in part through the use of verbs in the simple present tense. Also, being a 'fussy' eater may have connotations of childliness, so a self-description as 'not fussy' perhaps represents the speaker as less childly as well.

The following exchange between Leanne and her cousin Angela occurs when, as they peel the potatoes, their conversation turns to a discussion of the research in which Leanne is involved, with me, and Angela wants to know if she could perhaps make some recordings too. Leanne says that Angela would have to ask me, and Angela asks about me.

(8.8) Leanne (L) and Angela (A)

> A:    Al+ er is Alison nice?
> L:    Alison Sealey / she's okay
> A:    eh? you still on your first <u>potato</u>?
> L:    <u>but I</u> don't really know her that much do I / I mean
>       I've o+ I've only met her about three times / summat       5
>       like that anyway / probably about five times (maybe)
>       <u>and you do+</u>
> A:    <u>a few times</u> maybe about five
> L:    [laughs] well you don't really judge a person do you
>       li- when you- you need I think with me I need to get      10
>       to know people before I can like judge
> A:    <u>mm</u>
> L:    <u>on 'em</u> bit more // like see her every day / like now
>       I know that you're a snotty cow / because I see you
>       every day                                                 15

Here, again, Leanne offers a description of an aspect of what she is like, framed within an indication of her knowledge about the social world at large. She gives Angela a partial answer to her question about me (conscious, no doubt, that I will hear the recording), but passes on to a generalization about assessing people's characters. In doing so, she simultaneously makes a statement about what other people can be like, about her own stance – again presented as relatively fixed – and about where her way of making such judgements fits into a more general norm. In ll. 9–10, there are several false starts as her choice of pronoun changes. The first 'you' is apparently used in the sense of the generic 'one', positioning Leanne well inside the group of people-at-large who know to be cautious before forming opinions about others. Midway through the utterance she changes stance, and specifies how she, as an individual, prefers to reserve judgement. In describing herself in explicit ways, Leanne suggests that some of her characteristics confer membership of social groups, such as people who are not fussy about food, people who reserve judgement on the characters of others and so on.

## 8.4   Negotiating constraints

As was suggested in Chapter 3, published writing and recorded talk produced by adults are unlikely to adopt a childly perspective on experience, so it is not surprising if the major preoccupation found in news stories about children – the harm directed towards them – is not reflected to any great extent in these children's own recorded conversations. The topic did come up in my research when I was discussing with the children and their parents what kinds of contexts might be suitable for making recordings. These interviews usually touched on the limitations – primarily for their own safety – on what the children were allowed to do unaccompanied by adults. I could easily identify with these concerns, as the mother of a child of roughly the same age, and anxieties about the tension between fostering independence and responsibility while not exposing children to serious risks are also a theme of contemporary sociological literature on children – see Scott et al. (1998), for example.

However, from the children's own perspectives, it may be that any risk perceived by adults is less salient than the proscription on behaviour which is its direct impact on them. Thus many of the directives from adults to children, discussed in Chapter 6, could be seen as the immediate, situated outcome of less visible phenomena, such as parents' awareness of the threat of catching a cold (Example (6.8)) or suffering disappointment in competition (Example (6.9)). The danger to children from cars was alluded to in the radio broadcast about restrictions on children's play, reported in Chapter 3; these extracts from a recording made as Emma walked to school with Gemma illustrate the children's perspective:

(8.9) Emma (E) and Gemma (G)

> E: I could just say well I had to walk slow / because of erm
> G: the cars
> E: erm
> G: the cars held you up [*loud traffic noise*]
> E: eeow
> G: they never let you cross / shall we cross? cross
> E: let's go on the safe side and cross
> *a few minutes later*
> E: [sings] another road / [*fits this to a tune*] another road another road [*stops singing*] and yet again the cars won't let us cross over
> G: [sings]
> E: <u>try and sneak across while they're not looking</u>
> G: [sings]
> E: but don't get run over
> G: do you mind not holding my (finger)
> E: well that car was about to run you over / you should be thanking me
> G: (***)
> E: [*calling to her friend across the road*] Catherine will you wait for us / the cars won't let us cross over
> G: I think we can cross now
> E: can we? ooh
> G: no <***>
> [*they run across road*]
> E: oh we're saved

Cars are represented here as a potential danger – 'don't get run over'; 'that car was about to run you over' – but also as obstacles to the children's access to public space.

Several times in these extracts the girls use the formula 'the cars won't *let* us cross over' (emphasis added), a construction which occurs in other references to their restricted access to various spaces. Together with Gemma's 'try and sneak across while they're not looking', and the dramatic 'we're saved', reminiscent of a storybook escape, these representations of their experience depict the cars as intentional aggressors, while Emma's 'yet again' also offers a child's eye view of a world where it is routinely not possible to go where one wishes.

In a recording made at the swimming baths, Ian and his father discuss access to the pool-side. The exchange serves to differentiate the respective statuses of child and parent.

(8.10) Ian (I), 9, and his father (IF)

> IF:  Ian / you shouldn't be in there with your clothes on
> I:  **you**'ve sat there
> IF:  what?
> I:  **you**'ve sat there
> IF:  yes I know but you're not a lifeguard / only lifeguards are allowed on the side in here
> I:  well you are
> IF:  I know and that's why I can sit there / you can't

Within the domain of situated activity, this particular father and son generate an immediate exchange, which, like many of the directives discussed in Chapter 6, exemplifies relations between parents and children, including parental responsibility for children's socialization. The conversation is contextualized within the social setting of the swimming baths, whose own rules are more formal, linked (in ways with which adults are likely to be more familiar than children) with institutions like the law, council funding, procedures of certification and so on. Thus this brief series of exchanges represents both parent–child relations, and, in Ian's father's indirect quotation of the institutional rule, the micro-political reflection of larger scale distributions of power. Once again, implicitly, the identification by the speakers of themselves as 'I' and 'you' is not just of individuals, but members of groups occupying different social locations. Often the salient dichotomy for children is 'adults'/'children' (see the notices in public spaces in Part I), but here it may also be 'life-guards'/'pool-users'. But since children are clearly not eligible, as a group, for such responsibility, membership of the category 'children' rules out membership of many other social categories, especially those which confer responsibility and power.

When Jenny loses her ball over the wall, she rejects her grandmother's suggestion that she should go and get it by quoting her mother's proscription on her right to go into the neighbour's garden.

(8.11) Emma (E), sister Jenny (J) and their grandmother (EG) in the garden

> J:  Mum won't <u>let me</u>
> E:  <u>where</u> was <u>I / oh</u>
> EG:  <u>why not</u>?
> J:  she just won't let me go
> E:  won't let you go where? to get your ball from next door?
> J:  mm

As has already been suggested, the quoting of other people's speech is common in these dialogues, and is one means by which the children demonstrate their awareness of perspectives on, and locations in, the social world other than their own. Quoting from others will be explored further in Sections 8.6 and 8.7.

## 8.5   Speaking as a child

When a speaker says that someone 'won't let' them do something, or that they are 'not allowed' to do it, or appeals to what is or is not 'fair', there are strong connotations of childliness, as was indicated in Chapter 7. One of the reasons for this may be that it is often children to whom these formulations apply – and several of the extracts quoted so far include instances.

A number of other ways of speaking may be identified as distinctly childly, some of which, again, were identified by respondents to the elicitation study described in the previous chapter. One of these is the emphasis of individual interests and rights, contrasted with those of others. Examples given there included 'You always get more than me' and 'Well it's my ball anyway'. Exchanges consisting of assertion and counter-assertion combine to make an almost stereotypically childly formulation (Brenneis and Lein 1977; Maynard 1985). This is represented in the following authentic example from Goodwin's (1990) study of children in Philadelphia. Carl (aged 11) and William (aged 10) are making sling boards:

> William: You usin' my **nails**.
> Carl: I ain't use **none** a your nails.
> William: Did **so**.
> Carl: Did **not**.

> (Goodwin 1990: 166)

Although this kind of negotiation is fairly unsophisticated, it is important to note that, like appeals to what is 'fair', it relies on an intersubjective definition of what counts in terms of rights, even if the details are disputed (in this case whether the nails Carl has used do or do not belong to William).

Here is another example, from my own data, of an interaction involving a disputed interpretation of norms. Leanne is playing a skipping game with her cousins Angela and Marcie. Leanne has commented derisively on Marcie's nil score, which she repeats in l. 3.

> (8.12) Leanne (L), 9, with Angela (A), 12, and Marcie (M), 8

> M:   please (let me have an<u>other go</u>)
> A:   <u>no</u>
> L:   <u>none</u>
> M:   Angela had an<u>other go</u>

A:    I never had a go
M:    you had another go
A:    I never / I didn't <***>
M:    you two had chances
A:    no I never I couldn't
M:    yes you did
A:    I couldn't get my foot right
L:    yous two stop arguing man

This interaction exemplifies assertion and counter-assertion (this happened / no that happened), using the 'format-tying' discussed at length by Goodwin and Goodwin (1987) and Goodwin (1990): Marcie and Angela both incorporate 'had a(nother) go' into several of their respective turns, rather than simply substituting 'did' and 'one'. The argument also turns on the immediate conflict of interest between 'you' and 'me' – a contrast identified in Chapter 7 as typically childlike. Leanne's attempt at peacemaking in the final line contrasts herself, as non-protagonist, with her cousins, representing them briefly as being a group 'yous two', if only as co-combatants.

Although there is no explicit reference to what would be 'fair' in these circumstances, just as there is no explicit reference to why Carl would be wrong to use William's nails, each dispute implies an appeal to shared systems of property and rights. If Angela did have a second chance to score in the skipping game, then that is relevant, on the grounds of equity, to Marcie's claim to a second chance. Evaldsson (1993: 124) includes a very similar exchange in her account of children's skipping games (which are referred to by the American term 'jump-rope'), where the dispute is over whether a particular move with the rope 'counts' as a miss or not, and Goodwin (1998) describes the social significance among different groups of girls of the means by which violations of the rules of hopscotch are negotiated.

Various writers have noted the range of systems children employ for putting on record what procedures are to be followed, not only in games but also in how friendships are sealed, claims verified, promises made binding, and so on (e.g. Sutton-Smith 1982). Corsaro (1997: 95) refers to this as 'a stable set of activities or routines, artifacts, values and concerns that children produce and share in interaction with peers', while Opie and Opie (1959: 141) describe the 'ritual declaration[s]', which 'are verbal, and are sealed by the utterance of ancient words which are recognized and considered binding by the whole community'. They continue: 'This juvenile language of significant terms and formulas appears to be a legacy of the days when the nation itself was younger and more primitive.' As I explained in Chapter 6, the recordings made by the children in my study did not include many examples of ritual formulas (although the children may well have used them at other times), but references to friendship status, ownership of property, promising, lying and so on are found in my data. While some researchers stress the distinctiveness of the world of children's interactions, and others their role as preparation for full socialization into 'the adult world', it is also possible to see children's 'small-group society' as just that – a social grouping with variants on the same characteristics as any small social group. For Maynard (1985: 207), '... when disputing and arguing, children produce social organization, create political alignments, and thereby realize their practical interests within a changing set of social relationships'. The role of conflict among children in groups is also identified by Streeck (1986: 295), who claims that '[c]hildren ... like to fight over political issues such as ownership, alliances, status and power, social norms, prior agreements, and broken promises'. Van Peer (1988: 180) places less emphasis on conflict, but makes the similar observation that '[c]hildren's oral culture, even in what may be viewed as trivial genres such as counting-out rhymes, reproduces power relations and the prevailing method of coping with these'. Thus these aspects of 'children's oral culture' could be seen as speech acts whose illocutionary purpose is to make codes of conduct explicit and demonstrate individual and group adherence to them. If children are indeed engaged in social projects which are fundamentally much like those of adults, then, as van Peer claims (1988: 180), '[t]he apparent independence of children's oral culture from the world in which grown-ups live would seem to be an illusion'. However, if both children and adults use speech acts to put on record rules, promises, alliances and oppositions, a key difference between them, in terms of domain theory, is that children's words are not underpinned by the same social structures and contextual resources. They do not have the same reach, for example, as the sworn statement made in the social setting of a police station or court room, or the announcement of intention declared in the parliamentary chamber. This comparative fragility of the social order among children sometimes leads to appeals to the wider world where more substantial social authority is located.

## 8.6   Invoking the wider world

A respondent in the elicitation study suggested that a childish remark might be: 'If you let on I'll tell them about Woolworths', and the children in my study sometimes threatened to tell their parents of their siblings' misdemeanours. Of course it is often children who cite this particular performative speech act as a threat. Its childly connotations arise from its implicit recognition that the speaker's own power is not sufficient to enforce compliance by another participant,[1] and observers of children's interactions note that actually 'telling' on another child is a last resort (James 1993), a sign of cowardice (Evaldsson 1993) or 'the betrayal of one's kind' (Thorne 1993: 77). Adults in authority may reject 'tale-telling' or 'tattling' (Evaldsson 1993), because the official, explicit social order, where individuals have the

right and the responsibility to report wrong-doing to authority, oversimpli-
fies the ways in which social actors are actually rewarded in their negotiations of such matters: hence the code of 'honour among [adult] thieves'
which despises a 'grass'.

In children's interactions with each other, claims James (1993: 166), 'can
be seen the bare outlines of the ways in which identities and personhoods
come to be taken on through the negotiation of a set of shared cultural
meanings' – an idea echoed by Corsaro (1997: 173), who claims that negotiating friendships with peers, and playing to win objects such as marbles,
leads to children's 'developing notion of identity or self embedded in the
collectively produced peer culture'. Yet these immediate instances of situated
activity are encased not only in the relatively fragile peer culture but also in
the domains beyond. More persistent, less malleable norms and conventions
also frame children's experience. When Ian's father reminds his son that he
is prohibited from sitting by the pool (Example (8.10)), or Chris's mother
rejects his request for mint sauce (Example (6.12)), they are not simply
citing temporarily agreed rules about what counts as being 'in' or 'out' of
a game. Behind their injunctions are institutions and contextual resources
which are different in this respect from those we think of as most typically
childly. (Thus Chris's use of the precise football term 'free kick-in' in his
garden game with friends makes it sound less childly perhaps than Marcie's
bid for 'another go'.)

However, as well as involving (or threatening to involve) adults and their
authority in their own interactions, children can, as was illustrated in Chapter 6, assume alternative personas which allow them to cite this authority
verbally, as if to accrue to themselves some of its power. Examples (6.1),
(6.16) and (8.1) are of this type. In another example, Ian appears to occupy a
position part-way between his younger brother and his mother when he
seeks permission for them to have some sweets before dinner.

> (8.13) Ian (I), 9, at home with his brother Jason (J), 7. Their mother
> (IM) is preparing dinner
>
> I:      I'm just going to get some tissue // [blows nose] Jason /
>         want a polo?
> J:      we're not allowed
> I:      why?
> J:      don't know
> I:      I'll ask
> J:      it's nearly dinner time
> [Ian finds his mother in the kitchen]
> I:      can we have a polo?
> IM:     one (***)
> I:      okay // [Ian returns to Jason] what do you think the answer
>         was?

J:     yeah
I:     what do you think it really was?
J:     yeah

Ian's original question to Jason appears to have the function of an offer which would position Ian as giver and Jason as beneficiary, but Jason's response repositions them both as people who are 'not allowed' sweets at this time. Ian's 'I'll ask' is interpretable both as an initiative-seeking move on behalf of both brothers and an acknowledgement that permission is needed. He does not say who he will ask, which is understood as the boys' mother. Having had a ration granted to them both, Ian then capitalizes on his access to knowledge of the judgement by getting Jason to guess what it was – briefly, knowledge is power!

Citing and quoting the words of adults is not a simple and complete appropriation of a way of speaking. Corsaro (1997) writes of how even very young children at pre-school seek control of their own experience by making what Goffman designates 'secondary adjustments' to the official rules of the institution, evading involvement in cleaning up, for example, by following a different rule at the relevant time, and otherwise 'using legitimate resources in devious ways' (p. 133), and he also quotes a study from the nineteenth century which found that the dolls given to girls to foster maternalism were used to perform subversive actions, like sliding down the bannisters: 'the adult model was appropriated, not simply internalized' (ibid.: 111). In my own data is an example of a conversation between two friends about homework, where the simple facts of children being under an obligation to do homework (an obligation set by the school, thus associated indirectly with the state, and mediated by parental authority too) are reworked in conversation to express both the girls' individual attitudes towards the tasks and their awareness of other perspectives.

(8.14) Emma (E), sister Jenny (J) and friend Gemma (G)

E:     have you done your homework Gemma?
G:     yes / my boring homework / have you done yours?
E:     yes / I had four pieces of homework
G:     [mock? sympathetically] aaah
E:     filled up the whole section of my homework diary
G:     aah
E:     reading science erm / spellings and / something else
G:     yes / don't you just hate homework / they give I bet they
       just give it you 'cos they think [adopts a 'posh' accent and
       measured pace] oh no school's not school tomorrow and they
       won't learn anything
E:     [laughs]
G:     so we'd better give them some homework

E:    [laughs]

G:    and the weekend's supposed to be a day of r+ [laughs] it's supposed to be a time (of rest)

E:    <u>Sunday</u> is supposed to be a day of rest <u>but w+</u>

G:    (***)

E:    how can you rest when you've got to do homework

G:    I know

J:    and <u>on Sunday</u> (***)

G:    <u>and they say</u> [*adopts a 'posh' accent again*] <u>you've got</u> to live up to your religion / if you can't say the prayer don't say it [*reverts to usual accent and quicker pace*] // and I like saying like you've got to do what your religion says

E:    your religion <u>says</u>

G:    (***) Sunday's a day of rest / let's just have a rest

E:    [laughs] yeah

The child's subordinate status is implied by both the content and the manner of the talk in this extract. To be given homework is to be required to do what someone with greater authority determines. Once again, expressions such as 'supposed to' and 'got to' indicate the children's relatively powerless position. Yet the two girls collaborate in their construction of a hypothetically adversarial relationship with the teachers who set them work, supporting each other in much the same way as Maybin (1994) identified in her school-based study, particularly by completing and echoing each other's utterances. In this example, however, the children also use the linguistic resource of 'echoing' other texts for another purpose: to suggest the invocation of one kind of adult authority to be used against another. They play with the idea that, since teachers quote church teaching as a source of authority, they too may draw on the same quotation in their (pretended) defiance of homework-setting teachers. The referents for the respective pronouns are not made explicit, but their use creates an 'us' and a 'them', while demonstrating a sophisticated ability to empathize with the viewpoints of others – even ironically. Although the conversation is clearly that of children in both topic and the stance taken towards it, the girls' use and maintenance of available adult discourses illustrates the complex intersubjectivity involved as children use talk in the social world.

## 8.7    Whose language?

I have been arguing throughout this chapter that linguistic resources are used in patterned – but not exclusive – ways by children and adults respectively, and that both groups deploy them in ways that are not categorically different: to express individual and group needs and priorities, and to invoke social and cultural conventions and structures where such contributions are relevant. I have also been suggesting that language resources can sometimes be appropriated by speakers other than those with whom they are most centrally associated. In this section, I shall address once again the intersubjectivity of language and interaction, which can make it difficult to attribute the unfolding of conversation to single individuals, further undermining any theoretical dichotomy between adult and childly language.

Take, for example, Emma's words to her rabbit, presented in Example (6.15) (reproduced here for convenience).

> E:    [tuts] this calls for mummy (stuff) // this is how the mummies get her out [*in role as a mummy:*] get 'ere or I'll pull your ears off / come 'ere / ugh

Later in the same episode:

> E:    I'll get her / I'll get her / [*in a sing-song tone:*] now Clover you're being impolite to our guests / [*in a mock-threatening tone:*] get out / now come on / out you come

Emma explicitly quotes what she claims that 'mummies' do and say, using the rather unchildly expression 'this calls for', and signalling her adoption of adult style in 'this is how the mummies get her out'. She proceeds to deploy two quite different styles in this 'role' – one confrontational and threatening: 'get 'ere or I'll pull your ears off' (a formulation which followers of Bernstein might describe as a 'status-oriented' instruction); and the other more inclusive, or 'person-oriented': 'now Clover you're being impolite to our guests'. Where do these different styles in her repertoire originate from? In another of Emma's recordings, she tells me of the magazines about rocks and gemstones which she is collecting, and in the course of her explanation she says: 'issue three came free with issue two' and also 'and I got this display tray free with issue four', both of which are objective statements of fact, yet both have the ring of a promoter's slogan. The unease which parents may feel about popular culture impinging on children's lives was discussed in Part I (see also Postman 1985), yet children inevitably make use of ideas and expressions from television, advertising and other aspects of the mass media. It is perhaps ironic that a branch of research about children which takes their attitudes and perspectives particularly seriously is market research (Kline 1993; Seiter 1993), which sees children 'as highly informed and powerful consumers' (Corsaro 1997: 112). As I have observed, many of the roles played by the children in my study derived from popular television programmes and films, and gave children opportunities to speak with various accents and in a range of styles.

Sometimes the collaboration is exclusive of adults while still not the language 'product' of a single child. (There is a phenomenon in southern Europe known as the 'cantilena', an extemporized chant taken up communally by young children, often to the irritation of their parents (Corsaro 1997).) The following extract, which illustrates a particular kind of duetting, is from Chris's dinner-table talk with his younger sister. She has been promised strawberries for dessert and announces that she's looking for them in the kitchen. Their mother mishears her and asks what she means by 'strawberries on the choo choo train'. This nonsense idea is taken up and developed by both children over several utterances.

(8.15) Chris (C), 8, and Vicky (V), 5

    C:  you can laugh but you can't do that
    V:  [laughs]
    C:  but / y+ you can do the strawberries on the <u>choo choo train</u>
    V:  <u>strawberries on the choo choo</u> train [laughs]
    C:  [laughs]
    V:  [laughs]
    C:  it's not getting <u>f±</u>
    V:  <u>eyeballs</u> on the choo choo train [laughs]
    C:  [laughs] eyeballs on the choo choo train
    V:  [laughs]
    C:  why don't you say something like //
    V:  mummy on the choo choo train [laughs]
    C:  [laughs] why don't you say+ why don't you say something like Tom's on the inter-city or something
    V:  mummy on the choo choo train [laughs]
    C:  Tom's on the inter-city
    V:  Tom's on the in two city

Here, Chris almost seems to be speaking 'through' his sister, encouraging her to repeat what has made them both laugh, suggesting what she 'can' say, suggesting what she might say ('why don't you say...'), and they both repeat, modify and complete each other's utterances. In the recording made by Emma and Gemma on their walk to school, the two girls proclaim themselves members of 'the nutters club', alluding to the 'nutter calling card' and singing a nonsense song in unison: 'We're nutters and violets are red and as long as polka-dotted rabbits have bad breath we'll be nutters to the end of a giraffe's neck.'

Childly talk in both these instances is not the self-centred expression of one's own interests. Neither is it the rehearsal of age-old formulae or ritual. Rather, it seems to be a collaborative playing with language resources, where the manipulation of 'nonsense' entails distinguishing it from 'sense'. Language games like these, according to Meek (1985: 48), are played by children

. . . on the edge of what is socially tolerated. Thus they discover what is congruous or fitting and also what is incongruous and ill-fitting in language and behaviour. The experimentations are laced with the risk of being misunderstood or thought to be sense-less or stupid.

Constructing talk like this also demonstrates membership of a social group (quite literally in the 'nutters' refrain). Whitehead (1995: 45) describes a group of young children singing in unison the names of fast food restaurants. 'What was very obvious', she writes, 'was the strong social bond which this singing fostered in these little children . . . This apparently silly chant also highlighted the children's shared cultural experience. . . .' In such contexts, children can be members of a social group whose concerns are distinctly childly. The examples also recall the observation of the respondent in Chapter 7 who said 'a little fun or silliness helps to bind individuals together through humour'.

Another example, where it is hard to say who 'owns' the utterance, is from Emma's discussion with Gemma, as they walk to school, about Emma having had to make an Easter hat, even though she is really too old now for this to be an appropriate task.

(8.16) Emma (E) and Gemma (G)

    G:   well you've got a straw hat
    E:   I get a posh straw hat
    G:   <u>with a</u>
    E:   <u>with</u>
    G:   <u>yellow ribb</u>on on it
    E:   yeah and little posh chickens

This kind of collaborative talk is similar to that identified by Coates (1989, 1996) and Maybin (1994: 147), where 'meanings do not seem to be generated within one mind and then communicated to another through talk; rather, they are collaboratively and interactionally constructed between people'. Both these writers have commented specifically on the collaborative construction of *meaning*. In relation to examples of speakers – particularly women – completing each other's utterances, Coates (1989: 119–20) observes: 'this seems to be a clear example of the primacy of text rather than speaker', when 'the joint working out of a group point of view takes precedence over individual assertions'. However, in my own study, even where the function of some of the informal talk is apparently primarily phatic, rather than meaning-seeking, as it were, there are examples of 'duetting', such as repetitions and completions of an interlocutor's contributions. Sometimes the children seem to be using their informal talk to represent themselves as components of a collective 'we'. Instead of a 'primacy of text rather than speaker', this may illustrate a (temporary) primacy of collective rather than individual identification.

## 8.8   Summary and conclusions

This chapter has used some further examples of casual conversation involving children to illustrate how they, like other social actors, use such talk 'as a resource to negotiate social identity and interpersonal relations' (Eggins and Slade 1997: 9). But it has further suggested that children provide a particular illustration of the nature of the interplay in such negotiations between the possibilities of agency, on the one hand, and the constraints and enablements of social structures, on the other. Some examples of the children's self-identifications and self-descriptions were presented to illustrate how they align themselves discursively with different groups, as well as maintaining a unique 'I', in the context of rapid changes in the corporeal self and differentiated status associated with the different ages of childhood.

I suggested that the children's representation of the world and their experience in it has many features in common with the adult equivalents, but also reveals a perspective which derives from having relatively little power or status. Thus rules and conventions devised by adults (ranging from parents to the state), with goals such as the socialization and protection of children, may be experienced from a child's point of view as more saliently restrictions and constraints on what they can do. The chapter considered examples of the children's negotiations of rules and conventions in their own activities, and considered how, despite the apparent simplicity of these, a necessary prerequisite for them to work at all is some agreement about what is to 'count' as fair, as a rule and so on. Such intersubjective consensus is also crucial for the social institutions that affect us all, but whereas official versions of these are underpinned by powerful forces (the complex apparatus of law, government and, ultimately, institutionalized physical force), children can often only invoke local representatives of authority (parents, teachers) to back up their own claims to justice. Intersubjectivity was also important in considering how children can appropriate for their own purposes some of the ways of talking associated more typically with adults. In addition, examples of the implicit rejection of adult styles involved children co-operating in playful 'nonsense' talk, while these and other collaborative utterances could be seen as emphasizing that aspect of the human condition which is drawn towards 'connectedness' rather than 'separateness' (as discussed in Chapter 5, p. 106). All of these analyses can be related to the common ground, or 'blurred boundaries', between adults' and children's use of informal talk, while at the same time they point to some of the distinctive features of being a child in the social world. In the final chapter of the book, I shall attempt to draw together the themes which link children, language and the social world as explored in the first three parts, and consider what the implications may be for working with and researching children and language.

## Note

1.  The obverse of this is related to the connection between childly talk and intimacy noted in Chapter 7: a speaker who suspends his or her rights to adult status by talking like a child is made vulnerable, relinquishing temporarily the 'back-up' of social institutions.

Part

IV

# 9

## Conclusions and Implications

*Ideas about children directly impinge upon the experience of childhood which children themselves have.*

(JAMES 1993: 72)

## 9.1 The idea of the child and the realities of childhood

It is inevitable that the words used to denote any social group will be something more than monosemic labels. Even the apparently 'neutral' naming word *child* evokes a range of connotations, which are the products of: repeated language patterns in large numbers of texts; the aims and intentions of the institutions and individuals which generate these texts; and the immediate purposes and experiences of speaker and hearer, reader and writer. Some of the connotations of words and expressions connected with 'children' have been revealed in earlier chapters which analysed both specific instances and repeated patterns. As well as the dichotomous categories of 'cherub' and 'demon', which have long been noted by writers on the cultural significance of childhood, the analyses identified several other themes, including: children as ever-changing in their passage through the lifespan, both physically and psychically; children as victims and beneficiaries of deeds and goods controlled by others; children as repositories of both innocence and enthusiasm; and children as admirably or dangerously daring and wild.

As is the case with any stereotype or metaphor, for it to be effective there must be some truth in the linking of these themes to members of this particular social group. Obviously children do grow and change, and their physical presence in the world – its biological basis – is a 'brute fact'. Then, irrespective of how membership of the group labelled 'children' is determined, children must eventually cease to be members. 'Child' is thus the only (sociolinguistic) category to which all actors belong at some time, yet which is left by all when they become members of the group that is its antithesis. It is a 'social fact' that children have distinctive ('childly') needs and interests. To give just two examples:

1.  Since judgement about matters of danger and safety is partly a product of experience, children, with limited experience of life and few instances to refer to, could not successfully be left to attend to their own survival needs without great risk.
2.  By dint of other social facts in the West, children, unlike adults, are obliged to attend school, with practical consequences for themselves and their families if this law is broken.

However, the links between physical and social realities and cultural ideas are complex and changeable. The cultural and metaphorical significance of 'the child' can be carried into settings where no actual children are to be found, as is the case, for example, when adult lovers use childly speech in the evocation of playful, vulnerable or nurturing relations. Conversely, although well-established stereotypes of children and their language can have the force of 'social facts', there are many ways in which children's social location might be other than it is. This is not simply speculation: other societies in other places and at other times have been organized differently. Expectations of children as family members, in education and in the labour force, are far from universal.

## 9.2   Children, adults and the social domains

In this book I have tried to draw out similarities, as well as differences, between children and adults. One of my main claims is that, as human beings, children, as well as adults, occupy all the domains of the social world. Their location in the different domains is partly a product of their childhood, but is also related to other social groupings to which they belong. In spite of adult fantasies of childhood innocence, children are involved in the systems which structure the social world. They participate in the economy, both immediately and indirectly as consumers, and on the basis of the labour they invest in school work, whose organization and staffing, of course, are financed by society. Children are also consumers of society's cultural products. What is available to them is determined predominantly by market priorities (Kline 1993; Seiter 1993). We might wonder how the culture of childhood would be changed if more public texts other than advertising were addressed directly to children. The notion of a newspaper or television channel produced by children for children may seem quite bizarre, but it is worth considering whether this is because of the nature of childhood or because of the nature of politics and economics in this society at the present time. It does seem that children's voices are heard most clearly when there is money to be made from listening.

One of the main things which children do not share with adults is a basis for collective agency. As participants in social settings, they are rarely able to organize themselves *as children*, and they have minimal economic or political power.

## 9.3   Children, language and research

The enterprise of researching children and language takes place not in a vacuum but in social settings in the context of social structures, with features such as those just described. None of us is free from the influence of commonsense assumptions about how people are classified into groups, and in undertaking research for this book I have often been struck by parallels between the patterns I have found and those identified by research about language and gender. Claims about what is 'natural' or 'fitting' for women can be used to deny them speakers' rights, for example, and I think we should entertain the possibility that routine expectations about children could influence research about them and about language. For example, in encouraging readers to recognize that *any* talk by women may be thought ' "too much" by men who expect them to provide a silent, decorative background', Holmes (1998: 48) asks us to 'think about how you react when precocious children dominate the talk at an adult party'. If children are present, in what sense is it 'an adult party'? What do we mean by 'precocious'? Is *any* talk by children 'too much' in some contexts? Why?

As I said in the Introduction, I am not seeking to invent a 'childist' linguistics. There is, I hope, no need to resurrect arguments about whether 'language is sexist', or racist – or 'adultist'. It is people who use language; but certain 'angles of telling', certain patterns of discourse, and certain structures of power, can privilege the interests of adults and will represent children in particular ways.

What are the implications of these observations for the research process? One suggestion would be that 'children' need not always be assumed as a self-evident category in sociolinguistic research. We could suspend the adult–child dichotomy and explore the language of both groups, in a range of similar or equivalent discursive contexts, to discover how relevant a variable 'being a child' turns out to be (cf. Chapter 6 and Freed 1996).

Because of the differences between standard adult speech production and that of the beginning speaker, the child language research community has been influential in developing awareness of 'transcription as theory' (Ochs 1979). (The CHAT transcription system, associated with the CHILDES project – the Child Language Data Exchange System – was developed to take account of these differences.) Without embarking on a process of infinite regress, researchers could seek to go further in raising awareness of the language used in writing about children and language. Stephens (1992: 138) notes that in children's fiction, if a child character is said to have 'declared' something, this '. . . almost invariably has a pejorative association . . . , marking an utterance as opinionated or wrong'. Might there be other subtly nuanced ways of transcribing and describing how child speakers talk which reflect an unconscious adult bias? If the idea that women 'gossip' can influence sociolinguistic research (Coates 1989), what about children's tendency to 'whine'? Is a 'giggle' or a 'chuckle' gender- or age-specific?

If it is difficult to be aware of all the ways in which assumptions about children and language are acted upon, it may be worth while for professionals and practitioners to consider whether they are inadvertently patronizing children (see Chapter 7). In schools, particularly, there are routinized discourse styles which are not inevitable but are very well established, and teachers might be encouraged to explore, perhaps through action research, the nature of their classroom discourse and the potentially overaccommodating register used with children in primary schools. The language of educational policy documents and curriculum prescriptions is also usefully scrutinized for assumptions about children and about language (Sealey 1997, 1999b).

## 9.4 Suggestions for future research

In reading for this book, I have engaged with quite a wide range of disciplines, finding much common ground but also some significant differences. I hope that those contributing to knowledge about children and language from different disciplines will be able to become increasingly aware of each other's work, and to engage collaboratively in research projects.

The CHILDES database, probably the largest corpus of children's language, is very extensive and accessible to researchers, but there is as yet no equivalent corpus of spoken language organized to facilitate lifespan sociolinguistic research, including the middle childhood phase. Such an enterprise would be very worth while.

The involvement of children themselves in the research process is not without its problems (James et al. 1998; Leonard 1990; Qvortrup et al. 1994; Willow and Hyder 1998, and cf. Coupland 1997), but is another aspect of child language research that could be further explored.

How far there is evidence to support the knowledge we assume about children, language and the social world will be illuminated by contrastive research. There is a need for studies about representations of children in other languages (including other varieties of English), as well as in texts produced at other times. Similarly, there is still much which could be learned about children as social actors in different countries with different social institutions and different versions of 'the family', 'the peer group' and so on.

The discussions in this book about children, language and the social world cast doubt upon three perspectives, each of which has influenced research: the assumption that 'childhood' is linked with 'development', and that 'development' is necessarily an isolated, programmed and predetermined experience; the assumption that childhood is primarily a period of socialization, leading towards a predictable future; and the assumption that children occupy a separate, discrete, alternative culture. In place of these assumptions, I would propose that we should aim to locate any sociolinguistic analysis within all four social domains, and to see children's use of language as data which is relevant to that analysis. Children's experience of the social world, in this account, is emergent, partially predictable but also open-ended. Fundamentally, children have the same capacities and potentials as adults; they live in a world with the same linguistic resources, but in many contexts they occupy a different social location. Children have different experiences of the 'same' world in real time, but, as human beings, they are active participants in the same social and linguistic world to which we all belong.

# References

Adger CT 1998 Register shifting with dialect resources in instructional discourse. In Hoyle SM and Adger CT (eds) *Kids talk: strategic language use in later childhood*. New York and Oxford: Oxford University Press.

Aiken J 1977 Purely for love. In Meek M, Warlow A and Barton G (eds) *The cool web: the pattern of children's reading*. London: The Bodley Head.

Alanen L 1994 Gender and generation: feminism and the 'child question'. In Qvortrup J, Bardy M, Sgritta GB and Wintersberger H (eds) *Childhood matters: social theory, practice and politics*. Brookfield, VT: Avebury.

Allen R 1995 'Don't go on my property': a case study of transactions of user rights, *Language in society*, 24, 349–72.

Andersen ES 1990 *Speaking with style: the socio-linguistic skills of children*. London: Routledge.

Anderson H and Hilton M 1997 Speaking subjects: the development of a conceptual framework for the teaching and learning of spoken language, *English in Education* 31, 1, 12–23.

Archard D 1993 *Children: rights and childhood*. London: Routledge.

Archer M 1995 *Realist social theory: the morphogenetic approach*. Cambridge: Cambridge University Press.

Aston G and Burnard L 1998 *The BNC Handbook: Exploring the British National Corpus with SARA*. Edinburgh: Edinburgh University Press.

Attwood M 1997 *Alias Grace*. London: Virago.

Auwärter M 1986 Development of communicative skills: the construction of fictional reality in children's play. In Cook-Gumperz J, Corsaro W and Streeck J (eds) *Children's worlds and children's language*. Berlin: Mouton de Gruyter.

Avery G 1989 The Puritans and their heirs. In Avery G and Briggs J (eds) *Children and their books: a celebration of the work of Iona and Peter Opie*. Oxford: Oxford University Press.

Bain R, Fitzgerald B and Taylor M (eds) 1992 *Looking into language: classroom approaches to knowledge about language*. Sevenoaks: Hodder & Stoughton.

Bancroft D 1996 English as a first language. In Mercer N and Swann J (eds) *Learning English: development and diversity*. London: Routledge.

Barnes D 1988 The politics of oracy. In Maclure M, Phillips T and Wilkinson A (eds) *Oracy matters*. Buckingham: Open University Press.

Barnes D, Britton J, Rosen H and LATE (London Association for the Teaching of English) 1971 *Language, the learner and the school*. Harmondsworth: Penguin.

Bawden N 1989 [1963] *Tortoise by candlelight*. London: Virago.

Bell A 1991 *The language of news media*. Oxford: Blackwell.

Bergvall VL, Bing JM and Freed AF (eds) 1996 *Rethinking language and gender research: theory and practice*. Harlow: Addison Wesley Longman.

Bernstein B 1970 A critique of the concept of 'compensatory education'. In Rubinstein D and Stoneman C (eds) *Education for democracy*. Harmondsworth: Penguin.

Blank M and Solomon F 1972 How shall the disadvantaged child be taught? In Language and learning course team at the Open University (ed.) *Language in education: a source book*. London: Routledge & Kegan Paul.

Bloom L 1993 *The transition from infancy to language: acquiring the power of expression*. Cambridge: Cambridge University Press.

Blum-Kulka S and Olshtain E 1984 Requests and apologies: a cross-cultural study of speech act realization (CCSARP), *Applied Linguistics* 5, 196–213.

Board of Education 1921 *The teaching of English in England ('The Newbolt Report')*. London: Her Majesty's Stationery Office.

Bolinger D 1980 *Language: the loaded weapon*. Harlow: Longman.

Boston L 1977 A message from Green Knowe. In Meek M, Warlow A and Barton G (eds) *The cool web: the pattern of children's reading*. London: The Bodley Head.

Boyes G 1995 The legacy of the work of Iona and Peter Opie: the lore and language of today's children. In Beard R (ed.) *Rhyme, reading and writing*. Sevenoaks: Hodder & Stoughton.

Brenneis D and Lein L 1977 'You fruithead': a sociolinguistic approach to children's dispute settlement. In Ervin-Tripp S and Mitchell-Kernan C (eds) *Child discourse*. New York: Academic Press.

Brooks G 1992 The development of talk from five to eleven. In Norman K (ed.) *Thinking voices: the work of the National Oracy Project*. London: NCC Enterprises Ltd.

Brown P and Levinson S 1978 Universals in language usage: politeness phenomena. In Goody EN (ed.) *Questions and politeness: strategies in social interaction*. Cambridge: Cambridge University Press.

Bruner J 1983 *Child's talk: learning to use language*. Oxford: Oxford University Press.

Burman E 1994 *Deconstructing developmental psychology*. London: Routledge.

Burton H 1977 The writing of historical novels. In Meek M, Warlow A and Barton G (eds) *The cool web: the pattern of children's reading*. London: The Bodley Head.

Butt DG 1989 The object of language. In Hasan R and Martin JR (eds) *Language development: learning language, learning culture. Meaning and choice in language: studies for Michael Halliday*. Norwood, New Jersey: Ablex Publishing Corporation.

Cameron D 1996 The language-gender interface: challenging co-optation. In Bergvall VL, Bing JM and Freed AF (eds) *Rethinking language and gender research: theory and practice*. Harlow: Addison Wesley Longman.

Carter R (ed.) 1990 *Knowledge about language and the curriculum*. London: Hodder & Stoughton.

Carter R and Nash W 1990 *Seeing through language*. Oxford: Blackwell.

Central Advisory Council for Education (England) 1967 *Children and their primary schools (The Plowden Report)*. London: HMSO.

Chambers JK 1995 *Sociolinguistic theory: linguistic variation and its social significance*. Oxford: Blackwell.

Chang GL and Wells G 1988 The literate potential of collaborative talk. In Maclure M, Phillips T and Wilkinson A (eds) *Oracy matters*. Buckingham: Open University Press.

Clark K 1992 The linguistics of blame: representations of women in *The Sun's* reporting of crimes of sexual violence. In Toolan M (ed.) *Language, text and context*. London: Routledge.

Clark K and Holquist M 1984 *Mikhail Bakhtin*. Cambridge, Mass.: Harvard University Press.

Coates J 1989 Gossip revisited. In Coates J and Cameron D (eds) *Women in their speech communities*. London: Longman.

Coates J 1996 *Women talk*. Oxford: Blackwell.

COBUILD 1990 *Collins COBUILD English grammar*. London: HarperCollins.

Coe J 1994 *What a carve up!* London: Penguin.

Cook-Gumperz J 1977 Situated instructions: language socialization of school age children. In Ervin-Tripp S and Mitchell-Kernan C (eds) *Child discourse*. New York: Academic Press.

Cook-Gumperz J 1986 Caught in a web of words: some considerations on language socialization and language acquisition. In Cook-Gumperz J, Corsaro W and Streeck J (eds) *Children's worlds and children's language*. Berlin: Mouton de Gruyter.

Cook-Gumperz J, Corsaro W and Streeck J (eds) 1986 *Children's worlds and children's language*. Berlin: Mouton de Gruyter.

Cook-Gumperz J and Corsaro WA 1986 Introduction. In Cook-Gumperz J, Corsaro W and Streeck J (eds) *Children's worlds and children's language*. Berlin: Mouton de Gruyter.

Corsaro WA 1997 *The sociology of childhood*. Thousand Oaks, CA: Pine Forge Press.

Corteen K and Scraton P 1997 Prolonging 'childhood', manufacturing 'innocence' and regulating sexuality. In Scraton P (ed.) *'Childhood' in 'crisis'*. London: UCL Press.

Coupland N 1997 Language, ageing and ageism: a project for applied linguistics?, *International Journal of Applied Linguistics* 7, 1, 26–48.

Coupland N, Coupland J and Giles H 1991 *Language, society and the elderly: Discourse, identity and ageing*. Oxford: Basil Blackwell.

Coupland N, Coupland J and Nussbaum JF 1993 Epilogue: Future prospects in lifespan sociolinguistics. In Coupland N and Nussbaum JF (eds) *Discourse and lifespan identity*. London: Sage.

Coupland N and Nussbaum JF (eds) 1993 *Discourse and lifespan identity*. London: Sage.

Craib I 1998 *Experiencing identity*. London: Sage.

Crystal D 1987a *The Cambridge encyclopedia of language*. Cambridge: Cambridge University Press.

Crystal D 1987b *Child language, learning and linguistics: an overview for the teaching and therapeutic professions*. London: Edward Arnold.

Dahl R 1990 [1961] *James and the giant peach*. London: Unwin Hyman.

Davies B 1989 *Frogs and snails and feminist tails: preschool children and gender*. North Sydney, Australia: Allen & Unwin.

Davis H and Bourhill M 1997 The demonization of children and young people. In Scraton P (ed.) *'Childhood' in 'crisis'*. London: UCL Press.

de Villiers PA and de Villiers JG 1979 *Early language*. London: Fontana/Open Books.

Department for Education and the Welsh Office 1993 *English for ages 5 to 16 (1993). proposals of the Secretary of State for Education and the Secretary of State for Wales*. London: Department for Education.

Department of Education and Science 1975 *A language for life: report of the committee of inquiry into reading and the use of English (Bullock Report)*. London: HMSO.

Donald J and Rattansi A (eds) 1992 *'Race', culture and difference*. London: Sage.

Dunn J 1988 *The beginnings of social understanding*. Oxford: Basil Blackwell.

Edwards D and Mercer N 1987 *Common knowledge: the development of understanding in the classroom*. London: Routledge.

Eggins S and Slade D 1997 *Analysing casual conversation*. London: Cassell.

Ely R and Gleason JB 1995 Socialization across contexts. In Fletcher P and MacWhinney B (eds) *The handbook of child language*. Oxford: Blackwell.

Erickson F 1981 Timing and context in everyday discourse: implications for the study of referential meaning. In Dickson WP (ed.) *Children's oral communication skills*. New York: Academic Press.

Ervin-Tripp S 1977 Wait for me, roller skate! In Ervin-Tripp S and Mitchell-Kernan C (eds) *Child discourse*. New York: Academic Press.

Ervin-Tripp S, Guo J and Lampert M 1990 Politeness and persuasion in children's control acts, *Journal of Pragmatics* 14, 307–331.

Ervin-Tripp S and Mitchell-Kernan C (eds) 1977 *Child discourse*. New York: Academic Press.

Ervin-Tripp SM 1986 Activity structure as scaffolding for children's second language learning. In Cook-Gumperz J, Corsaro W and Streeck J (eds) *Children's worlds and children's language*. Berlin: Mouton de Gruyter.

Evaldsson A-C 1993 *Play, disputes and social order: everyday life in two Swedish after-school centers*. Linkoping: Linkoping University.

Fairclough N 1989 *Language and power*. London: Longman.

Fairclough N 1993 *Discourse and social change*. Cambridge: Polity Press in association with Blackwell.

Fairclough N 1996 Border crossings: discourse and social change in contemporary societies. In Coleman H and Cameron L (eds) *Change and language*. Clevedon: British Association for Applied Linguistics/Multilingual Matters.

Ferguson CA 1996 [1964] Baby talk in six languages. In Huebner T (ed.) *Sociolinguistic perspectives: papers on language in society 1959–1994*. New York and Oxford: Oxford University Press.

Ferguson CA 1996 [1971] Absence of copula and the notion of simplicity: a study of normal speech, baby talk, foreigner talk and pidgins. In Huebner T (ed.) *Sociolinguistic perspectives: papers on language in society 1959–1994*. New York and Oxford: Oxford University Press.

Fine A 1988 *Crummy Mummy and me*. London: Marilyn Malin Books in association with Andre Deutsch.

Fine GA and Sandstrom KL 1988 *Knowing children: participant observation with minors*. California: Sage.

Fletcher P and MacWhinney B (eds) 1995 *The handbook of child language*. Oxford: Blackwell.

Fowler R 1991 *Language in the news: discourse and ideology in the press*. London: Routledge.

Fowler R, Hodge B, Kress G and Trew T 1979 *Language and control*. London: Routledge & Kegan Paul.

Fowler R and Kress G 1979 Critical linguistics. In Fowler R, Hodge B, Kress G and Trew T (eds) *Language and control*. London: Routledge & Kegan Paul.

Freed AF 1996 Language and gender research in an experimental setting. In Bergvall VL, Bing JM and Freed AF (eds) *Rethinking language and gender research: theory and practice*. Harlow: Addison Wesley Longman.

Galton M, Simon B and Croll P 1980 *Inside the primary classroom*. London: Routledge & Kegan Paul.

Garvey C 1977 Play with language and speech. In Ervin-Tripp S and Mitchell-Kernan C (eds) *Child discourse*. New York: Academic Press.

Garvey C 1984 *Children's talk*. Cambridge, Mass.: Harvard University Press.

Gilbert SM and Gubar S 1979 *The madwoman in the attic: the woman writer and the nineteenth century literary imagination*. New Haven: Yale University Press.

Giles H and Coupland N 1991 *Language: contexts and consequences*. Buckingham: Open University Press.

Goffman E 1971 *Relations in public: microstudies of the public order*. New York and Cambridge: Harper & Row.

Goffman E 1981 *Forms of talk*. Oxford: Blackwell.

Goldson B 1997 'Childhood': an introduction to historical and theoretical analyses. In Scraton P (ed.) *'Childhood' in 'crisis'*. London: UCL Press.

Goodwin MH 1990 *He-said-she-said: talk as social organization among black children*. Bloomington: Indiana University Press.

Goodwin MH 1998 Games of stance: conflict and footing in hopscotch. In Hoyle SM and Adger CT (eds) *Kids talk: strategic language use in later childhood*. New York and Oxford: Oxford University Press.

Goodwin MH and Goodwin C 1987 Children's arguing. In Philips SU, Steele S and Tanz C (eds) *Language, gender, and sex in comparative perspective*. Cambridge: Cambridge University Press.

Gordon D and Ervin-Tripp S 1984 The structure of children's requests. In Schiefelbusch RL and Pickar J (eds) *The acquisition of communicative competence*. Baltimore: University Park Press.

Graddol D, Cheshire J and Swann J 1994 *Describing language*. Buckingham: Open University Press.

Grice HP 1975 Logic and conversation. In Cole P and Morgan JL (eds) *Syntax and semantics; Volume 3: Speech acts*. New York: Academic Press.

Grugeon E 1988 Children's oral culture: a transitional experience. In Maclure M, Phillips T and Wilkinson A (eds) *Oracy matters*. Buckingham: Open University Press.

Gumperz JJ 1982 *Discourse strategies*. Cambridge: Cambridge University Press.
Gumperz JJ and Cook-Gumperz J 1982 Introduction: language and the communication of social identity. In Gumperz JJ (ed.) *Language and social identity*. Cambridge: Cambridge University Press.

Halliday MAK 1975 *Learning how to mean: explorations in the development of language*. London: Edward Arnold.
Halliday MAK 1978 *Language as social semiotic*. London: Edward Arnold.
Halliday MAK 1989 *Spoken and written language*. Oxford: Oxford University Press.
Halliday MAK 1991 Corpus studies and probabilistic grammar. In Aijmer K and Altenberg B (eds) *English corpus linguistics*. Harlow: Longman.
Harré R 1992 What is real in psychology: a plea for persons, *Theory and Psychology* 2, 153–8.
Hasan R 1992 Meaning in sociolinguistic theory. In Bolton K and Kwok H (eds) *Sociolinguistics today: international perspectives*. London: Routledge.
Haynes J 1991 *A sense of words: knowledge about language in the primary school*. London: Hodder and Stoughton.
Haynes LM and Cooper RL 1986 A note on Ferguson's proposed baby-talk universals. In Fishman JA, Tabouret-Keller A, Michael C, Krishnamurti B and Abdulaziz M (eds) *The Fergusonian impact*. Berlin: Mouton de Gruyter.
Heath SB 1983 *Ways with words: language, life, and work in communities and classrooms*. Cambridge: Cambridge University Press.
Hoey M 1996 A clause-relational analysis of selected dictionary entries: contrast and compatibility in the definitions of 'man' and 'woman'. In Caldas-Coulthard CR and Coulthard M (eds) *Texts and practices*. London: Routledge.
Hogg MA and Abrams D 1988 *Social identifications*. London: Routledge.
Hollindale P 1992 Ideology and the children's book. In Hunt P (ed.) *Literature for children: contemporary criticism*. London: Routledge.
Holmes J 1995 *Women, men and politeness*. London: Longman.
Holmes J 1998 Myth 6: Women talk too much. In Bauer L and Trudgill P (eds) *Language myths*. London: Penguin.
Hood-Williams J 1990 Patriarchy for children: on the stability of power relations in children's lives. In Chisholm L, Buchner P, Kruger H-H and Brown P (eds) *Childhood, youth and social change: a comparative perspective*. Basingstoke: Falmer Press.
Hoyle SM 1998 Register and footing in role play. In Hoyle SM and Adger CT (eds) *Kids talk: strategic language use in later childhood*. New York and Oxford: Oxford University Press.
Hoyle SM and Adger CT (eds) 1998 *Kids talk: strategic language use in later childhood*. New York and Oxford: Oxford University Press.
Hughes M and Cousins J 1988 The roots of oracy: early language at home and at school. In Maclure M, Phillips T and Wilkinson A (eds) *Oracy matters*. Buckingham: Open University Press.
Hunt P 1984 Childist criticism: the subculture of the child, the book and the critic, *Signal* 43, January 1984, 42–59.
Hymes D 1972 On communicative competence. In Pride JB and Holmes J (eds) *Sociolinguistics: selected readings*. Baltimore: Penguin.

Hymes D 1974 *Foundations in sociolinguistics: an ethnographic approach*. London: Tavistock Publications.

James A 1993 *Childhood identities: self and social relationships in the experience of the child*. Edinburgh: Edinburgh University Press.

James A, Jenks C and Prout A 1998 *Theorizing childhood*. Cambridge: Polity Press.

James D 1996 Women, men and prestige speech forms: a critical review. In Bergvall VL, Bing JM and Freed AF (eds) *Rethinking language and gender research: theory and practice*. Harlow: Addison Wesley Longman.

Jenks C 1982 Introduction: constituting the child. In Jenks C (ed.) *The sociology of childhood*. London: Batsford.

Jones P 1988 *Lipservice: the story of talk in schools*. Buckingham: Open University Press.

Katriel T 1987 'Bexibùdim!': Ritualized sharing among Israeli children, *Language in Society* 16, 3, 305–20.

King-Smith D 1988 *George speaks*. London: Viking Kestrel (Penguin).

Kline S 1993 *Out of the garden: toys, TV, and children's culture in the age of marketing*. London: Verso.

Knowles M and Malmkjaer K 1996 *Language and control in children's literature*. London: Routledge.

Kress G 1997 *Before writing: rethinking the paths to literacy*. London: Routledge.

Labov W 1972 The logic of nonstandard English. In Language and learning course team at the Open University (ed.) *Language in education: a source book*. London: Routledge & Kegan Paul.

Lass R 1980 *On explaining language change*. Cambridge: Cambridge University Press.

Layder D 1997 *Modern social theory: key debates and new directions*. London: UCL Press.

Le Page RB and Tabouret-Keller A 1985 *Acts of identity: Creole-based approaches to language and ethnicity*. Cambridge: Cambridge University Press.

Leach P 1994 *Putting children first: what our society must do – and is not doing – for our children today*. New York: Alfred Knopf.

Lee D 1986 *Language, children and society: an introduction to linguistics and language development*. Brighton: Harvester Press.

Lee D 1992 *Competing discourses: perspective and ideology in language*. London: Longman.

Leonard D 1990 Persons in their own right: children and sociology in the UK. In Chisholm L, Buchner P, Kruger H-H and Brown P (eds) *Childhood, youth and social change: a comparative perspective*. Basingstoke: Falmer Press.

Levin EA and Rubin KH 1983 Getting others to do what you want them to do: development of children's requestive strategies. In Nelson KE (ed.) *Children's language, Volume 4*. New Jersey: Lawrence Erlbaum Associates.

Lurie A 1990 *Don't tell the grown-ups: subversive children's literature*. London: Bloomsbury.

Maclure M 1988 Introduction. Oracy: current trends in context. In Maclure M, Phillips T and Wilkinson A (eds) *Oracy matters*. Buckingham: Open University Press.

Maclure M, Phillips T and Wilkinson A (eds) 1988 *Oracy matters*. Buckingham: Open University Press.

Martin JR 1989 *Factual writing*. Oxford: Oxford University Press.

Maybin J 1994 Children's voices: talk, knowledge and identity. In Graddol D, Maybin J and Stierer B (eds) *Researching language and literacy in social context*. Clevedon: Multilingual Matters.

Maybin J 1996 Story voices: the use of reported speech in 10–12-year-olds' spontaneous narratives, *Current Issues in Language and Society* 3, 1, 36–48.

Maynard D 1985 On the functions of social conflict among children, *American Sociological Review* 50, 207–23.

Mayor B 1996 English in the repertoire. In Mercer N and Swann J (eds) *Learning English: development and diversity*. London: Routledge.

McCreedy L 1998 The effect of role and footing on students' oral academic language. In Hoyle SM and Adger CT (eds) *Kids talk: strategic language use in later childhood*. New York and Oxford: Oxford University Press.

McTear M 1985 *Children's conversation*. Oxford: Basil Blackwell.

Meek M 1985 Play and paradoxes: some considerations of imagination and language. In Wells G and Nicholls J (eds) *Language and Learning: an interactional perspective*. Lewes: The Falmer Press.

Meinhof U and Richardson K (eds) 1994 *Text, discourse and context: representations of poverty in Britain*. Harlow: Longman.

Menn L and Berko Gleason J 1986 Baby talk as a stereotype and register: adult reports of children's speech patterns. In Fishman JA, Tabouret-Keller A, Michael C, Krishnamurti B and Abdulaziz M (eds) *The Fergusonian impact*. Berlin: Mouton de Gruyter.

Mercer N 1995 *The guided construction of knowledge: talk amongst teachers and learners*. Clevedon: Multilingual Matters.

Mercer N, Edwards D and Maybin J 1988 Putting context into oracy: the construction of shared knowledge through classroom discourse. In Maclure M, Phillips T and Wilkinson A (eds) *Oracy matters*. Buckingham: Open University Press.

Merritt M 1998 Of ritual matters to master: structure and improvisation in language development at primary school. In Hoyle SM and Adger CT (eds) *Kids talk: strategic language use in later childhood*. New York and Oxford: Oxford University Press.

Meyerhoff M 1996 Dealing with gender identity as a sociolinguistic variable. In Bergvall VL, Bing JM and Freed AF (eds) *Rethinking language and gender research: theory and practice*. Harlow: Addison Wesley Longman.

Miller C and Swift K 1989 *The handbook of non-sexist writing*. London: Women's Press.

Milroy J 1992 The theoretical status of sociolinguistics. In Bolton K and Kwok H (eds) *Sociolinguistics today: international perspectives*. London: Routledge.

Milroy L and Milroy J 1992 Social network and social class: toward an integrated sociolinguistic model, *Language in Society* 21, 1–26.

Mitchell-Kernan C and Kernan KT 1977 Pragmatics of directive choice among children. In Ervin-Tripp S and Mitchell-Kernan C (eds) *Child discourse*. New York: Academic Press.

Morpurgo M 1987 *Conker*. London: William Heinemann.

Morrison B 1997 *As if*. London: Granta.

Newnham D 1997 *Walking a fine line. The Guardian.* London and Manchester.
Norman K (ed.) 1992 *Thinking voices: the work of the National Oracy Project.* London: NCC Enterprises Ltd.

Ochs E 1979 Transcription as theory. In Ochs E and Schieffelin BB (eds) *Developmental pragmatics.* London: Academic Press.
Ochs E 1983 Cultural dimensions of language acquisition. In Ochs E and Schieffelin BB (eds) *Acquiring conversational competence.* London: Routledge.
Ochs E and Schieffelin B 1995 The impact of language socialization on grammatical development. In Fletcher P and MacWhinney B (eds) *The handbook of child language.* Oxford: Blackwell.
Ochs E and Schieffelin BB (eds) 1979 *Developmental pragmatics.* London: Academic Press.
Ochs E and Schieffelin BB (eds) 1983 *Acquiring conversational competence.* London: Routledge.
Ochs E and Taylor C 1992 Family narrative as political activity, *Discourse and Society* 33, 301–40.
Opie I 1993 *The people in the playground.* Oxford: Oxford University Press.
Opie I and Opie P 1959 *The lore and language of schoolchildren.* London: Granada.

Painter C 1984 *Into the mother tongue.* London: Pinter.
Painter C 1989 Learning language: a functional view of language development. In Hasan R and Martin JR (eds) *Language development: learning language, learning culture. Meaning and choice in language: studies for Michael Halliday.* Norwood, NJ: Ablex Publishing Corporation.
Paton Walsh J 1977 The rainbow surface. In Meek M, Warlow A and Barton G (eds) *The cool web: the pattern of children's reading.* London: The Bodley Head.
Paton Walsh J 1978 *A Chance Child.* London: Puffin Books.
Perera K 1984 *Children's writing and reading: analysing classroom language.* Oxford: Basil Blackwell.
Phillips T 1985 Beyond lip-service: discourse development after the age of nine. In Wells G and Nicholls J (eds) *Language and learning: an interactional perspective.* Lewes: The Falmer Press.
Phillips T 1988 On a related matter: why 'successful' small-group talk depends upon not keeping to the point. In Maclure M, Phillips T and Wilkinson A (eds) *Oracy matters.* Buckingham: Open University Press.
Pinker S 1994 *The language instinct.* London: Penguin.
Postman N 1985 *The disappearance of childhood: how TV is changing children's lives:* W.H. Allen.
Potter J 1996 *Representing reality: discourse, rhetoric and social construction.* London: Sage.

Qvortrup J 1994 Childhood matters: an introduction. In Qvortrup J, Bardy M, Sgritta GB and Wintersberger H (eds) *Childhood matters: social theory, practice and politics.* Brookfield, VT: Avebury.
Qvortrup J, Bardy M, Sgritta GB and Wintersberger H (eds) 1994 *Childhood matters: social theory, practice and politics.* Brookfield, VT: Avebury.

Raban B, Clark U and McIntyre J 1994 *Evaluation of the implementation of English in the National Curriculum at Key Stages 1, 2 and 3 (1991–1993)*. London: School Curriculum and Assessment Authority.

Rampton B 1995 *Crossing: language and ethnicity among adolescents*. Harlow: Longman.

Romaine S 1984 *The language of children and adolescents: the acquisition of communicative competence*. Oxford: Blackwell.

Romaine S 1995 *Bilingualism*. Oxford: Blackwell.

Rose N 1989 *Governing the soul: the shaping of the private self*. London: Routledge.

Rubens B 1995 *Yesterday in the back lane*. London: Abacus.


Said EW 1978 *Orientalism*. London: Peregrine.

Sarangi S and Slembrouck S 1996 *Language, bureaucracy and social control*. Harlow: Addison Wesley Longman.

Saville-Troike 1989 *The ethnography of communication*. Oxford: Basil Blackwell.

Schegel J 1998 Finding words, finding meanings: collaborative learning and distributed cognition. In Hoyle SM and Adger CT (eds) *Kids talk: strategic language use in later childhood*. New York and Oxford: Oxford University Press.

Schieffelin B 1983 Talking like birds: sound play in a cultural perspective. In Ochs E and Schieffelin BB (eds) *Acquiring conversational competence*. London: Routledge.

Schieffelin BB and Ochs E (eds) 1986 *Language socialization across cultures*. Cambridge: Cambridge University Press.

Schiffrin D 1994 *Approaches to discourse*. Oxford: Blackwells.

Scott S, Jackson S and Backett-Milburn K 1998 Swings and roundabouts: risk anxiety and the everyday worlds of children, *Sociology* 32, 4, 689–705.

Scraton P 1997 Whose 'childhood'? What 'crisis'? In Scraton P (ed.) *'Childhood' in 'crisis'*. London: UCL Press.

Sealey A 1992 The Dazzlers' Dictionary. In Bain R, Fitzgerald B and Taylor M (eds) *Looking into language: classroom approaches to knowledge about language*. Sevenoaks: Hodder & Stoughton.

Sealey A 1994 Language and educational control: the construction of the LINC controversy. In Scott D (ed.) *Accountability and control in educational settings*. London: Cassell.

Sealey A 1996 *Learning about language: issues for primary teachers*. Buckingham: Open University Press.

Sealey A 1997 Models of language, models of childhood in the English National Curriculum, *Changing English* 5, 1, 69–81.

Sealey A 1999a 'Don't be cheeky': requests, directives and being a child, *Journal of Sociolinguistics* 3, 1, 24–40.

Sealey A 1999b Teaching primary school children about the English language: a critique of current policy documents, *Language Awareness* 8, 2, 84–97.

Searle JR 1995 *The construction of social reality*. London: Allen Lane.

Seiter E 1993 *Sold separately: children and parents in consumer culture*. New Jersey: Rutgers University Press.

Shotter J 1993a Becoming someone: identity and belonging. In Coupland N and Nussbaum J (eds) *Discourse and lifespan identity*. London: Sage.

Shotter J 1993b *Conversational realities: constructing life through language*. London: Sage.

Siegert MT 1986 Adult elicited child behaviour: the paradox of measuring social competence through interviewing. In Cook-Gumperz J, Corsaro W and Streeck J (eds) *Children's worlds and children's language*. Berlin: Mouton de Gruyter.

Simpson P 1993 *Language, ideology and point of view*. London: Routledge.

Sinclair J 1991 *Corpus, concordance, collocation*. Oxford: Oxford University Press.

Sinclair JM and Coulthard M 1975 *Towards an analysis of discourse*. London: Oxford University Press.

Snow CE 1976 The language of the mother–child relationship. In Rogers S (ed.) *They don't speak our language*. London: Edward Arnold.

Soothill K and Grover C 1997 A note on computer searches of newspapers, *Sociology* 31, 3, 591–6.

Speier M 1982 [1970] The everyday world of the child. In Jenks C (ed.) *The sociology of childhood*. London: Batsford.

Stainton Rogers R and Stainton Rogers W 1992 *Stories of childhood: shifting agendas of child concern*. Hemel Hempstead: Harvester Wheatsheaf.

Steedman C 1982 *The tidy house*. London: Virago.

Stephens J 1992 *Language and ideology in children's fiction*. Harlow: Addison Wesley Longman.

Streeck J 1986 Towards reciprocity: politics, rank and gender in the interaction of a group of schoolchildren. In Cook-Gumperz J, Corsaro W and Streeck J (eds) *Children's worlds and children's language*. Berlin: Mouton de Gruyter.

Stubbs M 1996 *Text and corpus analysis*. Oxford: Blackwell.

Sutton-Smith B 1982 A performance theory of peer relations. In Borman KM (ed.) *The social life of children in a changing society*. New Jersey: Lawrence Erlbaum Associates.

Sykes M 1985 Discrimination in discourse. In van Dijk T (ed.) *Handbook of discourse analysis*. London: Academic Press.

Taylor C 1985 *Human agency and language: Philosophical Papers 1*. Cambridge: Cambridge University Press.

Thomas K 1989 Children in early modern England. In Avery G and Briggs J (eds) *Children and their books: a celebration of the work of Iona and Peter Opie*. Oxford: Oxford University Press.

Thorne B 1993 *Gender play: girls and boys in school*. Buckingham: Open University Press.

Tizard B and Hughes M 1984 *Young children learning*. London: Fontana.

Trease G 1977 Old writers and young readers. In Meek M, Warlow A and Barton G (eds) *The cool web: the pattern of children's reading*. London: The Bodley Head.

Ure J 1987 *Who's talking?* London: Orchard Books.

van Dijk TA 1988 *News analysis: case studies of international and national news in the press*. New Jersey: Lawrence Erlbaum Associates.

van Leeuwen T 1996 The representation of social actors. In Caldas-Coulthard CR and Coulthard M (eds) *Texts and practices*. London: Routledge.

van Peer W 1988 Counting out: form and function of children's counting-out rhymes. In Maclure M, Phillips T and Wilkinson A (eds) *Oracy matters*. Buckingham: Open University Press.

Waksler FC (ed.) 1991 *Studying the social worlds of children*. London: Falmer.

Wall B 1991 *The narrator's voice: the dilemma of children's fiction*. London: Macmillan.

Wells G 1986 *The meaning makers: children learning language and using language to learn*. London: Hodder & Stoughton.

White J and Karavis S 1994 *The reading repertoire at Key Stage 2: a selective list of books*. Slough: NFER.

Whitehead M 1995 Nonsense, rhyme and word play in young children. In Beard R (ed.) *Rhyme, reading and writing*. Sevenoaks: Hodder & Stoughton.

Whitehead MR 1990 *Language and literacy in the early years*. London: Paul Chapman.

Wilkinson A 1990 Introduction: the concept of oracy – retrospect and prospect. In Wilkinson A, Davies A and Berrill D (eds) *Spoken English illuminated*. Buckingham: Open University Press.

Willes MJ 1983 *Children into pupils*. London: Routledge & Kegan Paul.

Willow C and Hyder T 1998 *It hurts you inside: children talk about smacking*. London: National Children's Bureau/Save the Children.

Wootton AJ 1986 Rules in action: orderly features of actions that formulate rules. In Cook-Gumperz J, Corsaro W and Streeck J (eds) *Children's worlds and children's language*. Berlin: Mouton de Gruyter.

Zentella AC 1998 Multiple codes, multiple identities: Puerto Rican children in New York City. In Hoyle SM and Adger CT (eds) *Kids talk: strategic language use in later childhood*. New York and Oxford: Oxford University Press.

# Index